LIFE *at* SEA

From Caravels to Cruise Ships

MONIQUE LAYTON

 FriesenPress

Suite 300 - 990 Fort St
Victoria, BC, V8V 3K2
Canada

www.friesenpress.com

ISBN
978-1-5255-0092-3 (Hardcover)
978-1-5255-0093-0 (Paperback)
978-1-5255-0094-7 (eBook)

1. TRAVEL, CRUISES

Distributed to the trade by The Ingram Book Company

PREVIOUS REVIEWS

The New Arcadia: Tahiti's Cursed Myth (2015)

"A layered and fascinating analysis of history and anthropology." *(Kirkus Review)*

"A vital and compelling picture of a conflicted island and its people." *(Clarion Reviews* – four stars)

"Engrossing." (*BC BookWorld)*

"A scholarly book, research-rich yet appropriate and interesting for the general reader." (Jury, Whistler Independent Book Award, 2016)

Notes from Elsewhere. Travel and Other Matters (2011)

"This wide-ranging book… reveals a singular voice and a capacious mind." (Eleanor Wachtel, author of *Writers and Company, Original Minds,* and *Random Illuminations)*

"A rich melange of philosophical musings and literary allusions…. A considerable reading pleasure…" (Elvi Whittaker, author *of*

A Baltic Odyssey, The Mainland Haole, the Silent Dialogue, Solitudes of the Workplace)

"Rich, sensory details… [Her] blend of historical, literary and political references throughout helps put her keen personal observations in context." *(Kirkus Review)*

ACKNOWLEDGEMENTS

I have by now run out of words to thank my first and vigilant readers, Elvi Whittaker and Lee Southern. They know my gratitude. I also appreciate Jane Cowan's reading of the manuscript and my FriesenPress editor's useful suggestions.

Some people have provided help in various forms and I wish to recognize their kindness: John Layton, for carting books from the Vancouver Public Library and back again for several years without a complaint, always keeping an alert eye for topics of interest; Lee Southern, again, for sending daily emails of encouragement and related articles; maritime historian Paul Brown, for suggesting additional readings and sending illustrations; Clare Sharpe, webmaster at the Esquimalt Naval and Military Museum, for offering the services of his institution; Hans-Jörg Pust, formerly of the *Anna Katrin Fritzen*, for giving me access to his story. My thanks are also due to several long-time cruisers who have commented on the nature and future of cruising, notably Patricia Flanagan, Wendy and Eric Dryden, and Linda Passin.

It is my great pleasure to use as cover for this book Margaret Meredith's photograph of the young apprentices on board the *Macquarie*, on her way to Australia in 1894. The young men once treated her and the three other ladies on board to tea, toast, and excellent jam.

As usual, this book is for John.   Vancouver, 2016

LIFE *at* SEA

From Caravels To Cruise Ships

Monique Layton

2016

By the Same Author

Non-Fiction

Street Women and the Art of Bullshitting (2010)
Notes from Elsewhere. Travel and Other Matters (2011)
The New Arcadia: Tahiti's Cursed Myth (2015)

Translation

Claude Lévi-Strauss. *Structural Anthropology II* (1976)

Table of Contents

Sailing is a noble thing, useful beyond all others to mankind. It exports what is superfluous, it provides what is lacking, it makes the impossible possible, it joins together men from different lands and makes every inhospitable island a part of the mainland, it brings fresh knowledge to those who sail, it refines manners, it brings concord and civilization to men, it consolidates their nature by bringing together all that is most human in them.

George Pachymérès (1242-c.1310), *Historical Relations*

Something magical happens. The ship almost becomes a being... Watching over all within, feeding, sheltering, giving warmth, and offering the rest of sleep. Though they might hate being there at times, all aboard feels like its children, will do anything for it, and will go where it goes, towards the goal they gain together. This feeling does not come from the ship's design, or with structure and function, but from this intricate, interwoven relationship between vessel and crew, built of time and intimate association.

C. W. Johnson, *Ice Ship* (2014)

No man will be a sailor who has contrivance enough to get himself into a jail; for being in a ship is being in jail with the chance of being drowned... A man in jail has more room, better food, and commonly better company... Men go to sea before they know the unhappiness of that way of life.

James Boswell, quoting Samuel Johnson (1709-1784)

The sea never changes, and its works, for all the talk of men, are wrapped in mystery.

Joseph Conrad, *Typhoon*

PROLOGUE

Some of my readings on eighteenth-century navigators for a book I was then writing *(The New Arcadia: Tahiti's Cursed Myth)* took place at sea. Watching the nodding of some grey heads rocked by the swell of an equally grey sea, I started wondering what connections existed between these elderly passengers on a cruise and the men whose adventurous early voyages I was discovering in my books. How did we evolve from sailing bravely on three-masted barques to cruising idly on vessels shaped like large apartment buildings with balconies, having for the most part forsaken the look of traditional ships? I was intrigued and decided to look into the ways of people at sea and consider how the events that shape a voyage have evolved over the centuries.

I wrote this book to address topics of personal interest, and I often digress as I wind my way along sea lanes. It is so vast a subject, and so many of its aspects have been so ably covered by others, that I felt quite unconcerned in indulging myself and satisfying my own curiosity. If readers are shown a side of sea life they find lackluster, perhaps the next one broached will pique their interest.

There are constant threads running through all voyages, in spite of their being guided by different motivations for sailing to far distant lands: the physical constraints on board, the treatment of illness, the vagaries of the weather, the importance of food—leading to various tactics for overcoming the limitations and isolation of sailing and the dangers met along the way.

Some things have changed over time. The voyages themselves have shifted purpose and focus from utilitarian (trade, exploration, transportation) to the futile (entertainment) and the essential (world economy), and benefitted from the enormous scientific and technological development now available on ships. Others have not. Seafarers are still violent, generous, foolhardy, vain, and heroic. We might observe that humans at sea are much like those on shore, only far more tightly bound to their mates and to their exceptional and inescapable circumstances.

The first three sections of this book address the positive aspects of sailing, including style, comfort, safety, food, and entertainment. The last two relate to the darker side of being at sea, like inclement weather, illness on board, the perils of sailing in dire circumstances and dreaded company, and the odds of surviving a shipwreck.

My sources include studies, encyclopaedias, and film and television documentaries dealing with older vessels and the evolution and improvement of navigation and facilities on board ships, from Columbus's *Santa Maria* to the French Line's flagship *Normandie*. Some consider the connections between the sea and the expansion of civilization, while others are more specifically concerned with piracy, slavery, emigration, or with customs born of the sea.

The travel log and photographs of my husband John's great-aunt Margaret Meredith on her eight-month return voyage to Australia in the 1890s helped illustrate the experience of sailing as a passenger on a packet-ship. This period is also abundantly covered in Deakes and Stanley's useful book, *A Century of Sea Travel* (2010). For background on modern liners and cruise ships, I have also relied on travel reports, guidebooks, conversations with passengers, and personal sailing experience.

Finally, I chose the Holland America Line as my main term of reference for modern cruising for two reasons: convenience and symbolism. The *Unofficial Guide to Cruises* describes those for whom HAL cruises are not recommended, including "swingers, party seekers, late night revelers, trend seekers, or pace setters." Their absence seems to suit those who end up feeling some affection for these ships. Their names all end in "dam," permitting their passengers to refer fondly to them as "those dam ships!" as if they had an intimate and teasing connection with them. These passengers seemed congenial enough to contribute reliable opinions on the nature of cruising. The second reason is that the logo of Holland America illustrates the theme of this book. It is a medallion showing, silhouetted against the much larger stylized shape of a contemporary liner, the outline of *de Halve Maen, (the Half Moon),* the small, three-masted Dutch barque on which Henry Hudson, an English captain unable to find backers at home, had sailed in 1609. The collapsing of the two vessels into a single image has become the symbol of some four centuries of continuity at sea and the token memory of a far more valorous past, when sailing had not yet understood what cruising would become.

I
PRELIMINARIES

A Eurocentric Vision

How Cruising Came to Be

Travel, Tourism, Cruising

Coastal Communities

Before following ships and their human cargo through time and space, it seems appropriate to dispose of a few ancillary topics. The ships mentioned here relate mostly to a European tradition of exploration, trade, and scientific discovery and to the elaboration of an essentially European and American cruising culture. Yet, other civilizations have a long seafaring tradition, and we recognize the substantial contributions to maritime history made by China's formidable fleet and the powerful outriggers of the South Pacific.

It also seems appropriate to relate the origins of the new taste for idle cruising to two entrepreneurs responsible for creating the parameters of organized tourism (Thomas Cook) and for transforming the earlier ordeal of transoceanic voyages into crossings that could finally be enjoyed by focusing on speed and comfort (Samuel Cunard).

We also consider the tricky topics of what makes travel what we intuitively sense it to be and how tourism and cruising relate to it. Cruisers (a term used throughout to describe cruise ship passengers) have set foot on every continent and many describe themselves as travellers, though non-cruisers might object to this self-identification. Finally, we briefly examine the part played by coastal communities as an extension of sea life.

With this hodgepodge of preliminary topics out of the way, we then focus on the basic aspects of spending time at sea, saving for later some of the harsher realities of sailing.

1 A EUROCENTRIC VISION

This book focuses on the evolution of European navigation, which is well documented and covers the history of a large part of the human experience at sea.

Wherever there has been a happy congruence of accessible shoreline, convenient supply of timber, and able workforce, ships have been built. Over time, they evolved from the dugout canoe sailing along familiar shores to the largest ship ever built, the tanker *Jahere Viking* (564,650 deadweight tonnage). Whatever their size and power, ships remain what they have always been: an extension of humankind's natural reach.

The enormous transformation of ships from coastal canoes to superships crisscrossing oceans results from three main factors: the modernization of the materials used in their construction, their means of propulsion, and the sailors' ability to determine their position at sea.

SHIPBUILDING

The humble canoe, made of wood and still found in many parts of the world, is unique in that its length to width ratio must remain fairly constant, and any tampering with it (as has occasionally been done to adapt it for special functions) renders it unseaworthy. This restriction applies to any wooden ship, as does the limitation of its waterline length of 80 metres (260 feet). Both constraints ruled shipbuilding right through the eighteenth century. By then, European industrial shipyards were finding the demand for timber starting to outstrip supply. Forests were depleted, wood was short-lived at sea, fire took a heavy toll, and vessels were needed in always greater number. Only countries with vast resources of timber (some European nations, North America, and Russia) could remain competitive.

There was tremendous sea activity between the fifteenth and the eighteenth centuries, with most European maritime countries involved in exploration, colonization, trade, war, and piracy. We will examine these in more detail later, but we should note the influence of two men on the maritime development of their nations: Henry the Navigator of Portugal (1394-1460) and Henry VIII of England (1491-1547). The former promoted the development of caravels from mere fishing boats to merchant ships with lateen sails on two masts (later three), initially facilitating the exploration of the West African coast, and becoming part of Vasco da Gama and Christopher Columbus's expeditionary fleets. For his part, Henry VIII was responsible for establishing the bases that enabled England to become Europe's foremost naval power. From the seven ships he inherited upon acceding the throne, his fleet grew to fifty-three, manned by some eight thousand sailors.

During his reign, the shipyards of Greenwich and Deptford were created, and many new shipbuilding skills were developed. Great Britain became a sea power to contend with under his influence, and *Henry Grâce à Dieu*, also known as *Great Harry*, then the largest warship in the world (1514), was the emblem of the kingdom's naval power. At over a thousand tons, with four pole masts and a complement of seven hundred men, armed with twenty-one heavy guns and 230 other weapons, she was deemed a sailing marvel—and contemporary illustrations do her justice.

At the same time, the demand for ships was ever increasing. Shipyards were flourishing from England to Venice, and the whole of Europe had their eyes fixed on the sea. However, there was still the matter of the constraints and vulnerability of wooden ships.

In May 1819, the *Vulcan* was launched from the banks of the Monkland Canal, near Glasgow. She was an experimental sixty-six-foot (twenty-metre) barge made entirely of iron, each piece forged by hand by two blacksmiths, making her one of the most labour-intensive ships ever built. Iron shipbuilding was the industry's most dramatic innovation, as the restrictions on size and proportions disappeared. The greatest commercial advantage of using iron was that doubling a ship's length resulted in an eightfold increase in her capacity.

The *Great Britain* (launched at Bristol in 1843) was the first large passenger ship built of iron. She was 322 feet (98 metres) in length with a propeller, and, the builders being inspired by Marco Polo's description of Chinese vessels, she was divided into compartments by watertight bulkheads. Accidentally stranded for a year after her first crossing, she remained in good condition, showing the merit of her design and construction. She remained in service for forty years, carrying six hundred passengers to Australia at one crossing.

The use of iron required new engineering techniques, leading in the 1860s to the incorporation of steel into shipbuilding. More susceptible to corrosion than iron, it was also stronger and lighter and increased a ship's cargo capacity even more. The *Rotomahana*, a merchant ship, became the first steel ocean-going vessel in 1879.

While the need for accessible timber favoured shipyards in forested countries, iron shipbuilding only required smelting facilities and technical knowledge, and thus it was more mobile. During WWI, British shipbuilding dominated the world, and American shipyards were also working full time. With the Depression came the slow decline of European shipbuilding, even as some of the star ships were being built, including *Empress of Britain, Normandie, Queen Mary*, and *Queen Elizabeth*.

Today, China, Korea, and Japan build most of the ships worldwide, with new techniques permitting larger sizes and new designs. The use of container ships had previously revolutionized commercial transport, and today's greatest changes are occurring in the tanker trade, allowing the transportation of enormous quantities of crude oil. The second area of growth is in the construction of cruise ships, as the number of passengers and the space allocated to them continue to increase. Both are modern versions of traditional seafaring activities (cargo and people transportation), yet they have evolved in a manner unimaginable a mere century ago.

PROPULSION

Originally, strong arms and favourable winds were a vessel's sole means of propulsion—from Greek triremes to Mediterranean galleys to Viking longboats. Larger ships and longer voyages required making optimum use of the wind and devising a sophisticated and efficient system of sails and rigging. So impressive is the sight of a ship in full sail that Margaret Meredith's first entry in her 1894 log was the name of all twenty-four sails on the *Macquarie*.

Simply put—particularly in the context of the complex system involved—the traditional rigging, consisting of all the fittings, ropes, chains used to support and operate the masts and sails, falls into two types. The first is standing, meaning it is fixed to support the masts and spars, and the second is running, which is adjustable to operate the sails. Sails are also of two types: those used in square-riggers, set on horizontal spars crossing the masts and supported by slings from the masthead, and those used in fore-and-aft-rigged vessels, set on masts.

Three- or four-strand ropes were originally made of hemp, which stretched and required constant adjusting and tightening. They were later replaced by steel wires. Similarly, the demanding skills of sail making and hand stitching canvas disappeared with the introduction in the 1950s of synthetic materials and sewing machines. Today, lighter material, such as Kevlar and Mylar, are used, and new methods for making and cutting sails use computer-generated moulds. The beneficiaries of these changes are tall ships, training cadets in the fine art of navigation, and private yachts.

Steam propulsion was introduced during the early nineteenth century, giving ships more speed and maneuverability. However, the early steamships were paddle steamers requiring huge storage of coal, to the detriment of the space allocated to freight and

passengers. The method was unreliable and for many years oceango-
ing ships continued to be also rigged for sailing. In her first attempt
to cross the Atlantic in 1819, the *Savannah* ended up stowing her
collapsible paddle wheels on deck and sailing most of the way. Ships
only started relying almost entirely on steam in the 1880s.

Rotary steam-turbine engines brought in a revolutionary level of
efficiency, particularly with the introduction of the propeller. The
British-built and aptly named *Turbinia* (1897) was the first vessel in
the world powered with steam turbines, which became particularly
popular with passenger liners. Concurrent with the appearance of
turbine engines was an experiment to replace steam with oil, and in
1905, the Royal Navy converted its warships to it. After WWI, most
passenger liners and merchant ships followed suit.

Diesel engines were introduced in the earlier part of the twentieth century, first for river and harbour craft, until they proved their
reliability. A ship we will later meet in polar navigation, the *Fram*
(1911), was the first ocean-going vessel to be so propelled. Since the
1980s, most commercial ships have been fitted with economical and
highly productive diesel engines, in spite of their high consumption
(over two hundred tons a day for a large vessel) of the potentially
highly toxic diesel oil when spilled into the ocean. The latest and
most efficient innovation in steam power is that of nuclear reactors
for icebreakers, aircraft carriers, and submarines (the first being the
USS *Nautilus* in 1955).

THE LONGITUDE AND THE CHRONOMETER

Today, we could not conceive of sailing while knowing only half
our position at sea. Yet, until the middle of the eighteenth century,
the only certainty was the course of the latitude. The compass had
long been accurate enough to permit sailing beyond the sight of
land, but navigation was still essentially a matter of guesswork. On
long voyages, the custom was to sail as far as possible along the
same latitude (determined by the elevation of the North Star above
the horizon, or by measuring the angle made by the sun with the

horizon at its zenith) in spite of adverse winds and currents and the tacking required. From Europe to the Americas, the route was "due south till the butter melts and then due west," following the same parallel. "Sailing the parallel" would have taken Columbus to his intended Far Eastern destination, had the American continent not stood unexpectedly in his path.

Captains and pilots mostly proceeded by dead reckoning, which consisted of throwing a log overboard and observing the speed at which the ship moved away from it. They noted its progress, the direction taken (calculated from the stars or a compass), and the time spent on a particular course (recorded with a sandglass or a pocket watch). Unfortunately, there were many potentially misleading factors, including unknown currents, erratic winds, and the frailty of human judgement, so they often missed the mark, which was sometimes an island with fresh water and food.

Tragically, they often failed to locate coastal rocks on which to founder. Such was the fate of Admiral Sir Cloudesley Shovell's fleet off the Scilly Isles on a foggy October night in 1707. Misjudging their longitude and unaware of their location, four of the five ships under his command sank with nearly two thousand men. The flagship *Association* was first to hit the rocks and went within minutes, with only the admiral reaching shore alive. He was soon dispatched by a beachcomber attracted to the emerald ring on his finger. The next three ships, following the *Association* too closely to change course, sank as fast as she did. There are undoubtedly many similar cases, where ignorance of their longitude led vessels to their destruction.

Another consequence of this inability to calculate longitudes was the captains' preference for following known sea lanes, with explorers, whalers, merchants, pirates, and others following the same busy and familiar routes. This made some ships vulnerable to predators. Such was the unfortunate fate of the Portuguese galleon *Madre de Deus,* returning from India and ambushed in 1592 by six English men-of-war near the Azores. In spite of her thirty-two brass guns, the Portuguese ship was soon made to surrender. Under her hatches were "chests of gold and silver coins, pearls, diamonds, amber, musk, tapestries, calico and ebony," and, even more valuable, nearly five hundred tons of spices, including pepper, cloves, cinnamon, and—particularly rare—mace and nutmeg. It was eventually assessed at about half the value of the entire English Exchequer. Such encounters between merchant vessels and rogue ships would continue as long as all were bound to the same sea lanes.

The fates of the *Association* and the *Madre de Deus* are merely anecdotal examples of the accumulated dangers brought on by sailing without knowing the longitude. It was a constant concern for navigators, equipped with only half the calculations they needed to find their position in oceans. Yet, longitude had long been understood and was already represented on maps drawn in 150 CE by Ptolemy who, in accordance with established calculations of natural laws, had also used the Equator as the zero parallel of latitude. Unfortunately, there was no such scientific basis for the longitude's position, and Ptolemy arbitrarily ran the zero-degree longitude line through the Fortunate Islands (today's Madeira and the Canaries), off the coast of Africa. This *ad hoc* location was successively replaced by other cartographers' whims and the start of the longitude was variously relocated to the Azores, the Cape Verde Islands, Rome, Copenhagen, Jerusalem, St. Petersburg, Pisa, Paris, and Philadelphia. Many navigators had also simply used their ports of departure as zero meridian for their calculations. Since any line drawn between the poles could serve, politics became the determining factor. The fifth astronomer royal, Nevil Maskelyne, settled the matter by issuing between 1765 and 1811 forty-nine *Nautical Almanacks* in which all lunar-solar and lunar-stellar calculations were based from the Greenwich meridian. This became the established custom, and Greenwich was officially recognized at the International Meridian Conference in Washington in 1884.

The major problem, beside the unaccountability of the zero meridian, was the lack of a simple mechanical device accurate enough to determine the time on board a ship and compare it to the time at another known longitude. The difference between the two times reflects the distance between the two locations and, as the rotation of the earth takes twenty-four hours, a difference of one hour between two sites (one known, the other being calculated) translates into one twenty-fourth of the rotation, or fifteen degrees. When navigators reset their clocks at noon, they compared it to the time their other clocks (set to the time of the known longitude) and could visualize the progress made. Naturally, latitudes must also be known for the calculation of the distance covered to be accurate, as those fifteen degrees of longitude vary between the Equator, where they are the longest, and closer to the poles, where the distance is significantly reduced. However, until reliable timepieces could be found, such calculations were impossible and much of navigation was still left to luck.

Coming on top of many similar incidents, the catastrophic sinking of the *Association* and her three companion ships in 1707, with the loss of nearly two thousand men, served to alarm public opinion, particularly as it had happened close to English shipping lanes. In 1714, Parliament proclaimed the *Longitude Act*, offering a prize of £20,000 for the solution to the problem of accurately measuring longitude. Isaac Newton, who sat on the Board of Longitude, illustrated the dire need for a consistently accurate time-keeping machine when he wrote in 1721, "A good watch may serve to keep a recconing at Sea for some days and to know the time of a celestial Observ[at]ion: and for this end a good Jewel watch may suffice till a better sort of Watch can be found out. But when the longitude at sea is once lost, it cannot be found again by any watch."

After many years spent developing models, an English clock-maker named John Harrison produced in the mid-1750s a reliable mechanism, easy to reproduce at reasonable cost: the chronometer. Its first buyers were captains of the Royal Navy and the East India Company, causing some to argue that John Harrison's discovery was the origin of Britain's supremacy at sea. In 1860, the Royal Navy had fewer than two hundred active ships, yet owned some eight hundred chronometers. Worldwide, they were so successful that their usage rose from just one in 1737 to about five thousand by 1815.

The chronometer brought a tremendous improvement to the safety of sailors, finally able to calculate their exact position. Had there been one on Commodore George Anson's ship, he would have avoided the dreadful events that befell him. The destructive effect of the storm he encountered had certainly been compounded by the treacherous currents that impeded the ships' progress, but more to the point and far more seriously was the Commodore's inability to track down their course and their location.

With seven other ships in his squadron, he set sail in September 1740 for the South Pacific on the *Centurion* to circumnavigate the globe and capture Spanish possessions. After crossing the Atlantic and reaching Cape Horn five and a half months later, his crew sick with scurvy, he met with a great storm that blew in from the west and dashed many to their death. The rain, sleet, and snow did not abate for fifty-eight days, during which time scurvy continued its ravages. Anson stayed on the same parallel for what he estimated to be some two hundred miles westward, intending to sail around Tierra del Fuego and aiming north towards the restorative island of Juan Fernández, where his ailing men could found food and water.

By then, his companion ships had vanished in the storm, some never to be seen again. As the haze cleared, he saw land immediately ahead—not Juan Fernández (still a few days away, according to his calculations), but Cape Noir, at the western edge of Tierra del Fuego. He was back where he had started. Unaware of the strong currents against his ship, he had more or less treaded water. From then on, the tale becomes even more frustrating. Heading north, then sailing along the Juan Fernández latitude, he did not know whether the island stood east or west of his course because he was unable to determine the longitude. He first opted to sail west but, after four days, decided he had been mistaken and veered back east, only to reach the intractable coast of Chile, forcing him once more to reverse his direction, realizing that he had earlier been very close to Juan Fernández. As a result of these two weeks of helpless zigzagging, another eighty men died of scurvy. Anson's voyage was one of the worst disasters to strike the Royal Navy. Of the 1854 men who had sailed with him, only 188 returned.

EARLY EUROPEAN NAVIGATION

Europeans were particularly well served by their interconnecting seas and navigable rivers, and it is not surprising that from antiquity, the Mediterranean should have been the scene of intense sailing activity. Among the first recorded Mediterranean cultures, the early Egyptians, the Minoans, and particularly the Phoenicians were renowned seafarers. From their city-states of Tyre and Sidon, and the many trading posts they had established by the ninth century BCE along the northern coast of Africa (Carthage noteworthy among them), the Phoenicians had widely exported their manufactured goods, including glassware, metalware, and textiles. They were the first to cross the Strait of Gibraltar and their sailors were sought after throughout the ancient world.

They were followed by the Greeks, whose galleys spread their activities to the Black Sea, and by the Romans, who "owned" the Mediterranean as *Mare Nostrum*. All plied their trade there, waged their wars, and imposed their power.

By the tenth century, the Mediterranean maritime trade had shifted to the Byzantine Empire and the Fatimid Caliphate in Egypt, with the ports in the Levant at its centre. They were later supplanted by the powerful Italian city-states of Genoa, Pisa, Amalfi, and Venice.

Venice's particularly close and exclusive relationship with the sea was symbolized by the *sposalizio,* the union celebrated annually in great pomp. The Doge, uttering the traditional formula, "We wed thee, Adriatic, as a sign of our true and perpetual dominion," dropped into the sea a gold ring blessed by the patriarch. By the middle of the fifteenth century, the Republic of Venice operated about three thousand vessels in the Adriatic, the Aegean, and the Black Seas. However, Vasco da Gama, sailing for Portugal, discovered new routes that would eventually signal the end of the Venetian supremacy.

Further north were the Vikings and their formidable long ships. These were slender vessels, with recognizable high bows and sterns, designed for coastal waters and fjords and inspired by the efficient Celtic vessels tested on many long-distance expeditions during the Early Bronze Age. The Vikings' merchant and war ships often raided the shores of Northern Europe, and one of their vessels, the knarr, was particularly designed for oceanic navigation. With a length of sixteen metres (fifty-four feet) and a hull capable of holding 122 tons, the knarr took them to Greenland, Newfoundland, the Black Sea, and possibly to the New World in the eleventh century. The Viking culture was imbued with the sea; even their chieftain's funeral rituals prominently featured ships, as both were buried together. While it is said they oriented themselves at sea with a sun-stone, said to show directions by polarizing light, it is more likely that their navigation was based on a traditional and quasi mystical knowledge, much like the Polynesians, a people also organically attuned to the sea.

Still in northern Europe, the intense marine trade resulted in the creation of a commercial and defensive confederation of powerful independent merchant guilds from the Baltic and the North Seas, the Hanseatic League. The league, which peaked between the fifteenth and seventeenth centuries, raised its own army and its vessels were always heavily armed. By the end of the sixteenth century, it found itself in a much weaker position and, with the rise of the Swedish Empire, gradually started losing control of the Baltic.

By this time as well, some European navigators such as Columbus, Magellan, and Vasco da Gama, far away from the North Sea and the Mediterranean, had started sailing on the great oceans. They later came from Spain, Portugal, the Netherlands, France, and England, mostly driven by their desire to find other accessible routes to the riches of the Orient, and went on to chart the coasts of Africa, discover the Americas and Australia, and dispel many of the ancient myths about the shape and nature of the world. Early navigators had opened the way and, following in their wake, eighteenth-century captains—particularly James Cook—mapped the world, while their scientists and naturalists revealed its nature to Europeans. These were, among others, Joseph Banks on *Endeavour,* Philbert Commesson on *Etoile,* Georg Foster on *Resolution,* Charles Darwin on *Beagle,* Joseph Hooker on *Erebus,* and Thomas Huxley on *Rattlesnake.*

SEAFARING IN CHINA AND POLYNESIA

This rough survey of enterprising European nations using the sea as a venue for commercial and political activities includes only one aspect of humankind's sailing history. There were other great maritime civilizations beside those evolving in the West, and the Chinese and Polynesian are particularly noteworthy. Rather than attempt to describe their evolution, we will restrict ourselves to a snapshot of their status when first encountered by Europeans.

Marco Polo's descriptions revealed to Europe the coastal trade and naval power of China between the thirteenth and fifteenth centuries. There had been in the eighth century a strong competition between the Chinese port of Guanzhou and the trade localized in Annam, and China had been eager to establish her superiority by increasing territorial expansion and welcoming embassies from neighbouring provinces and states. She had developed a thriving sea trade, importing exotic woods while mostly exporting luxury items (silk, ceramics, bronze bells, and paper).

Chinese shipbuilding and navigation were ahead of other countries' achievements. Throughout Southeast Asia, ships were built with several layers of thin planks bound together by ropes made from the bark of the coconut tree, using neither nails nor clamps for fear that heated iron might cause fires. Foreign sailors had seen the more advanced Chinese hulls successfully fastened with iron as early as the eighth century, but they did not introduce iron fittings in naval construction until the sixteenth century.

The Chinese had also long known the properties of the magnetized needle and towards the end of the twelfth century started using it as compass, the needle floating in a bowl of water. Zhu Yu, a contemporary specialist of seafaring practices, described China's navigational techniques, where sailors, familiar with coastal configurations, steered by the stars at night and by the sun in daylight. They used the common sounding lead, a hundred feet of line with a hook at the end, to take samples from the sea-bottom that would help them determine their location. In dark weather, they would rely on the needle pointing south.

Marco Polo drew an arresting portrait of the sophisticated naval architecture then existing in China and of the size of her navy, far superior to anything existing in Europe. China's four-masted trading ships, propelled by both wind and oars, often had as many as sixty small cabins for merchants. Remarkably, ships already had watertight compartments as a safeguard against damaging accidents, such as hitting a large rock or being struck by a whale, as sometimes happened. Chinese ships were double planked for extra protection, and were efficiently caulked with a viscous compound of quicklime, chopped up hemp, and oil from a particular tree that adhered better and longer than the usual pitch used to seal the seams packed in oakum, as was the tradition in Europe. These ships' crews numbered between 150 and 300, could hold up to six thousand baskets of goods in their cargo space, and had as many as ten small boats on board, used for fishing, carrying anchors, and other necessary tasks. It was said they could be at sea for as long as a year.

By the fifteenth century, Emperor Zhou Chu had embarked on a shipbuilding program of unprecedented ambition and the Chinese were building larger and more numerous vessels than ever. The shipyards on the Yangtze River near Nanking were doubled in size, and seven new dry docks were added, each permitting work on three ships at once. They build 1,681 new vessels, bringing the total of the fleet to 2,800 ships, 1,350 patrol vessels, and 1,350 combat ships attached to guard stations.

The main fleet, stationed near Nanking, consisted of four hundred large warships and four hundred freighters to transport grain, as well as 250 galleons, whose average complement grew from 450 men in 1403 to 690 in 1431, reaching a thousand men in the largest vessels. Finally, there were some three thousand merchantmen as auxiliaries, together with a large number of small craft used as dispatch boats or police launches.

The figures for this impressive naval force, reflecting China's size, technical advances, and superb self-sufficiency, clearly contrast with what we know of the European fleets of the time. Unlike the combined power of the Chinese fleet, European vessels came from several nations often at war with each other. On the other hand, these nations also found their progress stimulated by their constant competition for new venues for exploration and trade.

In the South Pacific, navigators Wallis, Cook, Bligh, Bougainville, and Boenachea, together with their naturalists and artists, discovered another sophisticated maritime civilization at the end of the eighteenth century: Tahiti, her islands, and their extraordinary outrigger canoes. The culture was entirely turned towards the sea and had reached and settled distant islands, eventually spreading north to Hawaii, east to Easter Island, and south to New Zealand, the outer limits of what became known as the Polynesian Triangle. They called themselves Ma'ohi.

The construction of their double-hulled canoes was new to eighteenth-century Europeans, but even more astonishing to them was how effectively the Polynesians sailed them over vast expanses of ocean without any navigational instruments. Their navigation seemed instinctive, mystical, and poetic, and appeared guided by the winds, the currents, the birds in flight, the clouds, and the will of their gods.

The canoes were built from tree trunks and carved with stone adzes and chisels made of human bone, or from boards joined with ropes of braided coconut fiber. The sails were woven from coconut or pandanus leaves, and in calm weather oarsmen would propel the canoes. The natives of Raiatea in particular were reputed for their canoe-building skills, using for timber breadfruit trees that were impervious to salt-worms, and building them large enough to carry up to three hundred people. Two would be lashed together for long voyages, joined with crossbeams to form a deck spanning the two hulls; a small hut built on this deck would shelter precious survival goods.

The Europeans were impressed, particularly Captain Cook and Joseph Banks, but none as much as the Spanish explorer Ignacio Andia y Varela, who had observed them closely while visiting the Society Islands in 1774. He had been particularly astonished by the enormous spread of sails on such narrow outrigger canoes, which could not be lowered and furled.

The Polynesians' ability to find their way at sea, relying only on their memory and their senses, puzzled the Europeans. Adding to Cook's observations, Andia y Valera described precisely how they calculated this path without a mariner's compass by dividing the horizon into sixteen parts, using as cardinal points those where the sun rose and set. Helmsmen constantly observed the many directions of the wind (aft, either beam, on the quarter, close-hauled) and of the sea (following, head, beam, bow, or quarter). Their other cues were the paths of the land birds fishing out at sea, the changes in swell patterns, the reflection of lagoons in overland clouds, and drifting vegetation. What had seemed an incomprehensible native aptitude to the Europeans used to relying on scientific instruments was only the Polynesians' profound knowledge of their natural environment and a superb sense of observation—allied to a deep faith in the guidance of their gods. Their knowledge also enabled them to predict the weather in ways lost to Europeans. This was also noted by Andia y Valera, confirming his admiration for the skills of this great maritime nation.

THE URGE TO SAIL

The contrast could not be greater between the powerful Chinese trading fleets and the far-reaching Polynesian outrigger flotillas, forcing us to marvel at the way that people's natural propensity to head off into the unknown always leads them out to sea. We think of the Age of Exploration as the great era of expansion and discovery of new lands, but the Stone Age may have been the greater purveyor of sailors. While the Polynesians colonized the Pacific between 5,000 and 3,000 years ago, they themselves came from an older seafaring tradition from Southeast and South Central Asia. Some had sailed southward across open water to reach Australia (around 45,000 years ago) and New Guinea (around 30,000 years ago); others had gone eastward into the Pacific to Polynesia; a third group, known as the Jomon, may have eventually sailed further east to the northern American shores of the Pacific, thousands of years before the Polynesians started their own great colonizing expeditions.

With islanders, and the Polynesians in particular, the question arises whether they were impelled into the ocean by overcrowding or starvation or whether they merely responded to what historian Clive Gambler has called their heroic tradition, inspired by a worldview of discovery that honoured the founders of new colonies, particularly when they could also make the return voyage.

The need to survive may have been one of the causes for setting forth to settle new islands, but it does not preclude this heroic inspiration. Gambler argues that the rate of exploration and continued migration in Polynesia could not be explained by unusual population explosions; instead, they may have been propelled by what we might see as inspired and innate wanderlust. Our modern presence on the oceans should be viewed within the context of this worldwide expansion by sea, dating almost from the origins of humankind. It is said that we came from the sea, and it should come as no surprise that we seem almost atavistically compelled to return to it.

2 HOW CRUISING CAME TO BE

The advent of cruising can be succinctly ascribed to the end of sailing as a means of transporting passengers. The first blow came with the waning of emigration, which had filled steerage space and cheaper cabins until the 1920s. The second came with the speed and convenience of aircrafts, turned to civilian use after WWII. Seventy percent of travellers between Europe and America were already flying across the Atlantic when commercial jets cut down the flying time even further to seven hours in October 1958. At that point, reduced to carrying only about four percent of passengers and unable to compete with speed, the shipping industry turned to leisure.

PASSENGERS

Passenger ships did not really exist until the nineteenth century. Much of what we read on the early inclusion of civilians on board ships whose primary mission was, depending on the times, exploration, conquest, or trade indicates that they had to make do as best they could, often providing for their own necessities. Given the adverse conditions on board during the long months at sea (close quarters, the constant fear of scurvy, short water rations, uncouth companions, unpredictable weather, perils of every nature, pirates, the occasional threat of mutiny), few sailed for the pleasure of the adventure. A small number did, but the majority only went by sea when travelling on land was not easier or safer.

Among those who sailed were merchants accompanying their goods, employees going to trade posts, government officials journeying to the colonies, preachers, families rejoining husbands and fathers settled abroad, and so on. Long and perilous as the voyages could be, they were sometimes safer than the land routes that, moreover, would have required far more organization than embarking on a ship. By the seventeenth century, both English and Dutch Indiamen had special cabins for these few civilians.

In the eighteenth century, many non-sailors joined European ships in their exploratory voyages, including naturalists, astronomers, geographers, map makers, and artists, to whom we owe our first glimpses of the extraordinary lands, populations, fauna, flora, and rituals they discovered. They sometimes had the same accommodations as the ship's officers, but even then, none compared in comfort to what land journeys might have afforded. Traders, missionaries, officials, families travelling together, and other civilians continued to sail occasionally, but few did so exclusively for pleasure.

Today, those who casually set out to sea, often on a frivolous pretext, are part of a modern concept, one we owe mostly to two nineteenth-century entrepreneurs, Samuel Cunard and Thomas Cook, before it developed into the tentacular ramifications of modern-day cruising and tourism.

Cruising is part of a natural evolution. Between the sixteenth century's caravels to today's behemoth cruise ships, the shipping industry has expanded as much as any other field of human endeavour, with both technology and purpose undergoing massive changes. The capabilities and amenities for carrying passengers has grown from the *Mayflower* and her 152 souls on board to such floating cities as Royal Caribbean's *Oasis of the Seas,* temporary home to 6,296 cruisers and 2,165 crew members. The earlier ships' strictly utilitarian functions of transporting people and cargo have partly made way to the concept of sailing palaces idly connecting picturesque ports of call for the pleasure of their holidaying residents.

Several social, economic, and technical factors led to this relatively rapid transformation of purpose. Some relate to greater prosperity and increased human longevity in developed countries; others derive from a stronger curiosity for other cultures following two world wars when soldiers fought overseas. Conversely, some nations were also determined to benefit from the economic boon of tourism and actively opened themselves to it. Finally, having fulfilled its role in the emigration of vast groups of people to the New World, the sailing industry was left to rethink its purpose and turn to a more leisurely trade, with a focus on comfort rather than speed.

Modern technology has made voyages so much safer that passengers never think they are putting their lives in danger. The technology guiding ships' progress at sea is so advanced that most accidents are due to unaccountable factors or avoidable human errors. Among the instruments available to the modern captain and crew are the radar, Global Positioning System, echo sounder (measuring depth), two types of compass (gyro- and magnetic), electronic charts, speed logs, auto-pilot (through a combination of hydraulic, mechanical, and electrical systems), rudder angle indicator, and many others that passengers with minimal scientific background simply trust will contribute to the safety of their passage. This sentiment is often reinforced by half-listening to overly technical dinner conversations between retired U.S. navy personnel bandying about extraordinarily technical terms while nodding wisely at one another and seemingly confirming their own trust in the ship's safety.

Some technical innovations also address comfort, particularly the fin-like ship stabilizers mounted below the waterline. They were gradually introduced in the 1930s and serve to reduce the ship's lateral motion, thus also reducing seasickness. Air conditioning is also much appreciated in the tropics.

THE COOK-CUNARD CONNECTION

Typical of the way some new companies evolved is the Peninsular Steam Navigation Company, started in 1822 by a sailor, Arthur Anderson, and a businessman, Brodie McGhie Wilcox. It began sailing to Scotland and Iceland in the summer, and Spain and

Portugal all year around. Within twenty years, it was also delivering mail to Spain and Egypt and had entered the opium trade (then a legitimate enterprise). It would eventually become the P&O (Peninsular and Oriental Steam Navigation), one of the largest passenger lines, famous for its comfort in first class.

The emergence and growth of civilian sailing and tourism resulted from newly acquired leisure time for some individuals. Samuel Cunard (1787-1865) and Thomas Cook (1808-1892) dominated popular travel for many years, and their organizations still flourish into the twenty-first century. Cunard provided regular, convenient, and safe passage between Europe and America; Cook created comfortable and safe tourism for everyone in the form of organized tours.

Until then, few ordinary people had conceived the notion of taking a holiday and visiting other regions of their own country and, even less, travel abroad to satisfy their curiosity. The somewhat limited pre-Edwardian travel experience in England mostly ranged from the educated middle class travelling through Italy, guidebook in hand, to the cockney families hoping for a day by the sea, eating shrimps and whelks.

Then came successively the Industrial Revolution, the luxury of leisure, and Thomas Cook. An English lay preacher and supporter of the Temperance Movement, Cook was concerned that people might not properly use their newly acquired spare time and created the packaged tour, making purposeful travel available for the masses. He organized land excursions to the Midlands, then across the Channel to continental Europe, and finally to the United States. After the opening of the Suez Canal, he led groups of travellers to the Middle East and the Far East. Modern mass tourism was born.

The contemporary cruise industry, constantly adding new destinations to an already impressive list, is merely an evolution of this organized mode of travel, for which we should also thank Samuel Cunard, a successful Nova Scotia entrepreneur. He bid for the right to run a transatlantic mail service between the United Kingdom and North America, resulting in the creation of the British and

North-American Royal Mail Steam-Packet Company in 1839. Thus started the Cunard Steamship Company, with the *Britannia*'s maiden voyage between London and Cunard's hometown of Halifax, Nova Scotia, on July 4, 1840.

Passengers commonly travelled between Europe and North America on what were known as packet-boats, or packets. Cunard's company was reputed to provide speed and reliability, but also focused on a newly emerging trend by making passengers' comfort a priority. The popular Atlantic passages organized by Cook to visit the battlefields of the American Civil War had been made possible by the recent improvements brought to navigation and ocean travel. Fifty years earlier, the same passages had been described as "thoroughly miserable affairs," being "cramped, sick-making, with terrible food and unremitting discomfort, often fear," and sometimes lasting well over a month. However, by the 1860s, the crossing had been reduced to a mere twelve days and offered the most revolutionary amenities. Passengers could now revel in all sorts of pleasures, "playing deck games, loping around the ample decks for exercise, enjoying the gas lighting and the hot baths, attending the nightly musical entertainment in the Grand Salon, and consuming excellent food, with plenty of champagne." This was the beginning of a new era for travellers, and we recognize in the details that turned these passages into a pleasant experience all the elements modern ship lines compete to provide in ever greater variety.

THE COMPETITION

While Cunard and Cook were key players in the growth of tourism and sailing, there had been a good deal of competition in offering passages to America. In the nineteenth century, a number of liners linked Europe to America and to Australia. They had started as packet ships, mostly intended to carry mail and a few passengers. My husband John's great-aunt, Margaret Meredith, on a four-month crossing to Australia in 1894, had sailed from England on the *Macquarie*, a 1867-ton, three-masted clipper with fourteen passengers on board and limited facilities. In addition to the passengers' cabins, there were only two common rooms, the "ladies' boudoir" and the "saloon." In spite of those basic amenities, they succeeded in making the most of the voyage through sheer ingenuity and sociability, a trait we often find in the manner resourceful passengers succeeded in transforming the monotony of their voyage into lively entertainment.

Shipping companies undertook to make passages faster and more comfortable and several threatened Cunard's prevalence in the transatlantic trade, such as the White Star Line of Boston Packets that first ensured the Britain-Australia trade. Starting in Liverpool with chartered sailing ships, it acquired in 1863 its first steamship, the *Royal Standard.* The company soon went bankrupt and was bought in 1868 by Thomas Ismay for the North Atlantic service. Renamed the White Star Company, it started running between Liverpool and New York in 1871. It was heavily engaged in transporting immigrants to North America and later became famous as the owner of the *Titanic.*

During the Great Depression, both the White Star Line and the Cunard Steamship Company were in financial difficulties and merged their North Atlantic operations, becoming in 1933 the Cunard White Star Ltd. In 1953, the name reverted to the Cunard Line and some ships still sail under that name today.

In this century, a new configuration has evolved with the mergers of shipping lines and two giant companies, the Royal Caribbean International and the Carnival Corporation, dominate the cruising industry. A third player, Apollo International, recently entered the competition. The once-distinctive lines that had transported people and played an important part in business, emigration, and tourism now report to one of the three.

The Carnival Corporation now owns Cunard, Holland America, Seabourn, Costa Cruises, P & O (including the Australian branch), and Princess Cruises. The Royal Caribbean International runs its namesake the Royal Caribbean Cruise Line, Celebrity Cruises, Azamara Club Cruises, and the former Spanish operator Pullamtur.

The third, Apollo International, owns Oceania, Regent Seven Seas Cruises, and part of a Norwegian line.

These mergers result from economic and political events that put enormous pressure on the cruising market, like the attack now universally known as 9/11 and the ensuing reluctance of Americans to travel abroad, as well as the 2008-9 economic downturn. During that period, six smaller cruise lines went out of business. For the other lines, consolidation was a way to stymie competition. To avoid cutting fares below an acceptable level, companies tried to attract passengers with additional services, such as unusual shore excursions or itineraries, special deals for children, free airfare, and so on.

In North America, the impact of these two events led to a greater focus on homeland cruising along both American coasts, as well as Mexico and Central America. Catering to this trade, Fort Lauderdale is now the largest passenger port in the world.

3 TRAVEL, TOURISM, CRUISING

Seen from space, our blue planet is bathed in omnipresent sea, and we should not wonder that ships have been part of human history since restless wanderers first settled on its shores. They are so entrenched into our mythological thought that the great quests of our Western culture have taken place at sea: Noah fleeing on his Ark under God's command and seeking a new life for humanity and the animal kingdom; Jason on the great ship *Argo* on his way to Cholchis, searching for the golden fleece in the company of other heroes who fill our western mythical pantheon: Laërtes (Odysseus' father), Orpheus (the rouser of dawn), Perseus (son of Zeus and slayer of Medusa), Theseus (son of Poseidon and slayer of the Minotaure); or the Irish voyages of St Brendan and his seventeen monks and Maelduin and his seventeen companions searching across the seas for his father's murderer.

In the aftermath of the Trojan War, two other mythical voyagers sailed in the Mediterranean, Odysseus and Aenneas. The former attempted to return home to Ithaca under Athena's protection, and the latter eventually settled in Italy and augured the birth of Rome. Their narratives set down the pattern for all journeys: the tempestuous excitement of adventure, danger, seduction, betrayal, fearsome enemies, the jealous interferences and ambiguous protection of the gods (or fate), and the weary but triumphant return to land.

Thus, humankind appears to have been drawn to the sea through myth and history, and most ventures have involved ships and oceans.

We need only think of trade among coastal nations, wars, exploration and the discovery of new worlds, invasions and conquests, the search for more favourable economic and political conditions, the expansion of knowledge, and the spread of religions through crusades, pilgrimages, and overseas missions.

Today, ships are still strongly engaged in trade and war. As bulk carriers, they shift between continents most of the merchandise consumed worldwide, and they participate in intimidation tactics or actual wars as monumental aircraft carriers or atomic submarines, with all the trappings of modern navies. However, their recent transformation into pleasure craft is barely over a century old. More than a transformation, it is a revolution in the way we consider sailing as a mere offshoot of tourism—travel's more passive imitator.

THE SCOPE OF TRAVEL

We may grasp intuitively the difference between travel, tourism, and cruising, but our perception often depends on where we personally stand within this range. The Concise Oxford Dictionary defines a connection between tourism and cruising (both organized and associated with holidays, on land and at sea), while travel has a connotation of duration, is more likely to take place abroad, and does not necessarily include the notion of leisure. In other words, travel is deemed serious business and the other two frivolous enterprises, one merely deriving from the other.

Naturally, there is an implied hierarchy. "Tourists don't know where they've been. Travellers don't know where they're going," wrote Paul Theroux as he kayaked his way through Oceania, leaving no doubt about the category in which he belonged. He couldn't imagine where cruisers might fit in this succinct evaluation of travelling modes. Indeed, cruisers end up having little direct experience of the places they visit, since they seldom venture far from their ships while in port.

Consider Genghis Khan, Alexander the Great, or Napoleon. They were not concerned with studying the countryside and the populations as they crossed continents, unless such observations were pertinent to their conquests, and it is doubtful that Attila did much informed sightseeing while riding and plundering his way through most of Europe. They forged ahead and conquered or were defeated. What of Charles I of Spain who, upon becoming in 1519 Charles V of the Holy Roman Empire, visited ten times the Netherlands, nine times Germany, seven times Italy, six times Spain, not to mention England, France, and North Africa? His travels were peaceful and usually intended to acquaint himself with his subjects, so one might expect him to have been aware of his surroundings and mindful of the people's way of life.

Should we think of these men as travellers? Based on the ground covered, it would be difficult to deny them the title, but perhaps as much as the extent of the journey an interest in seeing the world enters into it. Closer to our intuitive definition of travellers, the Greek historian Herodotus (c. 480-c. 425 BCE), the Venetian merchant Marco Polo (1254-1324), and the Moroccan pilgrim Ibn Battuta (1304-1377) kept an alert watch for unusual and interesting sights, encounters, and events along the way. Ibn Battuta and Marco Polo gave overwhelming evidence of the interest they took in their surroundings, from curiosity as much as a desire to pursue the purpose their journeys, and we suspect that, even with different purposes, their curiosity, their open mind, and their keen interest would have been the same. Herodotus, interested in religion, geography, and unusual fauna, described what he had observed across the Greek world and reported what he had been told, much as travel writers do today. However, all travelled on land, only crossing water when it was necessary, because it is only on land that such opportunities occur.

Later, the European navigators—whose realm of exploration for over three centuries was the world's oceans or, more specifically, the lands within these oceans—were tasked with finding an easier and shorter route to the Orient. They also conquered the New World, converted pagan natives, and sought *terra incognita*, Australia. While they deployed their talents and endured many hardships at sea, it is on land that they realized the true purpose of their voyages, as they mapped the shores, reported on the lands and the people they encountered, relying on their naturalists and artists to classify and illustrate the new animal and vegetal species they were discovering.

Travellers were once explorers, traders, pilgrims, colonists, soldiers, and missionaries, for whom confrontations and interactions with alien cultures, languages, and religions were an intrinsic part of the journey. Most were trained to deal with the unexpected, the perilous, and what they considered the outrageous. More to the point, their journeys had other purposes than travelling for the mere sake of seeing the world, and they would have been puzzled at what today passes for travel, particularly on cruise ships.

Today's travellers are usually drawn abroad by their professions, as were the earlier ones, but with perhaps lesser goals. They are often anthropologists, scientists, journalists, travel writers, workers from humanitarian or religious organizations, documentary filmmakers, musicians and artists, scientists, and so on, often personally seeking the alien, the challenging, the incongruous.

THE GRAND TOUR AND WOMEN TRAVELLERS

It became fashionable between the seventeenth and nineteenth centuries for some Europeans with personal wealth and sufficient leisure to feel they would personally benefit from visiting parts of the world reputed for their beauty or their interest. The Grand Tour became the thing to do, and it was soon the unavoidable consequence of belonging, or wishing to belong, to a certain social class. People travelled and wrote about their journeys, stressing their exotic character. The more they travelled, the greater became their interest for the change and excitement of visiting foreign countries, and the more other people wanted to emulate them. However, those were also journeys on land, a ship being only necessary to reach new and more exotic shores.

It did not take long for this personal and self-centred form of travel to give rise to the revolutionary concept of females discovering the world on their own. For the first time, it was economically and socially possible for them to do so, leaving behind the constraints of home and hungering for the freedom they found in travel. They left on their own, faced with admirable determination anything travel would throw at them, and emerged from their journeys by far the richer and the more enlightened.

Abigail Adams, the influential wife of the second American president, reflected the contemporary opinion on these women's incongruous behaviour when she wrote, "Women... are considered as Domestick Beings... [and] the Natural tenderness and Delicacy of our Constitutions, added to the many dangers we are subject to from our Sex, renders it almost impossible for a Single Lady to travel without injury to her character." Hers and similar opinions long prevailed, in spite of the rising evidence that women could travel alone, and did so mostly unmolested.

Unlike most other early women travellers, who were "wives of" or "daughters of" (Lady Canning, Lady Brassey, Lady Franklin, or Lady Burton) or travelled with a protective brother (Emily Arden), they set forth on their own. The advantage of escorted travel was to offer a male companion's protection and a remedy against the fearsome solitude that were thought to magnify the perils encountered along the way.

However, what the solitary women enjoyed most was precisely the solitude others deemed antagonistic to the safety and comfort required of travel. Several had suffered difficult conditions at home (emotionally destructive family situations, the care of sick relatives, their own ill health, unrequited passionate love), and all found liberation in travel. It is trite, but accurate, to say that they found themselves, which was certainly not the acknowledged purpose of their quest, but became a by-product of their experience on the rough roads on which they hiked, rode, or cycled. These women certainly discovered in themselves resources that enabled them to overcome the hardships and perils of travel, and revealed their true characters, previously unchallenged at home. A few may have been animated by a missionary spirit (such as Annie Taylor in Tibet), but most were only urged on by a sense of excitement.

Many could have figured here, but the following few illustrate convincingly the transformative experience of travel. They are Isabella Bird, Gertrude Bell, Lady Richmond-Brown, Mary Kingsley, Alexandra David Néel, Luisa Jebb Wilkins, and Dervla Murphy. Separately, they visited Hawaii, the Caribbean Islands, Panama, the Rocky Mountains, Japan, Persia, Kurdistan, Tibet, China, North and South America, Turkey, Syria, Arabia, Central Africa, Baghdad, India, Nepal, Ethiopia, and other parts of the world few Europeans, and certainly fewer European women, had ever visited, and all reported on their journeys in books, diaries, or letters home.

Isabella Bird (1831-1904) wrote, "It is so like living in a new world, so free, so vital, so careless, so unfettered... No demands of any kind... above all... no conventions." Clara Fitzroy Kelly Bromley, who spent part of the year 1861 nursing a yellow fever victim in Barbados, said, "The year I spent on the other side of the Atlantic was the happiest and most peaceful of my life." Alexandra David-Néel (1868-1969), reflecting on her walk through Tibet in the depths of winter dressed as a man, explained that it had been "the most blessed existence one can dream of, and I consider as the happiest in my life when... I wandered as one of the countless tribes of Tibetan beggar pilgrims." Luisa Jebb (1845-1925), who "once did crochet work in drawing rooms," joined in a wild dance on her way to Baghdad. "The men seized me, and on we went, on and on with the hopping and turning and stamping. And soon I too was a savage, a glorious free savage under the white moon." The crochet must have been highly symbolic of feminine propriety, since Mabel Sharman Crawford wrote in 1863, "If exploring the foreign lands is not the highest end or the most useful occupation of feminine existence, it is at least more improving, as well as more amusing, than crochet."

Finally, Lady Richmond-Brown (1885-1946) put it best when asked in 1924 whether she would again travel alone under primitive conditions. She replied, "Weighing the intense thirst and burning heat, the fever and the mosquitoes, the not being able to take off clothes for days on end, even the shortage of food, I can truly say 'Yes', for I was not the same being—sex had disappeared."

There were certainly exceptions to their exultant feeling, and others were dismayed to find themselves in a brutal environment they had not anticipated when setting out to follow the fashion of the time. One Emeline Lott, travelling in Egypt in 1866, wrote about being "unaccustomed to the filthy manners, barbarous customs, and disgusting habits of all around me; deprived of every comfort by which I have always been surrounded." There is almost a sense of betrayal in her reaction to the realities of travel and having to face what she sees as another culture's abhorrent manifestations.

By the end of last century, the world discovered by these intrepid travellers had changed radically. The women who today are their counterparts in courage and determination are instead engaged in extreme sports and adventures. Women have long flown planes (Amelia Earhart, Jacky Cochrane, Jacqueline Auriol), some climb mountains, and others will no doubt explore the stars and the depths of the oceans. There are also those who focus their passion on the sea, like sailboat racers and single-handed sailors, facing extraordinary hardships and successes, usually alone. They include Isabelle Autissier, sailing solo four times around the world and declared World Sailor of the Year (Female) in 1991 by the International Sailing Foundation after completing the longest race of the BOC Challenge (later renamed Around Alone). Samantha Davies came fourth in the fiercely competitive Vendée Globe race in 2009; Anne Davison was the first woman to have completed a solo crossing of the Atlantic in 1952; and Ellen MacArthur was declared the fastest solo circumnavigator in 2005.

The remarkable thing about these pilots and sailors' exploits is that, unlike their predecessors, they no longer sought the broadening of views provided by land travel and the enrichment of meeting different populations. Instead, they chose the intense focus of solitary or near solitary flying and sailing, with the sea, sky, and wind their sole companions and antagonists. Their common link is the need to test their limits; the first in travelling to foreign countries and discovering foreign cultures, and the second in measuring themselves against foreign elements. Only the first could justifiably call themselves travellers.

THE NATURE OF TRAVEL

There may be almost as many definitions of travel as there are travellers. Some relish the discovery of unknown people, lands, languages, manners of thought, as well as the desire to unravel them. Such a definition addresses the realities of early travel when the world was mostly unexplored. By contrast, Paul Theroux remarks that merely being there and looking hard also constitutes travel. Purpose, determination, and focus with the appeal of the unknown, are for him at the root of the yen for travel. However, these could equally apply to active tourism, which is frowned upon by purist travellers.

It is also said that travel is a means of finding ourselves, which we do by first losing ourselves in other cultures and distancing ourselves from our egocentric concerns. This powerful transforming effect of travel is what we saw happening with the women travellers mentioned, even when not originally driven by a desire for personal transcendence. Other definitions are more common and evident, for instance that travel broadens the mind by exposing us to different experiences and peoples—precisely the way R. L. Stevenson felt on his way to America. "Travel is of two kinds; and this voyage of mine across the ocean combined both," he wrote. "I was not only travelling out of my country in latitude and longitude, but out of myself in diet, associates, and consideration. Part of the interest and a great deal of the amusement flowed, at least to me, from this novel situation in the world." The lively bunch of dancing and singing emigrants he met on board stood in for the travel abroad he would have equally enjoyed.

Paul Theroux also proposes an anti-escapist travel definition, appealing to those who seek the familiar wherever they go. It is less a rejection or denial of the unknown than a form of reconnection or continuity with the past. For instance, I once walked with an Englishwoman on the small dry hills outside Kamloops, in British Columbia's tumbleweed country, where we both lived at the end of our separate journeys to Canada. We stood, our eyes closed, inhaling the dryness of the land while on an imaginary return to the past, she to the odorant countryside of her childhood in India, and I to the *bled* aroma of my arid Moroccan one. Our joint experience indirectly supports Theroux's allegation that, "Travel, which is nearly always seen as an attempt to escape from the ego, is in my opinion the opposite. Nothing induces concentration or inspires memory like an alien landscape or a foreign culture. It is simply not possible (as romantics think) to lose yourself in an exotic place."

Travellers, because they sometimes feel dislocated, may indeed experience the need for reconnection. What they perhaps unknowingly seek elsewhere is often themselves in other guises. Theroux continues, "Much more likely [than losing yourself in an exotic place] is an experience of intense nostalgia, a harking back to an earlier stage of your life...But this does not happen to the exclusion of the exotic present. What makes the whole experience vivid, and sometimes thrilling, is the juxtaposition of the present and the past." Were we to adhere to this conception of travel, each trajectory would be personal, with little commonality of perception among individuals witnessing the same scene. Indeed, leaving it to nostalgic and egocentric memory to interpret sensorial perceptions, every experience would be entirely personal. Yet, people continue to travel, claiming an interest in the different, the exotic, the unique, the never encountered, and the alien for its own sake. But they cannot help telling each other, "Do you remember? It was just the same in Cairo" (or Toledo, or Gdansk, or somewhere else), their personal experience seemingly the main connection between these different places.

For others, such as anthropologist Wade Davis, the purpose of travel is being open to "the wonder of the other," being "sensitive and respectful of the differences that lend meaning to a journey." These differences may also be a cause of conflict, as Davis believes that tourists usually take along their values (however discordant) to foreign places, while travellers adopt those of the countries they visit and respect "the local spirit" as the only appropriate one. There would then be a difference of attitude between tourists and travellers, with the latter able to distance themselves from their customary manner of thinking and adopting a value-free interpretation of what they perceive—even going as far as espousing what was once foreign, and divesting themselves in so doing of their natural ethnocentricity. The tourists, on the other hand, would remain unchanged.

Adopting Davis's distinction would automatically eliminate a number of people from the travellers list, including most of the early explorers, missionaries, and settlers, who definitely lacked empathetic vision and were hell-bent on converting heathens to the true faith, pillaging their valuable resources, and destroying their civilizations. The philosophical interest in discovering the many faces of humankind (including that of the almost mythical and always elusive Noble Savage) did not really emerge in Europe until the Enlightenment and then only in those influenced by its ideals.

From a practical point of view, the real value of Davis's argument resides in distinguishing between two mindsets: seeing ourselves as spectators as we move about the world or willing to be participants to the extent allowed us. We also seem to attach a value to these two frames of mind, leading to the clear implication of a moral hierarchy between them and putting tourists well below travellers.

Tourists (and cruisers), who often find little favour among both "real" travellers and the populations they visit, should be defended at least for being indirectly blamed for the phoniness of the staged events they attend, when they would undoubtedly have preferred a more authentic cultural experience than the one presented to them. On sufferance wherever they go (for their clumsiness, their comparative wealth, their innocence, and even their good will), could tourists be the least appreciated visitors? Far from it, thanks to the fleeting presence of the even more despised cruisers, ashore and back on their ships almost in the glimpse of an eye.

CRUISING

Even in the sailing world, cruisers rate lower than those who cross the oceans as part of a journey, in spite of their similar activities. John Maxtone-Graham, an authority on sailing, offers this distinction: "On ocean crossings there is a feeling that the passenger, crew, and ship are going somewhere, not drifting around." Although he immediately springs to the defense of the charms of cruising, the unfavourable distinction is clearly made. Apparently, old Cunard hands also discriminate between "crossing" and "cruising", which, commented Simon Schama while sailing on the *Queen Mary 2*, has not prevented Cunard from having been sold to "the mother of all cruise companies," Carnival Corporation, and from ensuring that the whole day is filled with activities in accordance with the corporation's abhorrence of a vacuum.

I should now reveal my identity as a cruiser. In 2004, John and I decided to discover the Panama Canal by sailing through it. A later accident limited my ability to travel as we once did, and our cruising experience has since grown to eight months spent on Holland America's ships. From walking and hitchhiking alone through Europe in my youth to cruising the world in my old age, I have acquired a sense of the different travel modes available to people on the move. Let us consider the pros and cons of cruising when compared to them, and whether all cruises and cruisers are equal.

The Pros

Travelling at twenty, my endless concern was finding accommodations for the night, particularly since I was always short of cash and often with an insufficient grasp of the language. Even the far more experienced traveller Philip Glazebrook expressed the same concern in his adventurous *Journey to Saars*. He wrote, "What is most essential in reality for peace of mind on a journey is a watertight attitude towards your next night's lodging." Cruisers always know where they will spend the next night and assume it will continue to be watertight. Gone also is the tedium of packing with every move, best illustrated in the land equivalent of cruising, the guided coach tour, which stops each night at a different hotel. Cruisers pack, unpack, and repack only once.

Generally speaking, cruising is among the safest and most convenient manners of travel. Short of hitchhiking and living off the land and strangers' generosity, it is also among the cheapest, if the cruiser chooses the more modestly priced cabins or takes up one of the frequent sales available. Having a light meal at a café on shore reminds us how expensive it would be to pay separately for each service received on board as part of a package.

It has a number of other advantages beyond the pecuniary one. Elderly people can attest to the benefits of prompt, patient, and courteous service, often proffered with apparent kindness and respect, all for a cost similar to that of a comfortable private nursing home. Thus, it is not surprising to hear that some retired people decide to cruise most of the year. Longer stays may also engender additional benefits and prestige, from free laundry to priority boarding.

It gives lonely people a chance to mix socially and the self-confident plenty of opportunities to shine in front of captive audiences. The gourmets have seemingly sophisticated menus to pore over, while the gourmands can satisfy their appetite almost around the clock. Those who need to be continuously entertained can attend conferences, movies, Broadway-style shows, performers' acts, bingo games, cooking and other demonstrations, music recitals, Trivial Pursuit games, treasure hunts, visits to the bar and the casino, shore excursions, and so on, throughout the day and part of the night. For many, it is an artificial and controlled reconstitution of village life, enriched by the service of an attentive staff who spare them from having to perform tedious domestic tasks.

Another attraction is the casual companionship that can develop among cruisers. Having mostly been assigned to share dining-room tables with Canadians, Americans, and Australians (sometimes of various ethnic origins, but long implanted in their adopted lands), John and I have never experienced any of the culture shocks that can bring so much interest to travel, and felt instead that we were sailing with variously distant cousins. There is even an occasional connivance deriving from our common experience, as when the elderly American on our 2006 Baltic cruise told our group of Canadians and Australians with a small grimace and no necessary explanation, "I never voted for Bush!"

The Cons

Cruising is the epitome of "bubble" or "cocoon" tourism, implying much isolation from the realities of being abroad and, with little opportunity to meet local people, much ignorance of life in the countries visited. Comfortable beds, plentiful and appealing food, built-in entertainment, controlled temperature, organized tours, and all the pleasures of the resort are there, without any of the indigenous discomfort or strangeness. Ensconced on board, cruisers perform short touristic forays while in port, and then return to their ships, where they are often greeted with "Welcome home!"

Surprisingly pleading for the merits of superficial encounters, zoologist and ethologist Desmond Morris wrote what amounts to an advertisement for the cruising industry. "It's amazing how much you can learn about a country in a single day on your first visit there. Now, I only have to hear someone say the word 'Samoa' or 'Guatemala' or 'Brunei' and all kinds of vivid details resurface in my brain, even though I have spent no more than a day in each of those places." All cruisers do, and clear images also pop into my mind when I hear "Cartagena," "Gdansk," or "Nuku Hiva." However, they are nothing more than a few impressions gathered in a short time, and constitute a minimal introduction to the countries we briefly glimpse while cruising.

Unlike interested tourists, cruisers do not visit their foreign surroundings at leisure and tentatively attempt to share in the activities performed around them, eat the local food, and stay at family-run bed-and-breakfast places. The speed of shore excursions argues against any discovery, except of a superficial nature. Travel writers explain that during the eight hours spent in port on a Baltic cruise, you could "paddle a kayak on a Norwegian fjord, stroll in Copenhagen's car-free Stroget, gaze at the Rembrandts in St Petersburg's Hermitage, and walk in Lech Walesa's footsteps in the shipyards and cobblestone streets of Gdansk." It is true, in theory. On our own Baltic cruise, John and I simply ambled along in the smaller towns and, in larger cities, we would take a tourist bus in the morning to see their outlay and spot places we wanted to revisit on our own in the afternoon. We ended up with a vague sense of the place, but never felt that we had even scratched the city's surface. These visits were merely a smorgasbord of soon forgotten nibbles, rather than the satisfying feast travel could be when each dish is enjoyed at leisure. It could be described as impressionistic tourism.

The realities of travel, sometimes quite harsh, are nowhere to be found on cruise ships. Some may see this as an asset, but I do not, thus revealing my bias. Even the elements are banned from disturbing the passengers' peace as they bask in the sun beside the pools. At the first inkling of a cloudburst, the mechanical roof closes over the deck and, presto, nature has been eliminated. On a recent cruise, as we consistently faced rough seas and bad weather, the captain apologized for it and sent champagne around when he could not safely allow us to land on an island. The ocean's true nature—changing, stormy, and unpredictable—was treated as a rogue event.

Cruise Ships

Cruisers' preferences are often guided by the culture specific to certain lines. Guidebooks list the characteristics that would appeal to different passengers, sometimes disguised as counter-indications. It is then easy to sort out the fun-seekers from the quieter and (by

implication) more refined passengers. For instance, Carnival Cruise
Lines are not recommended for those "seeking a quiet cerebral
travel experience" or "who consider Martha's Vineyard their ideal
vacation spot." Potential Costa Cruise Lines passengers are warned
that these ships are not intended for people "who prefer to travel
with Americans." And how could one resist the snobbish injunctions
that Crystal Cruises ships are not for "Anyone uncomfortable with
or uninterested in sophisticated ambience," or the Cunard Line's
for "those uncomfortable with elegance, who prefer a casual or
nonstop party atmosphere." Finally, for the utmost in elegant travel,
the expensive Seabourne Cruise Line warns that their voyages are
not intended for "Those unaccustomed to luxury or a sophisticated
environment; anyone uncomfortable in a fancy restaurant or five-
star European hotel; flashy dressers; late-night revelers; inexperienced travellers; children."

Their clear bias indicates the type of cruising experience these
lines hope to provide. Whether the overt snobbery is only that of
the guidebooks' authors or relates to the ambitions of the cruise
line, the message is clear: cruising aspires to be a sophisticated experience. This picture may be attractive but the reality is different, and
a far cry from the time when cruising seemed reserved for a certain
elite able to indulge in exotic voyages. Today, the cheap deals
offered to passengers no longer require them to belong to society's
wealthy sophisticates. Instead, cruising has become a melting pot of
people trying to have a good time because that is, after all, the point.
Still, it is useful to know that some lines cater to noisy partygoers, a
characteristic they would probably depict as "fun-filled."

The Cruisers

Those people of roughly the same generation, similar in looks,
dress, and conversation, certainly seem to constitute a cohesive
group united by the superficial bonds of a cruising culture, where
every moment of life on board is organized in an apparently purposeful series of leisurely events. It often seems that merely being

on board and being taken care of at reasonable cost constitutes for them a desirable, if temporary, way of life, with only superficial attention paid to the itinerary. However, most make the distinction between cruises taken with family or friends, where the ship actually is the destination, and cruises that take them to outstanding locations worthy of all their attention.

For some, quantity seems to prevail in the retelling of their voyages, and Desmond Morris fits in well when he states, "My wife and I have become cruise addicts, making fourteen voyages in the past fifteen years and visiting more than a hundred different countries." By serious cruisers' standards, these numbers may actually be rather modest, and we should not be surprised to discover the odd case of cruising fatigue.

Such was probably the case with a passenger overheard saying that he would not bother going ashore in Helsinki, where we had anchored, because he had already done it on two previous cruises. It was also perhaps the case with the four people intently playing cards on deck, with the exotic French Polynesian vista in the background. They had done so throughout the preceding two weeks (and would continue to do so for the next three), eyes on the cards, the table, and each other, unmoved by the scenery or whatever thoughts the mythical South Seas islands could have otherwise evoked for them. Or with the two middle-aged and elegant couples familiarly exchanging desultory remarks. One woman said, "I've been everywhere in the world and I don't remember a single place." There was no response, and her words vanished into the breeze.

Even if, occasionally, the cruise is itself the experience and the journey—a form of travel where the means have almost entirely replaced the end—the cruisers' progress complies with the definition of travel, to "go from one place to another; make a journey, esp. of some length and abroad." However, the term "travel" is emotionally and intellectually endowed with a context of physical and cultural distance, intellectual quest, adventure, unusual events, freedom of movement and response, unexpected encounters, and personal discoveries of other cultures, all worth acknowledging, relating, and mulling over. In the controlled environment of a cruise, it is impossible to reach this extra dimension—assuming it was even desired. On the other hand, how could we tell someone who has twice sailed around the world that he or she has not travelled?

4 COASTAL COMMUNITIES

Coastal communities are usually ports, presuming the presence of many types of vessels, from fishing boats to pleasure crafts. Ports may also imply active trade, with much loading and unloading of merchandise. They offer sailors respite from their work and all types of entertainment. These communities usually live by and from the sea. They have also been connected with some exclusively maritime behaviours, from wrecking to rescuing.

Wrecking, a source of income in many impoverished parts of the world where it persists today, flourished as a legitimate business between the sixteenth and the nineteenth centuries. Many coast-lines, such as Denmark, Devon, Cornwall, and Brittany were so rocky that ships sometimes foundered within a short distance of shore. Salvaging was so vital to the local economy that rumours naturally spread about the forced wrecking of ships.

One of the methods reputedly used to lure ships closer to the dangerous shore was placing fake lights (signaling safe anchorage) to decoy the crews. Another, found in Nags Head, North Carolina, was to attach lanterns to mules (or nags) and make them walk back and forth on the beach to simulate the lights of anchored ships. These imaginative ways of making a living off the misery of others have apparently never been proved, even while authorized wrecking activities continued in earnest.

On the other hand, what has consistently been demonstrated is the helpful and courageous behaviour of coastal people in coming to the rescue of foundering ships or stranded passengers. There is a particularly touching scene in *David Copperfield* where Ham, a rope tied to his waist, tries to swim out in the storm to rescue a man struggling to escape from a sinking schooner, with the distraught villagers gathered on the beach. Ham knowingly risks his life and dies in the attempt.

In the same heroic spirit, Walter Pidgeon, playing Mrs. Miniver's husband in the popular film, is shown piloting his tiny pleasure craft on his way to Dunkirk and back, properly exhausted after days ferrying rescued soldiers. Between May 27 and June 4, 1940, a large number of vessels from the Navy and the Merchant Marine were involved in rescuing 338,226 Allied soldiers from the advancing German forces. They were accompanied by a disparate flotilla of small fishing boats, pleasure crafts, and speedboats, privately gathered in Ramsgate for this mission.

In 1915, when the *Lusitania* was torpedoed off the Irish coast, her lifeboats of little use, the first to arrive to the rescue were the fishing boats *Brock, Bradford, Sarba, Heron, Bluebell,* and *Flying Fish,* before the arrival of the larger tug boat *Stormock.* They rescued many from the sinking ship, even if they failed to save over eleven hundred men, women, and children.

In the tragic sinking of the Canadian Pacific *Princess Sophia* on her way from Skagway, Alaska, to Victoria, British Columbia, in October 1918, a little fleet hastily gathered in dreadful weather near Vanderbilt Reef, where the *Princess Sophia* had foundered, hoping to rescue the 353 people on board. They were the *Peterson,* a US Army harbour boat; the *Estebeth,* a mail and passenger boat from Juneau; the *Amy,* a small freight and passenger boat also from Juneau; and the small fishing boat *Lone Fisherman.* Unfortunately, they could not approach the *Princess Sophia* and all on board perished, including the twelve infants whose parents had paid $2.50 for their passage.

The most recent such incident in our own Pacific Northwest was on October 25, 2015, when the whale-watching ship MV *Leviathan* II capsized near Tofino. Local First Nations fishermen and others from Tofino immediately sailed to the rescue and succeeded in saving twenty-one of the twenty-seven people on board. As usual in such circumstances, the whole community rallied to provide warm clothes, food, and comfort.

These almost amphibian sites have a special status, as they partake both of the safety of the land and the adventure of the sea and benefit from the economic advantage of their juncture. On the other hand, they will be the first to suffer the brunt of naval invasions, bear the battering of cyclones, and respond to any emergency at sea—whether properly equipped to do so or not.

II
STYLE, SAFETY & COMFORT

Ships That Struck the Imagination

The Class System and Segregation

Yachts

Great varieties of people go to sea for an equally great variety of reasons. On earlier voyages, passengers endured exceedingly long crossings and bore the prospect of uncertain elements, chancy navigation, tight spaces, various illnesses, declining rations, inimical people, the crew's incompetence, and a host of other potentially unpleasant and life-threatening events. Today, all expect their sailing to be safe and comfortable.

Some passengers obviously enjoy far more amenities than do others. Originally, established hierarchy and the nature of the work demanded that some individuals be provided with more space and better cabins than others, thus the captain, the ship owner, or the chief merchant were given preferential quarters. As sailing evolved to include more passengers, distinctions among ranks became obvious. When commercial shipping lines started relying on paying passengers for their profits, these passengers' means and status were clearly reflected in their accommodations and in the service they received.

These differences were most evident on liners, specifically built and equipped for transporting a variety of people, from elite travellers with a full complement of servants to emigrants hoping for a better life on a new continent. Reflecting the hierarchical structure of society, their levels were formally stratified into three classes: first, second, and steerage (a term initially used on the transatlantic route and changed to third class at the turn of the twentieth century). The interaction of these disparate groups on board also merits examination, as do the utmost in sailing luxury and discrimination: the yachts.

5 SHIPS THAT STRUCK THE IMAGINATION

Two early voyages illustrate the contrast with later crossings. The passengers were persons of rank and quality, and the improvement in their travel conditions is described in two reports, written a century apart. The first was by a distinguished judge in the Spanish colonial law courts, Don Eugenio de Salazar, who sailed with his wife Doña Catalina and their children on *Nuestra Señora de los Remedios* from Recife to San Domingo in the late 1500s. He kept a running commentary throughout their crossing and, lurking in the background, we catch glimpses of lesser passengers travelling under even worse conditions. He may exaggerate a little, but his narrative tells us how he spent his time on a long voyage in a small ship with an inexperienced captain, a crew of thirty, and the most basic accommodations. He is often quoted here on food, table manners, seasickness, and boredom at sea, and constitutes an unofficial reference in matters of passengers' experience in the early days of long voyages.

This is how he describes the passengers' cabins. "The dwellings are so closed-in, dark, and evil-smelling that they seem more like burial vaults or charnel houses. The entrances to these dwellings are openings in the deck, which they call companionways or hatches, and anyone who goes through them can say goodbye to the order, the comfort, and the pleasant smells of dwellings on earth."

The second voyage is related by Captain Charles May, Master of the *Terra Nova*. The Duchess of Albermale, recently widowed, embarked on his ship in Port Royal (Jamaica) on Christmas Day

1688, about a century after Don Eugenio's crossing. Her accommodations were luxurious. She came on board with her two brothers and fifteen servants, bringing her own costly furnishings to the Great Cabin: "Rich hangings, curious chairs, large looking glasses, and all other choice goods," including "a large chest so heavy that five or six men could but just draw it along the deck, full of pigs of silver, bags of pieces of eight, and some gold." They also provided for themselves, as was the custom, and "laid in plentiful stock of all manner of provisions, as sheep, hogs, turkeys, hens, &c. with a sufficient quantity of Indian wheat, and others sorts of grain to feed them during the passage, according to all probabilities." After an epically disastrous crossing, not much of this luxury remained when the *Terra Nova* finally reached Plymouth in mid-April 1689. As the ship consistently faced violent storms, every superfluous weight (including the duchess' furniture) had to be jettisoned, while the livestock drowned.

While the *Terra Nova* and *Nuestra Señora de los Remedios* are no longer remembered, other ships have indelibly marked our memories because they were deemed to be the best of their kinds and times, because of their daunting fates, or because they are part of our history. Between 1492 and 1668, four such vessels took part in the early days of discovery, trade, and settlement, changing the known world or suffering memorable losses: the *Santa Maria,* the *Mayflower,* the *Batavia,* and the *Nonsuch.* In the twentieth century, four passenger ships became noteworthy for their technical innovations, size, luxury, or sudden and tragic ends: the *Titanic,* the *Lusitania, Normandie,* and the *Andrea Doria.*

Selecting these eight outstanding vessels does not mean others are not worthy of notice. For instance, the *Queen Mary 2,* launched in 2004, the Cunard Line's current flagship, possesses several unique features, including the largest library and ballroom at sea, and the only planetarium, and is also the last liner to accept passengers' pets on board, once a common practice. She crosses regularly between Southampton and New York, yet kowtows to today's economic pressure by offering an annual eighty-one-day cruise around the world.

However, she is not memorable in the manner of the European vessels listed, nor is the largest cruise ship so far built, which is *The Harmony of the Sea*. Size and luxury notwithstanding, they both lack the historical dimension of the others.

LA *SANTA MARIA* (wrecked in 1492)

La Santa Maria de la Inmaculada Concepción, sailing under the protection of the Virgin, formed with the *Pinta* and the *Niña* the trinity to which we owe the discovery of our New World. We know enough about contemporary shipbuilding to imagine her appearance, and many replicas have been proposed. Whereas the expedition's two other ships were the smaller caravels, the *Santa Maria* was a middling nau or carrack of some 100 to 150 tons, measuring about 75 feet (23 metres) in length, with a 20-foot beam and a draft of 6 feet. These approximate dimensions were about standard for her type and period. She had a single deck, three masts, five sails, and a round bow, with the so-called "mackerel" shape popular for long distance navigation until the seventeenth century. She carried four 90 mm-bombards and 50 mm-culebrinas (or culverins, a lighter and smaller type of cannon).

Her still enormous mainsail (their size would gradually be reduced) produced all the driving power, while the smaller lateen and foresail were mostly used for trimming. Reproductions of these ships show a great number of ropes maintaining the masts in place, with others used to handle the sails. Because of its considerable weight, the yardarm would only be lowered in cases of emergency; it would normally stay in place, supporting the main and used when the sail was furled.

The *Santa Maria* was the flagship of the expedition, captained by Columbus himself. A crew of thirty-eight, mostly from Spain, sailed with him from Genoa. Of the three, she was the one Columbus liked least, finding her "a dull-sailer and unfit for discovery." She was also ill served by luck. While Columbus was asleep, the watch officer entrusted the tiller to an untrained sailor who ran her aground off the coast of Hispaniola (Haiti) on Christmas Day, 1492. She had to be abandoned, and only seventeen of her crew survived the wreck: Columbus himself, the vessel's master and owner, the pilot, the physician, one boatswain, the comptroller, the Royal steward, Columbus's servant, a cabin boy, the converted Jew who served as interpreter, and seven sailors. By then, forty-three men from all three ships had already died. Disease was rife on long journeys, with scurvy a constant fear and deadly reality, and the conditions of life generally appalling. We might then suppose that the casualties died from an illness; however, the records indicate that most were "murdered by natives."

The level of comfort on board was even inferior to the usually dismal conditions of life on shore. According to some historians, "all the ships leaked; even with regular use of the pumps, water was constantly sloshing in the bilge, which was further fouled by the casual sanitary habits of the age." Only the master and the pilot had proper sleeping quarters, while the sailors slept on or below deck, wherever they found space, soaked to the bone in their canvas clothes. There were also roaches and rats, the latter supplementing the diet in times of starvation.

While the conditions at sea were dire for everybody, they were even worse for long-range navigators. Unlike traders and fishermen, they contended with greater distances and unknown destinations, and the consequent restrictions on food and drink. They ate dried and salted meat and fish, rice, dried peas, cheese, onions, oil, and drank water and wine, with the constant hope that landings would refresh their supplies. Later ships would be more crowded, often conveying soldiers, settlers, and merchants in addition to the crew.

The length and uncertainty of these long voyages created unrest among the crew. Columbus partly solved the problem by keeping two sets of records and forging the distances covered to allay the men's discouragement and fear at the unforeseen length of the voyage. These early ships had little entertainment to offer, apart from forbidden gambling. Sailors attended religious services, and there were often musicians on board who would entertain the company—a rather thin fare on voyages that would last for many months.

THE *MAYFLOWER* (historical voyage of 1620)

The *Mayflower* set out for the Colony of Virginia in September 1620, carrying seventy-four male and twenty-eight female passengers, among whom the English Puritans known as the Pilgrims. A companion ship, the *Speedwell,* carrying church members from Holland, sprung a leak and returned to port, leaving the *Mayflower* on her solitary course to the New World.

She was an ordinary English merchant ship, some 100 feet (30 metres) long and about 25 feet wide, her keel plunging about 12 feet below the waterline. Her captain and part owner, Christopher Jones, had sailed her as a cargo ship for many years in the Channel, the Mediterranean, and the Baltic, but never across the Atlantic. His crew of either thirty or fifty (numbers vary with the reports) included the master and pilot John Clarke, who had previously sailed in the Caribbean; three master's mates; the recently qualified barber-surgeon, Giles Heale; a cooper, in charge of the hogsheads, the ship's barrels holding food and drink; four quartermasters, the carpenter, the cook, and the master gunner. The boatswain, in charge of the riggings and sails and of the crew "before the mast," was known to be "a proud young man who would often curse and scoff at the passengers, but when he grew weak they had compassion on him and helped him." He died during the first deadly winter, when they remained anchored assisting the passengers as they settled in. She returned to England in April 1621 after suffering great loss of life.

The passengers consisted of Pilgrims, members of the Leiden Congregation from Holland with their servants, and a number of other people who merely intended to settle in the new colony with their own servants. Thomas Weston, of London Merchant Adventurers, had recruited them and organized the joint crossing to America.

The first group already had a history of emigration. A Puritan sect from the English town of Scrooby, the Separatists had gone to Leiden, Holland, in 1607 seeking a more welcoming environment. Others joined them, but employment was scarce in Holland, and their children were forgetting the English language and culture. They decided to leave for America, where they could find work and worship freely, and where their children would once more live in an English environment. This group included several families with their children, often escorting other relatives. There were also three childless couples, three men with their sons, and a handful of single men. Among the thirteen servants listed, five were children between the ages of four and eleven. Four of these were of the same family and had been entrusted to Thomas Weston, who had in turn assigned them as indentured servants to Pilgrim families. Two of them would die during the first winter.

The second group included five families, with twelve children altogether (one born at sea); eight single man; and three couples, among them Rose and Myles Standish (Myles, hired as military advisor for the new colony, remained a man of eminent standing until his death in 1656). All were from England, as were the six servants they brought along.

The three-masted *Mayflower* had three levels: the main and gun decks, and the cargo hold. At opposite ends of the ship stood two high constructions: the forecastle with the kitchen and stores, and the poop house with the captain and master's living quarters and below it the cabin where the crew took turns sleeping. These superstructures, built for the benefit of the crew, rendered the ship difficult to maneuver when sailing against the wind.

On the steerage room deck stood the helmsman, unable to see the sail from this position and taking directions from a man above him on deck. He used a vertical stick called a whipstaff that was attached to the tiller to gain leverage, since no man would be able to steer manually in bad weather. Below were the gun deck, about eighty feet (twenty-four metres) in length and the gun room, which contained all the ammunitions and supplies for the cannons and guns, and was off limits to the passengers. The remaining part of this gun deck, also known as the "tween" deck because of its location between the upper deck and the cargo hold below, was mostly reserved for the 102 Pilgrims; its available space has been estimated as being roughly 58 feet by 24 feet (17 by 7 metres) at the widest part.

To promote a sense of privacy during the sixty-six days of the voyage, they built flimsy divisions to create little cabins. The ceiling was only about five and a half feet high (around 1.65 metres) and many passengers must have been unable to straighten up properly. In good weather when they would not get in the sailors' way, they would go on the upper deck, reached by a ladder passing through the gratings. The facilities were basic, with neither latrine nor privy. The crew faced the elements, as was customary, and in lieu of chamber pots the passengers used buckets affixed to the deck to prevent spillage.

A number of hatches provided access to the cargo hold below, where the passengers stored all their supplies (food, drink, tools, personal effects, weapons, and the equipment and utensils required for their new homes) and a thirty-foot single-sail boat to be reassembled upon arrival. They had also brought along small livestock (sheep, goats, and poultry) and a few animals of company, including two dogs, a few cats, and birds. The large cattle would come later.

By all accounts, the voyage was miserable. Huge waves crashed against the top deck, until finally a structural piece of timber broke. Thanks to the equipment they had brought to build their future homes, the passengers were able to assist the ship's carpenter in making the repairs. They passed the time reading or playing cards and games, and the women prepared the meals using a firebox resting on a tray filled with sand. The diet was poor, with no fresh vegetables and fruit, and it did not take long before several suffered from scurvy. Two died before arriving, and a good many would not survive the first winter.

THE *BATAVIA* (launched and shipwrecked, 1628)

The *Batavia*, sailing from the Dutch Republic to the Indies in 1628, was unparalleled in her days—something that would also be said of the *Titanic* and *Normandie.* Displacing 1,200 tons and measuring 160 feet (almost forty-nine metres), she had four decks, three masts, and carried thirty guns. A flagship of the United East India Company *(Verenigde Oost-indische Compagnie: VOC),* she was known as a *retourschip,* built to carry passengers and cargo to and from the Indies.

She featured outstanding protection against the elements and shipworm, with her thick double hull lined with waterproof tarred horsehair and a third outer layer of pine. Her hull was further studded with thick iron nails and coated with a mixture of resin, sulfur, oil, and lime used as repellent. Several hundred hides of cattle tacked onto the pine hull protected the waterline. She could carry six hundred tons of supplies and trade goods.

The best quarters were naturally reserved for senior people among the *VOC* agents and the merchants travelling with their goods. The Great Cabin on the upper deck, the largest room on the ship, had good lighting and a long table for twenty people, used for the senior officers and merchants' meals and for transacting their daily business. The other merchants were lodged in a number of smaller and more spartan cabins on the deck above. The officers' quarters were located in the stern, while the junior officers and *VOC* clerks shared a cabin below the steerman's station. These quarters had no heating, little ventilation, and were no wider than "the span of a woman's arms." On the other hand, they contained unusual luxuries, such as bunks (rather than the more common sleeping mats), a writing desk and chair, and cabin boys to bring in meals and take away chamber pots.

The further they progressed towards the bow, the more primitive the quarters became, although exception was made for those who were not expected to stand watch or work at night, including surgeons, sail makers, carpenters, and cooks. They occupied more spacious berths on the gun deck. The situation was different for the ordinary seamen and the soldiers, who were confined separately when not at work. Their segregation served two purposes. The first was to reinforce the difference of status between officers and men and to guard against mutiny; ordinary seamen were relegated "before the mast" and the officers' quarters in the stern were fortified. The second objective was to separate the Dutch sailors and the German soldiers, notorious for not getting along.

The soldiers were particularly ill favoured, living in dreadful conditions two decks below the orlop—known as "cow decks" on Dutch ships, and part of the hold. It was too close to the water line to allow for vents or portholes, and the roof was so low that the men could not stand straight. Soldiers were often confined to these dark airless quarters, except for two thirty-minute periods a day, when they were brought up under escort for a taste or fresh air and to relieve themselves.

On the *Batavia*'s maiden and final voyage were some special passengers: a preacher, with his wife, their seven children, and their maid, and a young woman on her way to joining her husband in the East. These passengers complicated the usual assignation of living quarters, and they were lodged in the cabins usually reserved for the *VOC* merchants and employees.

Doomed by a chaotic fate of shipwreck and murderous assaults, the passage became a dreadful ordeal, rather than the customary, if arduous, voyage it would normally have been. The *Batavia*'s fate will figure again in our section on mutineers. Suffice it to say that there had been twenty women and eighteen children among the passengers, but only two children and seven women safely reached Batavia, the other twenty-nine having either been killed by the mutineers or died of thirst or illness on shore. Of the men, both *VOC* personnel and soldiers, it is estimated that 110-120 were killed by the mutineers, 82 died from illness or drinking seawater, or drowned trying to swim ashore. The *Batavia*'s wreck was discovered in 1963, renewing interest in a long forgotten story that dominated public opinion in the seventeenth century.

THE *NONSUCH* (voyage of 1668)

The voyage of the *Nonsuch* helped create the Canada we know today. A British ketch, probably intended for coastal trade or short crossings to Western European ports, she was chosen to sail to the Arctic Ocean because she could easily be hauled on shore to avoid the crushing ice of winter. Smaller than the *Santa Maria* and the *Mayflower*, she was a mere fifteen feet wide, measuring only thirty-seven feet on the keel, with an overall hull length of fifty feet (fifteen metres). She had two masts, a tall main and a mizzen, both with square sails. In peacetime, her crew was usually twelve, which was doubled in wartime, and she carried six small cannons.

She had a checkered career before she sailed for Hudson Bay in 1668: a merchant ship, probably built in 1650, later bought by the Navy, captured by the Dutch, recaptured by the Navy, then sold to a merchant who, in turn, sold her to a group headed by Sir William Warren, who was interested in exploring the possibility of opening the Canadian fur trade. On board for this expedition were Captain Gillam of Boston and Médard Chouart des Groseillers, explorer and trader with Hudson's Bay who had been put in charge of selecting anchorage, setting up a fort on shore, trading with the Indians, collecting samples of minerals, and seeking information about potential routes from the bay to the Pacific. The crew consisted of two mates, a French surgeon, and seven or eight seamen.

Their fare was the usual hard biscuits and bread, dried peas and oatmeal, and pigs half the size of their modern counterparts. Other provisions included raisins and prunes, sugar and spice, malt, oil, vinegar, lemon juice, and "small beer" for the crew. There was as well some brandy, intended for trading with the Indians—the Cree being by then acquainted with it.

Forty-four days after sailing from the Faroe Islands, the *Nonsuch* arrived on August 1, 1668, in Labrador, off Resolution Island in the mouth of Hudson Strait. Under Groseillers' direction, Captain Warren then proceeded farther into Hudson Bay, passing through Belcher Islands and to the south end of James Bay, having difficulty navigating among the shoals and islands. By the end of August, the weather had turned and they decided to haul the ship from the water at a place the Indians had shown them and build a cabin there to spend the winter months.

In April 1669, having successfully spent their time establishing good trading relations with the Indians (furs for goods and *wampum*), they also succeeded in negotiating a treaty and purchasing the land from them. In June, they were ready for their return journey, their hold full of prize beaver pelts. They returned after fifteen months, having substantially profited from the adventure. The investors in the project received on May 2, 1670, their charter as "Governor [Prince Rupert, King Charles II's cousin] and Company of Adventurers of England," trading into Hudson's Bay. The company's charter made them "the true and absolute Lordes and Proprietors" of 1,400,000 square miles within what was to become Canada.

A replica of the *Nonsuch* was built in 1967 to celebrate the Company's three hundredth anniversary, following the original method and using the same materials: solid English oak, hand sewn sails from navy flax canvas, hemp ropes for riggings, oakum caulking. She sailed for four years to various parts of the world before being donated by Hudson's Bay Company to the Province of Manitoba, unfortunately as far away from any ocean as she could possibly rest.

THE *TITANIC* (launched and sunk in 1912)

The White Star Line's *Titanic* ("unsinkable" and "Queen of the Ocean") was not a ship expressly built for speed. Rather, she boasted her safety, technical advances, comfort, and luxurious appointments. She struck an impressive profile with her size (an imposing 546 feet or 166 metres in length), her four chimneys (the fourth only there for aesthetic reasons), and her nine decks. With an emphasis on luxury, the ship was designed to provide for 833 passengers in first class, 614 in second, and 1,006 in third. Thankfully, on that fatal maiden voyage, the numbers were much lower, with only 325 first-class passengers, 277 in second, 706 in third, 908 crew members, and 8 musicians. While some 1,520 lives were lost on April 15, 1912, the number could have been much higher.

A tour of the *Titanic* from top to bottom reveals a clear division of the classes, determined by horizontal levels, vertical partitions, and some two thousand dollars' difference in fares (about $50,000 today) between the extremes. At the top, on the Boat Deck, were twenty lifeboats as well as the first-class gymnasium, equipped with the latest exercise machines. Below, the Promenade Deck was exclusively reserved for first-class passengers and contained their cabins, lounge, smoking room, and reading room.

On the Bridge Deck below were six luxurious staterooms with their own promenade, and two restaurants reserved for first-class passengers, "A la Carte" and the "Café Parisien." On this deck as well were the second-class smoking room and, towards the stern and separated from it, the 106 foot-long Poop Deck, which was reserved as a promenade for third-class passengers, where many of them stood as the ship sank.

The Middle Deck was for second- and third-class cabins, together with compartments for the crew, the third-class dining room, and the swimming pool and Turkish baths exclusively frequented by first-class passengers. Finally, in the Orlop Decks and Tank Top at the inner bottom of the ship's hull were located the boilers, engines, turbines, electric generators, and cargo spaces.

The ship was subdivided into sixteen compartments, themselves divided by fifteen bulkheads. Moreover, eleven watertight doors could seal the different compartments in case of emergency. They worked only too well in the end.

The fashion was then to decorate transatlantic liners with a rather heavy hand, and reproduce for them the atmosphere of an English manor house. The *Titanic* went against the grain and adapted to the ship's physical constraints the style of grand hotels, particularly the Ritz, the reference point for all that European hotels could offer in comfort, elegance, and sophistication. Each suite and first-class cabin was decorated in a variety of styles (Renaissance, Victorian,

Bourbon, Jacobean, Georgian, Tudor, Regency, Old Dutch, etc.), and most of them were equipped with a cozy fireplace. The different styles also partly extended to second-class cabins. The intention was to recreate the mood and style of a palace. Ladies in first class had their own reading and writing room, while gentlemen could enjoy their private smoking room. There were elegantly appointed restaurants, and the ship's best-known feature was the majestic Grand Stairway.

Each suite had its bathroom, but first- and second-class cabins had to share them. In third class, there was only one common bathroom for men and one for women, but many cabins were equipped with a washbasin, an uncommon luxury in 1912. Indeed, the *Titanic* and other White Star Line were known to have improved their lower-class accommodations and, whereas most other ships only offered dormitory-style sleeping arrangements in third class, the line provided separate cabins for two to ten passengers. The sexes were still segregated, with single men's cabins located at one end of the ship, while single women, couples, and families stayed at the other end.

Naturally, the fares reflected these differences in comfort. The 357 first class well-appointed accommodations were about £900 ($93,400 today) for a parlour suite and £150 ($15,500) for a stateroom; the fare for the 674 second class cabins £70 ($7,250), and passage for 1,026 in third class around £8 ($830). As a means of comparison, the charge for the first-class passengers' dogs was around £2 ($207).

No official list of passengers on the *Titanic*'s inaugural voyage has survived, apart from those occupying the suites and first-class cabins. These were mainly British aristocrats and American millionaires and socialites, with their servants and children's nurses in attendance and their dogs in the kennels. Their names filled Debrett's *Peerage and Baronetage* and the American *Who's Who,* and their loss had enormous consequences on both sides of the Atlantic.

Travelling in second class was the usual assortment of middle-class English and American families, members of the clergy, some academics, and ordinary tourists. They too had their own library and had access to an enclosed promenade. The musicians, whose memory lives on in books and films, were also located in second class.

Finally, in third class, were emigrants from all over the world, travelling alone or in groups, as well as wives and children rejoining in America their husbands and fathers, no doubt rejoicing at having secured more comfortable accommodations than were available on other ships.

The tragic endings of the *Titanic* and the *Lusitania* will figure in a later chapter of this book.

The *LUSITANIA* (launched 1907, torpedoed 1915)

For the *Lusitania*, another luxury Cunard ship, the decorators had also done away with the fussy old-fashioned décor and had chosen a more modern Georgian elegance, giving passengers the impression they were staying in a first-class hotel, such as Ritz or the Waldorf Astoria. While the Saloon cabin and suites were particularly elegant and comfortable, even ordinary cabins for one or two passengers were richly carpeted, contained mahogany wardrobes and desks, with thick eiderdowns on the beds. All had electric fans, individual heating, and basins with running water. Even when privacy could not be assured, shared bathrooms and lavatories were adequate, with a comfort not usually found on ships. On the ship's last voyage, there were 290 passengers in First and Saloon Class.

Second Class was also quite comfortable, with cabins for four, a men's smoking room, and a ladies' library available on Promenade Deck B. Their dining room was furnished with long tables and fixed swivel chairs, and offered two sittings. On her last voyage, there were 601 Second Class passengers.

Third Class cabins were plain, but more comfortable and spacious than on other ships of the day. There were a Ladies' Room and a Men's Smoking-Room, as well as access to a sheltered deck between these two rooms. The first to board because they were accompanied by so many children, these passengers numbered 373 in May 1915.

The costs naturally reflected their respective levels of comfort and luxury. The one-way passage for the two Regal Suites fetched about $2,250 ($56,250 today), the Parlour Suites approximately $1,500 ($37,500), while a typical First Class fare began at roughly $1,150 ($28,750), and a Second Class at $70, reduced for this voyage to $50, ($1,250).

NORMANDIE (launched 1935, sunk 1942).

Normandie was variously called *"le Ritz-sur-mer,"* "the ship of lights," *"la bête flottante,"* or even *"le plus grand bateau monté aux contribuables,"* which, thanks to the pun on the word *bateau,* could be translated as either "the largest ship paid for by taxpayers" or "the largest hoax mounted against taxpayers." Maxtone-Graham, an authority on ocean liners, saw her as the quintessential vessel of this type: "beautiful, fast, huge interiors, the likes of which have never been duplicated, stunning décor."

From the start, she had been conceived as the most luxurious ship in the world, and no expense had been spared to make her so. Passengers embarked at the Paris Gare St. Lazare on one of the three trains taking them directly to the Gare Maritime of Le Hâvre, specially built for the inauguration of *Normandie*. On board, there was glass by Lalique (particularly the sumptuous torchière in the Dining Salon), Pierre Patou, Henri Pacaud; decoration by Jules Leleu, a recognized master of the Art Deco period; Aubusson tapestries; and only the most precious woods were used for the furniture. She was intended to be a floating museum celebrating French art and craftsmanship. Particularly noteworthy was the Grand Salon, a large gallery, ten metres high and suitable for dancing. Many thought *Normandie* the most beautiful vessel in the world, and she remains the most powerful steam turbo-electric propelled liner ever built.

The kitchens were presided over by Chef Gaston Magrin (whose salary was reputed to be the same as the ship's captain) and the menu offered over seventy dishes to the seven hundred passengers who could dine at a single sitting. For her maiden voyage in May1935, many personalities were among her 1,216 passengers, such as Colette, Hemingway, Saint-Exupery (who was yet to write *Le Petit Prince* and spent the crossing shooting clay pigeons), and Jean de Brunhoff (Babar's creator). *Normandie* crossed in four days and three hours at a speed of thirty knots and, rivalling the *Queen Mary*, won the famous Blue Riband rewarding the fastest ship on the North Atlantic run.

The machine room caused much admiration and the writer Blaise Cendrars spent most of the crossing there. However, not everything was perfect on board and in 1937, the propellers had to be replaced. They created such a vibration that a caustic British journalist wrote, "*Normandie* was so well built that the barman did not even have to use his cocktail shaker."

Most ships offered a majority of accessibly priced cabins, but on *Normandie* the focus was on the luxury accommodations. There were four suites, each with a sitting room, a private dining room, four bedrooms, and a terrace, at a cost of $1,400 ($25,000 today). Next came 848 large first class suites, with access to a covered swimming pool, a sun deck for tennis and golf, a shuffle board, and a modern sauna and bar. The 665 second-class or "tourist class" cabins had fewer amenities but the passengers still had access to a smaller open air pool. Finally, third-class cabins only numbered 458 with more limited facilities but reasonably good standards. Dogs travelled for $20 ($350) and cats for a modest $5 ($90).

New Yorkers would long remember her tragic end on February 9, 1942. Coming two months after the attack on Pearl Harbor, the inferno ignited on *Normandie* was immediately attributed to sabotage. We should remember the political context of the time, and the sequence of events. When *Normandie* left France in August 23, 1939, for her 138th crossing, Europe was still officially at peace. After England and France declared war on Germany, the ship remained in New York, docked at Pier 88, specially built for her. In June 1940, France surrendered and her new Vichy collaborationist government seemed friendly to Nazi Germany and Fascist Italy and, as such, a potential enemy should America also enter the war. After the decisive attack on Pearl Harbor on December 7, 1941, the United States declared war on the Axis. *Normandie*, still docked in New York and a valuable spoil of war for the Americans, was seized on December 16, 1941.

The luxurious and fast ship had an obvious part to play in the conflict as an invaluable troop transport. She was renamed USS *Lafayette*, her 113 French crewmen were confined to the Seamen's House and the YMCA in New York, and the intensive work on her reconversion began. With the prospect of conveying ten thousand soldiers and their equipment to the European front, the wonderful Art Deco embellishments had to be removed to create space and lighten the weight of the ship. The plans called for artillery pieces on the upper deck, and anti-air guns and heavy machine guns throughout the other decks. The plans also called for an unrealistic two-month completion date for the work, hence the intensive rate of the conversion. The labour force of two thousand was mostly composed of recent immigrants from Europe, whose allegiances were unknown and always suspect in this climate of conflict.

The official version of the accident, to which we will adhere, although others were raised, is that on February 9, 1942, at around 2:30 p.m., a workman soldering and dismantling a large chandelier in the Grand Salon sent a spark onto a pile of kapok-filled life jackets. The highly inflammable material immediately caught fire and when all available New York firetrucks and fireboats reached the ship, the inferno had become incontrollable. The immediate concern was to prevent the fire from spreading to the pier and the adjacent buildings, and six thousand tons of water were poured over the ship. This immense weight, restricted by the ship's configuration mostly to one side of the upper decks, caused her to capsize. Unlike many nautical victims of fire, water eventually destroyed *Normandie*.

THE *ANDREA DORIA* (launched 1951, sunk 1956)

On July 25, 1956, newspaper headlines read, "2 Liners Crash off Nantucket; Andrea Doria Abandoned; Hundred are Picked up; Stockholm's Bow Crushed; Fog Hampers Rescue; Over 2500 Passengers on Stricken Vessels."

Unlike many shipwrecks, the loss of life was relatively low at forty-two from both ships. However, the advances of technology should have prevented a collision in the fog. The *Andrea Doria* boasted the most recent navigational aids, including two radars, and the most modern ship building techniques, surpassing even the specifications of the 1948 Convention for the Safety of Life at Sea (SOLAS). With her double hull, she was deemed to be among the safest ships afloat and had also been dubbed unsinkable.

From the time the *Stockholm*'s prow rammed her, both ships going full speed ahead, it took her eleven hours to submerge, permitting the rescue of all who had survived the impact. Flying over the ship, the CBS correspondent Douglas Edwards reported her final moments. "There below, on glasslike water, water strewn with wreckage and oil, was the *Andrea Doria*, listing at a 45-degree angle and taking water by the minute... A few minutes past ten o'clock... the ship's list was at 50 degrees. Her funnels were taking water... the boiling green foam increasing... Three minutes later, the *Andrea Doria* settled gracefully below the smooth Atlantic—a terrible sight to see.... At 10:19, it was all over, the *Andrea Doria* was gone."

Built soon after Italy's defeat in WWII, the *Andrea Doria* had helped restore the country's national pride. Rather than aspire to be the largest or the fastest ship in the world (records held by the *Queen Elizabeth* and the *United State*, respectively), she was designed for luxury by the modernist architect Giulio Minelotti. She was deemed as elegant and well-appointed as *Normandie*, the *Queen Eizabeth,* and the *Queen Mary*, and was particularly known for her artwork and décor.

Her length was 700 feet (213 metres), her beam 90 feet, her tonnage 29,100, and she was powered by steam turbines, achieving speeds between 23 and 26 knots. Usually sailing in the clement weather of the southern Atlantic, she had three swimming pools for passengers in all classes—the third now renamed tourist. She was known for the safety of her construction (a double hull divided into eleven watertight compartments) and had enough lifeboats for all passengers and crew. However, there were problems with her stability as she tended to list when hit sideways, particularly at the end of voyages when the fuel tanks were nearly empty.

She was making her hundredth crossing, with 190 passengers in first class (notably two Hollywood actresses, Ruth Roman and Betsy Drake, the mayor of Philadelphia, and the song writer Mike Stoller), 267 in cabin class, and 677 in tourist class, and a crew of 572 when tragedy struck. Travelling in heavy fog fairly close to the coast of Nantucket, she collided with a smaller Swedish liner, severely damaging the *Stockholm*'s bow.

Several factors probably contributed to this tragedy, including the heavy fog in a busy shipping corridor, the colliding course of the two vessels, the Swedish ship captain's ignorance of weather conditions ahead, a possible misreading of the radar, and other errors from both ships. Nevertheless, it was puzzling that two ships equipped with modern instruments did not avoid each other in the fog. The succession of events still remains uncertain, as there was no trial, and neither the settlement between the two shipping companies nor the attribution of responsibility for the collision were made public.

Why did the seriously damaged *Stockholm* keep afloat while the Italian ship sank? She had first capsized. Shipbuilders had not considered the possibility of leaks above deck after a collision, as happened on the *Andrea Doria*. The *Stockholm*'s bow penetrated and flooded the *Andrea Doria*'s deep starboard fuel tanks, located above her double bottom. The crew attempted to counteract the initial list by pumping ballast water into the port tanks, suddenly flooding some five hundred tons of water into the ship's ruptured tanks. Because of her initial list, the centre of gravity of the port tanks was higher than on starboard, and the crew's efforts had the opposite effect, causing her to list immediately some twenty degrees to starboard.

Luckily, it took the vessel so long to sink that rescuers were able to save everyone, apart from the thirty-seven passengers who had died at the point of impact. The *Stockholm*'s bow had penetrated through five passenger decks, affecting all ships levels. In first class, six passengers lost their lives, but lower in tourist class, the casualties were greater and thirty-one people, mostly immigrants, died. On the *Stockholm*, five of the crew were killed in the collision.

The decision to abandon ship was made within half an hour of the impact. When the crew started lowering the lifeboats, they discovered that those on the port side were inaccessible because of the ship's list and could only be reached with rope ladders or by using fishing nets to catch passengers. There were a few lapses, and the crew of the *Stockholm,* assisting in the rescue, were surprised to see the *Andrea Doria*'s first three lifeboats filled with Italian stewards and waiters. On the other hand, the officers and sailors showed great efficiency in their evacuation operations.

Other ships rushed to the scene, notably the *Ile de France,* arriving only three hours after the collision and sending her lifeboats to fetch passengers. By then, the fog had cleared and the rescuers could approach the damaged ships safely. The final low number of casualties came as a great relief, considering the usual heavy losses in such accidents.

All the vessels considered in this section had unique features, related to the circumstances and purposes of their times. Whether they sought to explore, provide basic passage on perilous routes, meet the demand of massive emigration, or afford luxurious crossing to a social and financial elite, ship owners and captains tried to adapt to the requirements of their era. The same vessels often provided passage to very different classes of individuals and it is worth examining their interconnections.

6   THE CLASS SYSTEM AND SEGREGATION

It would be tempting to see the class system prevalent on steamships as merely reflective of the intrinsic snobbery of the times. However, it resulted from sound business practices and the ship owners' decision to provide accommodations adapted to every purse. From the wealthy in their luxury suites, to those seeking modest comfort and privacy in their second-class cabins, to penurious immigrants occupying dormitories in steerage, everyone could cross the oceans according to their means.

The word *steerage*, lowest within the shipboard hierarchy, refers to some cheap berths' location near the noisy steering mechanism, with the quieter mid-ship section reserved for cabin passengers. Similarly, the word *posh* reflects the extra comfort provided to the more expensive cabins' occupants; the acronym P.O.S.H. was stamped on VIPs' tickets and meant that these privileged people enjoyed shady cabins on their passage to and from India: **P**ort side on the way **O**ut, **S**tarboard side coming **H**ome. However, some locations were misguided, such as the higher decks reserved for the most expensive staterooms, since this elevated location caused a higher pitch and more pronounced rolling from side to side in bad weather.

Generally speaking, each class corresponded to clear-cut variations in economic conditions and reflected different levels of elegance and comfort. However, while first class ensured the best accommodations on board, second class and steerage could vary a great deal in the amenities afforded to passengers, even on ships of the same line.

The *Titanic* illustrated almost to perfection the stratification of Edwardian society by replicating it through her construction, and rigidly enforcing the rules separating the liner's three levels. The vertical partitions on the ship meant that, while different classes of passengers used the same deck, they were actually separated from each other. For instance, on the Saloon Deck could be found the first-class Reception Room and Dining Saloon, the second-class Dining Saloon, as well as cabins in all three classes, yet there was no real connection between these various sections. On the Upper Deck, mostly reserved for cabins, all three classes had their quarters in different parts. Since it had the longest corridors, first-class passengers often walked their dogs there, passing the third-class cabins to whose occupants they usually had nothing to say.

The public spaces and the decks were not extensive on most ships, considering the numbers of passengers, so how strict was the segregation among the classes, other than inherent to the ship's construction? Normally, first-class passengers could go wherever they pleased, second-class passengers could only visit the third class, and those in third class were confined to their quarters. R.L. Stevenson, sailing to America on the *Devonia* in 1879 in pursuit of Fanny Osbourne, his future wife, described the visit paid by first-class passengers to the steerage quarters, "picking their way with little gracious titters of indulgence, and a Lady Bountiful air about nothing. It was astonishing what insults these people managed to convey by their presence."

These restrictions of movement among the three classes existed on almost every ship, with some lines well known for enforcing them. However, there were some exceptions to this rule, particularly the one ensuring that first-class passengers need not be forced to encounter their lesser co-travellers. Christadelphian author Robert Roberts, sailing from Sydney to San Francisco in 1898 on an American ship, the *Alameda,* was struck by some differences with English ships. The head steward even told him, "We have no red tape here." What Roberts had experienced on English ships was "a rigid adherence to System, from which one finds it difficult to depart." He was pleasantly surprised to see that on American ships, "there is no hard and fast line between the classes that exists on English vessels," although he admitted that, while "in theory, the Americans are all one class, in practice 'birds of a feather' flock together. Still, it is not the awful sacrilege that is on board an English ship if one of the steerage people should be found straying beyond the limits." However, in spite of having seemingly done away with the strict barriers and boundaries of English ships, there was little actual intermixing of the classes on board the American ships (no more than would have occurred on land in the American society of the 1890s).

The relaxing of the draconian discipline on board some ships appealed to Rudyard Kipling, who had travelled on both the P&O and the British India Lines. "Give me the freedom and cockroaches of the British India, where we dined on deck, altered the hours of the meals by plebiscite, and were lords of all we saw. You know the chain-gang regulations of the P&O: how you must approach the captain standing on your head with your feet waving reverently."

What did first-class passengers discover on their sightseeing tours of steerage, or even second class? We have descriptions that throw a more personal light on the travellers' experience than do ship plans and official reports. William Morris, on the *Moravia* in 1874, a ship mostly carrying emigrants to Canada (79 first class cabins, 52 intermediate, nearly 850 spaces in steerage), found the men in steerage sleeping "in hammocks over the table on which their food was served." Most of the cabins had two berths, but some had four "trays or shelves." To prevent the occupants of these shelves from falling off in their sleep, they were enclosed by a foot-deep board. Some cabins were far more commodious and included some proper furniture. They were "a square space of about ten feet, boxed off and lighted either by a small round porthole or a piece of glass let into the roof" and contained "a sofa or lounger, a washstand and a looking glass." Morris appreciated these small luxuries.

R. L. Stevenson described the steerage spaces he often visited on the *Devonia,* as "a triangular section lined with eight pens of sixteen bunks each double tiered... At night, the place is lit with two lanterns, one on each table. From all around the dark bunks, the scarcely human noises of the sick joined into a kind of farmyard chorus... The stench was atrocious." He also noted how the various sounds made by the steerage passengers ("the rattle of tin dishes as they sit at meals, the varied accents in which they converse, the crying of their children terrified by this new experience") penetrated though the thin partitions of his own second-class cabin.

There often seemed to be little difference between the two. The fare was six guineas for steerage and eight for second-class cabins, but since steerage passengers had to provide their own dishes and supply their own bedding, the difference between them seems more symbolic than real. The food in both sections (dinner of soup, roast beef, and potatoes) was much the same, although the potatoes in second class were rumoured to be of a superior brand, according to Stevenson.

If curiosity might drive privileged passengers to go slumming, this was not the case for those travelling second-class, many barely issued from the emigrant class themselves. Annie McPherson, in cabin class on the *Moravia,* describes her fellow passengers as "mercantile men going out or returning home on business, ... families, including a plentiful supply of children, ... a few married couples going out to start new homes for themselves in Canada," as well as young men who, "having established themselves there have returned to their old sweethearts in England, and are now taking them out as their wives." There was apparently little exchange between those who had already succeeded and the emigrants who hoped to do so.

Even if there was often little distinction between second class and steerage, there were semantic markers denoting class stratification among the three levels. For instance, Stevenson remarked that, "In the steerage there are males and females: in the second cabins ladies and gentlemen." Similarly, Alex Blascheck, on the *Ballaarat* in 1889, noted, "The second class had their dinner at 1:30, while the first class have lunch at 1 p.m… After dinner we all loafed until teatime, 6 p.m., then first class had dinner at 7:30." Both travelled in second class, mid-way between the extremes. The meal nomenclature revealed by Blascheck, while less precise today, would still be recognized by modern Britons as denoting class distinctions.

Far from visiting the lower classes as a form of entertainment, the higher ones sometimes developed a tacit coalition against them, as V.S. Naipaul relates while sailing in 1960 on the *Francisco Balboa* with a load of West Indian emigrants. From his cramped and dirty first-class cabin, going down lower and lower into their quarters, he found "choked little cabins," containing "four bunks, each dotted with a head emerging out of sheets, and many suitcases," with both men and women "hurrying to and from lavatories." While passengers "travelling tourist" (a euphemism for second class) took their meals in their canteen below deck, the nine first-class passengers ate their meals in comfort in their near-empty dining room. When the emigrants embarked, the second-class passengers rejoined the nine first-class occupants in their dining room. Whereas the original dichotomy had been between the first and second classes, once the emigrants came on board, all the class passengers rallied against the newcomers, and superficial barriers broke down when faced with a common invading force.

Passengers did not necessarily opt for the more expensive class, even when they could afford it. Here are two such examples, both from the 1930s, but resulting in a different travelling experience. Evelyn Waugh, the English novelist and journalist, was advised to travel second, rather than first class, on the *Ranchi*, because a lot of "first-rate people were travelling second class since the war, particularly on ships from India." He was soon disillusioned. "It was not that my fellow passengers were not every bit as nice as the Port Said residents had told me they would be, but there were so many of them, there was simply nowhere to sit down. The lounge and smoking rooms were comfortable and clean and well ventilated and prettily decorated and all that, but they were always completely full." He had not anticipated that, at the beginning of the hot season in

India, officers' wives would be taking their children back to England "in shoals." One of the few pleasures was the six o'clock visit from the band that came down from the first-class deck to the second-class saloon to play Gilbert and Sullivan tunes. Unfortunately, this visit coincided with the bath time of children who "shrieked their protest till the steel rafters and match-board partitions echoed and rang. There was no place above or below for a man who values silence."

His second-class companions were mostly "soldiers on leave or soldiers' wives, leavened with a few servants of first-class passengers, some clergymen, and three or four nuns," a slice of society one would have expected to find there. Also noticeable was the dress code adhered to by first-class passengers and lacking among the others. "On the other side of the barrier, we could see the first-class passengers dressed very smartly in white flannels and parti-coloured brown and white shoes."

At about the same time, French anthropologist Lévi-Strauss and his team were doing fieldwork in South America, always sailing on ships of *La Compagnie des Transports Maritimes*. As with Waugh, the question of class arose: second-class berths on the only luxury liner on that route, or first-class berths on more modest vessels? "Social climbers opted for the first alternative, hoping to rub elbows with ambassadors or some such and expecting problematic benefits." The others, including Lévi-Strauss, chose the mixed cargo and passengers boats, taking six days longer and stopping along the way, but where they were "top dogs." After several crossings, they had started to feel at home on board, with familiar stewards and eating meals "worthy of Pantagruel." He particularly enjoyed the "extraordinary luxury and regal privilege of being among the eight or ten passengers who, on a boat built to accommodate hundred and fifty, had the deck, the cabins, the smoking room, and the dining-room all to themselves."

Both men confirmed that, for some, the absence of crowded conditions on board constitutes the ultimate luxury—one always denied the lower ranking passengers, and the deeper these passengers went into steerage, the less space and privacy they could rely on.

Are there class distinctions on ships today? What tended to unite earlier passengers of different nationalities (and distinguish between them) was their social class. Wherever they came from, the poor easily recognized each other, and the rich knew who they were. Today's distinctions are far more tentative in the great social amalgam of the cruising clientele, which no longer includes the extremes of society on the same ship.

The passage from hierarchical liners to egalitarian cruise ships came about in the aftermath of WWII, when air travel became more common. Flying was then a novel and glamorous affair, offering a speed of travel and a convenience that ships are unable to match. For a while, liners held their own across the Atlantic, but by the late 1950s, seventy percent of travellers were flying between America and Europe. When the first commercial jet took off from New York to Paris on October 26, 1958, drastically cutting flying time from twelve to less than seven hours, the liners' decline was irreversible, and the number of those who chose to sail eventually dwindled to a mere four percent. As Maxtone-Graham put it, "White elephants almost overnight, the great liners were quickly taken out of service, or shifted to the bland pursuit of cruising."

The great transatlantic liners (the *Queen Mary,* the *QE2,* the *France*) and so many lesser ones, are now gone. Several had attempted to survive with the comfort, service, and luxury only they could offer, but only one now remains, the *Queen Mary 2,* and she too must resort to cruising once a year. The former rigid class stratification had been transformed on these modern liners. With emigration to the United States curtailed in 1920, the money-making steerage and its social pariahs lodged in dormitories made way to "tourist third" cabins. The three classes were the prevalent divisions during the 1920s on Atlantic crossing liners until the changing economic conditions of the 1930s caused the intermediate second class to disappear.

Upon the launching of the *Queen Elizabeth 2* in 1969, Sir Basil Smallpeice, a senior director at Cunard, asserted that, "in travel, separate class distinction as a reflection of a hierarchical social structure is clearly out of date... All passengers can walk from end to end without let or hindrance." This statement is perhaps slightly disingenuous, for the free-spirited ramble it suggests hides another reality. Passengers could indeed walk from end to end, but only because ships had now substituted their former vertical class compartments for horizontal ones. Later widely adopted, the change had been initiated in 1959 by Holland America for its new flagship, the *Rotterdam*. First and tourist class had their respective facilities on a single deck, one above the other, described as "a class sandwich" running the entire length of the ship.

Cruise ships go by different rules. The Depression's alarming impact on the shipping industry resulted in the conversion of many luxury liners into ships dedicated to leisurely cruising in warmer seas. From its inception, the guiding principle of cruising has been an egalitarian one. It was assumed that cruise ships' passengers would be united in the mellowness of a relaxed holiday mood, without the stress and potential friction of having to observe class distinctions. As with the earlier philosophy of providing passage to everyone, whatever their means, today's intent is to fill all cabins with happy people at reasonable cost. Thus, observes Maxtone-Graham in the 1980s, "Just as numbers of Atlantic vessels in the past were designed exclusively for immigrants or Cabin Class, so shipboard today is restricted to one amorphous cruising class." This is still true today. No one is made to feel inferior on board, as no overt class system is in place, although there are obvious advantages to lodging in the more expensive and spacious staterooms, with free access to the best restaurants.

However, as social animals, we crave hierarchies and know that sailing on the same ship no more erases social differences than does living in the same city. As cruising becomes one of the most affordable holiday options, distinctions have to be created to sort the wheat from the chaff. Particular ships are reputed to offer outstanding levels of comfort for a select few among their passengers. One of the latest is the Norwegian Cruise Lines' *Norwegian Escape*, which boasts outstanding facilities (named the "Haven") for a restricted 250 guests equipped with a gold card that gives them exclusive privileges.

Those who cannot afford these distinctions but still hope to achieve status can fall back on the number of cruises they have taken. Many reviewers of *Cruise Critic* (written by cruisers for cruisers) are not shy of bandying about large numbers. Some have cruised several times on almost every line and can explain the merits of respective ships and lines, and many of us have sat for lunch beside someone who had sailed around the world once and perhaps even twice. In an effort to promote what marketers call brand fidelity, cruising status is sanctioned with a star system (at least on Holland America): two stars reward thirty cruise days, three stars seventy-five days, four stars two hundred days, five stars mean at least five hundred days at sea, and at the very top sits the almost unattainable membership in the President's Club. Naturally, this rating system provides benefits and discounts, with the stars evident on the cards that serve as passes for all transactions on board. The progressive number of stars is even marked with the granting of medals (bronze, silver, gold). The stars constitute the only rating that could presumably justify a sense of superiority among some cruisers, since there is theoretically little else to distinguish between them. Thus, the most obvious differentiating factor among ordinary cruisers is "seniority" reflected in the number of days they have spent at sea.

Cruising is here to stay. Port Everglades/Lauderdale, among the busiest cruise ports in the world, has processed on several occasions more than 50,000 passengers in a single day, and is currently home port for the two largest cruise ships ever built. Cruising could not pretend to be anything but what it is: a mass-produced form of relatively cheap entertainment. As a reaction against it and bucking the initial trend and levelling philosophy of cruising, a few lines offer the exclusive sailing experience of glamorous suites, the most exotic destinations, and world-class entertainment for those who seek to escape from the general spirit of democratization prevalent on more broadly based cruise ships. As we consider future trends for the cruising industry, we can already predict a parting of the ways between mass cruising and more sophisticated attempts at exclusivity.

7 YACHTS

The peak of hierarchical sailing is, undoubtedly, owning one's own ship. Our son's thirty-five-foot catamaran is not what I have in mind, a proviso that in no way implies that love of sailing is proportionate to the size of the vessel owned.

"Salt-Water Palaces" Maldwin Drummond called them in his book of the same name, prefaced by a keen yachtsman, Admiral of the Fleet Earl of Mountbatten of Burma. Apart from sailors and servants, there was no more allowance for ordinary people on yachts than in the great houses on land they replicated at sea. With their wealth of refined details and gilded ornaments, their beautifully carved figureheads, the precious woods of their panels, their finest Persian carpets, their elegant furnishings, they displayed the elevated status and fortune of their owners and afforded magnificent occasions for entertaining friends and attendants.

The history of yachting in England starts with Charles II and continues to gain momentum into the Victorian era. The main goals of this pleasurable exercise were, according to the king, racing, cruising, and advancing the knowledge of the ships and the sea. In some cases, prizes earned in races helped with the huge expense of maintaining a yacht. At the king's death in 1685, yachting suffered a lengthy lapse, royal patronage being necessary for the sport to continue. It was not until 1801 that George III made yachting popular again. English naval history was made during this period, particularly with Nelson's destruction of the Franco-Spanish fleet at Trafalgar in 1794.

Famous among the latter yachts was the *Royal George*. Launched in 1817, she served four sovereigns, from George III to Victoria, and was described by a contemporary as "the most elegant [vessel] ever seen. The cabin doors are of mahogany with gilt moldings, and the windows of plate glass. Ornamental devices in abundance are placed in various parts... producing a superb appearance." She was succeeded by three yachts called the *Victoria and Albert*. The first was a twin-paddle steamer, and the third, put into service in 1901, was used by the royal family until 1939. Finally, the *Britannia*, probably the best-known royal yacht, carried on the tradition under George V and, eventually, the present queen.

Photographs of the interiors of these ships show the utmost refinement, in the taste of the period. The dimensions were truly on a royal scale, and forty-four could sit for dinner on the *Victoria and Albert*. Naturally, the glossy mahogany table rested on the finest Teheran carpets, the curtains were of silk, and the chairs were covered in morocco. The ship also boasted a twin, semi-circular, white and gold companionway staircase, in Georgian style described as very impressive.

The substitution of steam for sail was not a welcome one; purist yachtsmen resented the smoke, coal dust, and waste of space wholeheartedly. Yet, steam-powered pleasure yachts made their insidious progress into the entries in the Royal Yacht Club registers. They began with 30 in 1863, growing to 140 ten years later, and to 466 in another ten years, an enormous increase over such a short period. With further progress diesel replaced steam, providing a cleaner and more manageable fuel.

Yachts were involved in other endeavours than leisure and racing, and some even joined arctic expeditions, such as the *Pandora*, which searched for the Franklin expedition and joining in the quest for the Northwest Passage. Many yachts were put into service during WWI, among them Lord Dunraven's *Grianaig*, which became a hospital ship.

However, having a good time was the focus for most, and the *Cetonia*, in particular, was reputed for the parties held on board.

Passengers on the larger vessels could go fishing in the Norwegian fjords or hunting on the Greek and Albanian coasts. The often dangerous conditions on shore added to the pleasure and excitement of hunting. In Greece, for instance, a stimulating addition to the exercise was the lack of safety, the local populace being, as one owner put it, "a cut-throat-looking community, and not above a bit of brigandage."

Special cabins for ladies only appeared on yachts in the latter part of the nineteenth century. Yachts under fifty feet were usually deemed unsuitable for women, as they could not accommodate special quarters for them. To illustrate the ambiguity of women's presence on board, we should turn to a 1912 limerick,

> There was a young girl called Bianca,
> Asleep on a ship while at anchor;
> But she awoke in dismay,
> When she heard the mate say,
> "Let's haul up the top'sheet and spanker."

There was definitely an air of luxury and idleness (if not occasional debauchery) attached to the yachting life. Yet, Elizabeth Rigby, writing in the *Quaterly Review* in 1845, reminds us that yachts were sea-going vessels facing the vagaries of the elements and their owners and passengers did likewise. "For though yachts may be furnished with every luxury [she lists them], yet the winds will blow, and the waves toss, and the sun beat down, and the dust rise up, and the rain soak through, and hunger, and thirsts, and fatigue, and things their delicacy knew not of before, assail."

In 2014, our ship was moored for two days in Papeete, Tahiti, beside a beautiful little vessel, which I first mistook for a government training ship because of her battleship-grey colour, the small helicopter with its fitted canvas cover sitting on the aft deck, and the trim uniforms of the seventeen men and women on board. One man seemed exclusively attached to polishing the teak banisters, while others seemed equally busy with other tasks.

Naturally, she evoked much interest on our own ship. Debating on the owners' identity, we eventually opted for Russian billionaires. Navy men had pertinent (or so we imagined) things to say about her capabilities and the cost of running her, but since there were many different opinions, not much credence would be attributed to any. What made a great impression on us was her utter idleness—not that of her crew, constantly preoccupied with her maintenance, but of herself, anchored in Tahiti, waiting. This costly idleness was by far the greatest testimony to the owners' wealth.

Modern "superyachts" recently came up in the news, when Peter Munk (of Barrick Gold Corporation), in association with even wealthier yachtsmen, created the Porto Montenegro development to provide luxurious mooring in the Adriatic, at the very spot where Byron had marvelled at "the most beautiful encounter between the land and the sea." Such a port, with the usual accompaniment of luxury hotels, a golf course, and helipads, is naturally of much benefit to impoverished Montenegro, but let us particularly remark on the yachts themselves. Lest we thought the eras of the regal British salt-water palaces and the Greek shipping magnates Aristotle Onassis and Stavros Niarchos were things of the past, we should be reassured that the taste for outlandish private vessels is alive and well.

Munk's own *Golden Eagle*, forty-three-metres (141 feet) long with merely three decks and a crew of seven, is dwarfed by some of her neighbours, among which the *Ocean Victory*, five-story high and seventy-six-metres (250 feet) long, that boasts a beach club, a helipad, a cinema, and several other amenities. Built by Fincantieri, she is (reputedly) owned by the Russian billionaire Viktor Rashnikov. Journalist Eric Reguly believes that it is difficult to ascertain the current ownership of some of these behemoths, which are frequently traded for bigger and better vessels.

The future of luxury yachts is safe. Among the 850 berths planned for the project, 120 will be devoted to yachts over 30 metres (98 feet) long. Among those recently or currently moored are the 97-metre (318 feet) *Carinthia VII*, owned by the Horten family of Germany, and the 75-metre (246 feet) long *Enigma,* belonging to the Barclay family, owners of *The Telegraph* newspaper. There is still a way to go for owners wishing to outdo their neighbours, as the largest berth planned for Porto Montenegro will accommodate a 180-metre (590 feet) yacht. As a means of comparison, the Halifax-class frigate in the Royal Canadian Navy is 124.49 metres (408 feet 5 inches) long.

III
FOOD

From Scurvy to Entertainment

At the Dinner Table

8 FROM SCURVY TO ENTERTAINMENT

THE KILLER ON BOARD

It plagued the voyages of Vasco da Gama and Magellan and for centuries would continue to kill seafarers in appalling numbers. Until the middle of the nineteenth century, one of the major concerns of those engaged in long distance navigation was scurvy. Also known as *purpura nautica*, its effects and the devastation it inflicted have often been described, particularly the suppurative wounds covering the body, the bleeding or rotting gums, the putrid blood, the painful and swollen gangrenous limbs, the unstoppable diarrhea, and the bodies sewn into spare bits of sailcloth and tossed overboard after an agonizing death.

Scurvy killed more seamen than did sea battles, accidents, and shipwrecks combined during the first centuries of transoceanic navigation; estimates suggest that more than two million sailors died of it between 1500 and 1800. Every ship from every nation was affected as they rounded Africa or sailed to the New World. Captains were sometimes known to take on twice as many sailors as they actually needed in anticipation of the death toll. The haunting story was told of the first Dutch voyage to Indonesia. Half of the 249 men who sailed off in four ships in April 1595 were ill or dead from scurvy by the time they reached Madagascar in September, and the 87 who survived the rest of the voyage were so weak that they could not even lower the anchors when they arrived home two years later.

Schoolmaster Pascoe Thomas, aboard the *Centurion* during Commodore George Anson's 1740-44 voyage, where two-thirds of his men died of scurvy, described his own deteriorating condition. His legs and thighs became "as black as a negro," with "excessive pains in the... knees, ankles and toes." Then, his teeth became loose and his gums, "over-charged with extravasatated blood fell down almost quite over [his] teeth." With scurvy, old wounds often reopened and bones previously set fractured again, all of it accompanied by extreme lethargy.

The deterioration and shortage of food were common on long voyages. One of Magellan's sailors reported the condition on board.

> We ate... powder of biscuits swarming with worms, for they had eaten the good. It stank strongly of the urine of rats. We drank yellow water that had been putrid for many days. We also ate some ox hides that covered the top of the mainyard... and had become exceedingly hard because of the sun, rain, and wind. We left them in the sea for four or five days, and then placed them for a few moments on top of the embers, and so ate them, and often we ate sawdust from the boards. Rats were sold for one-half ducado apiece and even we could not get them.

Consumed as an unappetizing last resort, rats are able to synthesize vitamin C and were a source of protein. The actual cause of scurvy, a deficiency in vitamin C required for the synthesis of collagen in the human body, was not discovered until 1927. However, most captains and ship surgeons had realized that the sailors' deadly sickness was likely due to some lack in their diet. Sir Richard Hawkins had already proposed in 1593 "sower oranges and lemons" as a remedy for this sickness. On English and Dutch ships, lemons were commonly used as a remedy (rather than prevention) by some naval surgeons, but without understanding the reason for their success. John Woodall's *The Surgeon's Mate* of 1617 refers to citrus fruits as a precious and well-tried medicine, best taken every morning on a cold stomach to fight the disease, believing that scurvy was "an obstruction of the spleen, liver and brain." Barley water with cinnamon water was another recommended remedy, whenever citrus fruit was believed to dangerously thicken the blood.

Other possible causes were also entertained, notably noxious sea air. Navigators' logs sometimes mention the miasmic nature of the air at sea and how improvement was expected from short visits ashore—usually not observing that such visits also coincided with an intake of fresh food loaded with vitamin C. Nevertheless, it was eventually acknowledged that diet was partly responsible for the condition.

Before citrus fruit became officially part of the diet on European ships, some captains attempted to devise their own prevention methods. James Cook was convinced that clean conditions on board and a proper diet would be effective measures against scurvy, and he believed in the efficacy of the sauerkraut juice prescribed by the *Endeavour*'s surgeon, Mr. Monkhouse, accompanied by wort, a decoction of malt. He encouraged his officers to consume them as an example for the reluctant sailors who hated the taste. He also insisted on replenishing his ships with clean water whenever they reached shore, and on gathering berries, wild cabbage, wild celery, and any other green vegetables and fruits they could find. In spite of his preference for sauerkraut juice over lemons and limes, richer in vitamin C, Cook was credited with much success in reducing the cases of scurvy among his men. After his second voyage, he reported his methods in a letter to the president of the Royal Society and was awarded the Copley Medal. It was the first time this prestigious scientific award had been granted for a study on nutrition, indicating the importance accorded to any attempt at dealing with the dreaded affliction.

While ship surgeons and captains struggled haphazardly to prevent scurvy from decimating the sailors' ranks, Dr. James Lind of the Royal Navy put to test the theory that citrus fruit were the remedy for the disease. He designed and conducted the first clinical trial, proving that a group given a supplement of oranges and lemons fared much better than others who were fed a variety of other diets. He published his findings in 1753, but it took time for his results to be recognized and for his recommendations to be implemented. Eventually, they were rewarded with resounding success. Until then, seamen had to resort to whatever experience dictated, making do with any plant they knew to have beneficial powers, such as the humble "scurvy grass" *(oxalis enneaphylla)* and the healing capability of its leaves and flowers.

Noteworthy among the eighteenth-century navigators who struggled with the problem and tried to find a solution was Thomas Forrest (c.1729-1802), who sailed mostly in South-East Asian seas. He recommended the use of tea, coffee, and chocolate (rather than the usual "strong liquors and pernicious grog"). Noticing how well a Bengali crew did on a diet of vegetables and fish, he strongly (but unsuccessfully) requested that his sailors be provided with "onions, sour crout, French beans, and small cucumber pickles," instead of meat.

Observing local customs served others well. For instance, it was known that, unlike Arctic explorers, Inuit did not get scurvy in spite of a diet lacking fresh fruit and vegetables (apart from berries and a few plants during the summer, and the undigested vegetal contents in the stomachs of their prey). Artic explorers learned to imitate the native customs, realizing that the raw meat and blubber of the animals they hunt contain the precious Vitamin C they craved.

PROVISIONS FOR THE VOYAGE

In the early days, provisioning for long voyages relied on guess-work about its duration and was limited by practical constraints, as salting meat and fish and drying legumes were the only ways of conserving food. Those responsible for securing the victuals for long voyages were mostly concerned with keeping the crew alive and strong enough to work, the captain's table being the only attempt at some limited refinement in this domain. At least, such was the theory. In practice, many shortcuts were taken in procuring provisions, as the cost of food cut into the profits of the voyage. Even in the Royal Navy, the prospects were often dim.

In the early seventeenth century, European seamen lived essentially on cask meat, legumes, and hard tack, a dry biscuit that needed dunking in liquid before being eaten. Twice baked, it could keep indefinitely in normal temperatures, but when moistened became a choice habitat for weevils tunnelling chambers for their larvae. Every sailor had learned to tap his biscuit against the sides of the ship to dislodge the insects before eating it (a gesture similar to the automatic tapping of a cigarette against its case to dislodge the bits of foreign matter sticking to cheap tobacco during WWII).

Preserved fish, gutted and air dried to extreme hardness, needed softening before being stewed with dried legumes. Meat was cured by either rubbing it with salt or hanging it to dry, or by immersing it in boiling brine or vinegar. However, a cheaper method consisted in dipping freshly slaughtered animals in cauldrons of boiling seawater. When cooked in brine, this salty meat caused sailors to suffer from raging thirst. Despite these shortcomings, the seamen's meals included meat three or four times a week, a far superior diet to that of men working on land, who were lucky to eat meat once a week. They ate in their sleeping quarters, sitting on their sea chest and eating from wooden bowls and spoons.

A surgeon serving on Dutch Indiamen between 1639 and 1687 described the meals. "Every morning a full dish of hot groats, cooked with prunes and covered with butter or some other fat; at midday they get a dish of white peas and a dish of stockfish, with butter and mustard; save on Sundays and Thursdays when they get at midday a dish of grey peas and a dish of meat and bacon." As supplies lasted, they received weekly rations of four pounds of biscuit, a can of beer daily, and a reasonable supply of olive oil, butter, brandy, and vinegar. Passengers and officials on the same ships were served hot meals three times a day, with tablecloths, napkins, pewter plates, and tin spoons, giving a touch of refinement and normalcy, while stewards served wine and cabin boys brought in the food. Efforts were made to serve fresh vegetables grown in a little hutch serving as greenhouse and meat from the goats, pigs, and chickens travelling along. Fish would sometimes be caught and served fresh at the captain's table.

In England, the standard fare seemed to have been established at one pound of meat (which could be salt beef, otherwise known as "Irish horse," pork, bacon, or even fish) four times a week, with some cheese, peas, butter, and biscuit. The drink rations consisted of wine, brandy, small beer, or rum. All supplies were expected to be of acceptable quality. A typical seventeenth-century ship captain's standard provisions to feed 190 men for three months before rotting food, starvation, and scurvy took their toll—or before they found a propitious landfall to reprovision their ships—would have included "8,000 pounds of salt beef, 2,800 pounds of salt pork, a few beef tongues, 600 pounds of haberdine [salt cod], 15,000 brown biscuits, 5,000 white biscuits, 30 bushels of oatmeal, 40 bushels of dried peas, 1 ½ bushels of mustard seed, a barrel of salt, 1 hogshead [large cask] of vinegar, 11 firkins [small wooden casks] of butter, 10,500 gallons of beer, 3,500 gallons of beer, 2 hogshead of cider." The captain's store included "cheese, pepper, currants, cloves, sugar, aqua vitae, ginger, prunes, bacon, marmalade, almonds, cinnamon, wine, rice."

The typical daily ration of Captain Cook's sailors consisted of one pound of meat, one pound of hardtack biscuit or oatmeal (often worm-eaten), some rancid butter, and one gallon of beer. The Navy's Victualling Board responsible for outfitting ships had provided Cook's *Endeavour* with 45,000 lbs of bread and flour, 130 bushels of oatmeal and wheat, 10,000 pieces of pork and dried and salted beef, with suet, raisins, oil, vinegar, and salt for added taste and preservation. Drinks consisted in 1,200 gallons of beer, 1,600 of spirits, as well as an order to buy more wine in Madeira or the Canary Islands. As well, consistent with Cook's fight against scurvy, the board had ordered 7,860 lbs of sauerkraut, together with 40 bushels of malt (later doubled to 80 bushels) to make wort.

The hope of finding fresh food to supplement the sailors' diet was not always fulfilled, even when land was in sight, as treacherous waters or hostile natives would sometimes thwart their attempts to land. Yet, opportunities occurred, such as in the South Pacific, where Captain Cook made the most of them. "Some hands were employed picking celery to take to sea with us... I have caused it to be boiled with portable soup and oatmeal every morning for the people's breakfast... and I look upon it to be very wholesome and a great antiscorbutic."

By the end of the eighteenth century, fresh food was deemed to be a right for seamen in port, and at sea whenever possible, replacing salt meat with fresh meat and biscuit with fresh bread. Otherwise, the main foodstuff consisted of bread, salted beef and pork, dried peas, flour, and brandy. Stockfish was being phased out as it was hard to preserve and unpopular with the men. There were some variations, according to time and place (and authors, as well), but we have a general idea of the diet fed to sailors at the time. Interestingly, the anti-scorbutic value of some fresh food, still somewhat derided by contemporary medical science, had by then become well known among seamen.

Resourceful seafarers would add to their diet through a compendium of exotic foods, such as the adaptable turtle (fried, boiled, roasted, baked, or stewed), fishy-tasting booby birds, sea cows, seals, and penguins. They used these to supplement their diet as best they could, whether food restrictions were due to their captain's deliberate and economical shortages or to circumstances. The model for Robinson Crusoe, Alexander Selkirk, stranded for five years on a desert island, was able to survive because of the skills he had acquired as a seaman.

Similarly, the crew celebrated an officer's birthday on the *Endeavour* with a feast of dog meat. They dined on the animal's roasted hindquarters, its forequarters baked in a pie, and its guts turned into haggis. This choice of protein was due to meat shortage on board rather than gustatory preference, and the same dish was served to Cook, desperately ill while sailing near Easter Island. "A favourate [sic] dog belonging to Mr. Forster fell a Sacrifice to my tender Stomack; we had no other fresh meat whatever on board and I could eat of this flesh, as well as broth made of it, when I could taste nothing else, thus I received nourishment and strength from food would have made most people in Europe sick." By then, far from making them sick, dog meat had been tasted by English sailors as a delicacy in Polynesian feasts.

During this period, the same conditions prevailed in the French navy, with the same successes and failures in ensuring a proper diet. Bougainville, the first successful French circumnavigator (1766-1769), thought he had provided well for his crew with the usual complement of oxen, pigs, sheep, and poultry. Believing that greens could prevent scurvy, he had included sauerkraut, chicory, and some lemons in his provisions, trying as well to grow sorrel in barrels on deck. Unfortunately, the poor quality of the food was no match for the length of his voyage and his men were eventually reduced to eating rats.

Fictional Navy captains were also concerned with providing an adequate diet for their sailors, and food and drink figure prominently in C. S. Forester and Patrick O'Brian's novels. Forester composed ideal provision lists for Horatio Hornblower's frigate and Patrick O'Brian relates how, on festive occasions and after a landing, the captain and his officers might dine on venison and, perhaps, a suckling pig. Favourite dishes were soused pig's head and feet, drowned baby, jam roly-poly, cabinet pudding, and treacle-dowdy. Captain Aubrey also enjoyed spotted dick (a boiled suet pudding) and figgy dowdy, the latter's preparation requiring the following steps: "Take a ship's biscuit, put it in a stout canvas bag... pound it with a marlin-spike for half an hour... add bits of pork fat, plums, figs, rum, currants... send it to the galley and serve with bosun's grog."

In reality, whatever the amount and quality of the food, we can safely assume that sailors complained about it in any century. Unflattering nicknames were given to their rations and the men even jested that the victims of two notorious murderesses, Fanny Adams and Harriet Lane, had been tinned and sold as meat to the Navy.

In spite of its lack of appeal, food was produced and consumed in all circumstances, even in the middle of storms lasting days without respite. Their aftermath must have been scenes of utter confusion, but the crew of the *Terra Nova* (1688) on her way to Plymouth demonstrated how it could be done with fairness and efficiency. After the storm had abated, they took stock of the meat and found that the hogs, the sheep, some goats, and dozens of hens had washed overboard, only leaving behind three dozen drowned hens and turkeys. After feeding for two days on the latter, "which was dainty fare," they realized they needed to ration themselves, since they did not know how long this situation would prevail. They shared what was left of the bread, a mess bowl for every six men, which they ate with sugar, but were soon reduced to eating Indian wheat spoiled with seawater. They also shared boiled stockfish, small bites of beef, and a little flour for pudding "made with salt-water, and boil'd in the same, as were the stockfish, and eaten without any oyl, butter, or other thing whatever." Every group of six men received their food allowance equally, sight unseen and navy-style, "by which means we had no dispute about victuals." Their precious allowance of drink was "a small coco-nut-shell a-man," or about half a pint, doled out every night by the captain.

By the time of Margaret Meredith's passage to Australia in the mid-1890s, fear of scurvy was a thing of the past. Being of an abstemious nature, she did not comment on the meals served on board. However, when the ship stopped on the island of Saint Helena on their return journey, she noticed the many farms scattered around Jamestown, "where good butter is made, and poultry and eggs are plentiful. There is an abundance of good water... In some parts there is good pasture, and in others sweet potatoes, lemons, bananas, and green vegetables of all kinds are grown." By then, the *Hesperus* had been ten and half weeks at sea and, no doubt, the fresh provisions bought in Jamestown were very welcome.

Saint Helena had actually long been a favourite of English seamen on the East India route. Many contemporary writers remarked on the salubrious and restorative climate, as well as "plentiful arak wine, fine fishing, medicinal herbs, a clean breeze, and fresh fruit and food" to be found there. Francis Roger described it as "one of the most healthful places in the world" and wrote that many men "nearly dead with the scurvy and other diseases... when carried ashore here, recover to a miracle, rarely any dying though never so ill when brought ashore." William Dampier noted that men so sick that they were carried ashore in their hammock were soon able "to leap and dance."

Today, passengers take for granted the presence of large quantities of fresh and frozen food on board. Modern ships have become floating villages, with their own facilities and resources. Moderate size ships serve about twelve thousand meals a day, and the logistics required for preparing and serving them is reflected in the number of kitchen and dining room staff. Cruise ships usually organize guided tours to their kitchens, knowing that what the passengers are shown surpasses their expectations.

The provisions for these meals bear no resemblance to the seventeenth-century captain's list we read earlier. For instance, the average weekly requirements for *Statendam*'s cruise to French Polynesia in October 2014 notably included 12,500 lbs of meat, meat products, and poultry; 4,500 lbs of seafood; and 7,500 lbs of fresh fruit and vegetables. Dairy, eggs, sugar, flour were in similarly high quantities, as well as 2100 lbs of rice for the crew. These amounts seem standard when compared with others on cruises of similar duration and ship size. Provisions for one of our cruises also listed 12 lbs of caviar, and no doubt some such extravagance can be found on most ships for their elite passengers.

These lists show that provisions taken on board are no longer intended to merely sustain life, but constitute one of the sources of entertainment for the passengers. Crews on harsh assignments can also benefit from special pampering. For instance, on the *Fram*, a Norwegian ice vessel destined for long months of isolation (1893-1912), hearty meals were awaited with much anticipation and were so plentiful and enjoyable that several crew members put on weight during their months on the ice.

LIVESTOCK

Fresh meat did not keep long, so live animals were taken on the voyage. The custom endured to the end of the nineteenth century, until the introduction of refrigerated meat. According to the instruction of *The Ship Steward's Handbook,* these animals had to be deprived of food during twelve hours before being butchered but needed to be abundantly watered "to prevent the blood from being load with an excess of food matter," which would have caused the meat to deteriorate more rapidly.

We know the Duchess of Albermarle (1688) provided for herself and her retinue by bringing on board the *Terra Nova* "sheep, hogs, turkies, hens, &c." and enough food to keep them alive. Joseph Sams on board the *Northumberland* from London to Australia in 1874 wrote, "We have two cows on board, several pigs, ducks, geese, poultry and sheep in abundance, several dogs and parrots, and the forecastle is like a young farmyard." German naturalist Ernst Haeckel, en route to Ceylon on the *Helios* in 1881, mentioned, "the forepart contains … the stalls for our floating cattle farm including a few cows and calves, a flock of five Hungarian sheep with long twisted horns, and a large number of fowls and ducks." A passenger on the P & O wrote that he "woke up in the morning to the crowing of cocks, cackle of geese and bleat of sheep" and was inclined to think he was on an English farm.

By 1892, John Acland, sailing on the same route as Joseph Sams and his floating farmyard eighteen years earlier, could write, "All the meat, milk, butter, etc. comes out of course with us in the frozen state, the mutton and lamb being usually New Zealand, but butter, milk, and cream no doubt very English." No longer was it necessary to carry livestock to ensure appropriate rations of meat. There was naturally a period of transition, particularly on long crossings, when some livestock was still in evidence. Such was Robert Roberts's experience on his way from Auckland on the *Alameda* in 1897. "We had a flock of sheep penned away on deck at the stern… where there is the greatest heave of the vessel. I spoke to them frequently during the voyage. They were quietly responsive with ear and eye to the voice of sympathy. They thinned in number as the time wore on. Yesterday, they were all gone. I asked what had become of them. 'We have eaten them,' was the answer."

Interested in the passengers' wellbeing, Samuel Cunard installed a cow on board, quite a noteworthy event, as she was not intended to provide fresh meat along the way but only fresh milk. This aura of pastoral farmyard was much more acceptable to sensitive modern passengers than the once usual evidence of stockyard and slaughtering would have been.

While the animals carried on board were usually meat on the hoof, emigrants sometimes brought along pets. Noteworthy were the British settlers led by the Rev. Isaac Barr, who left for Canada in 1903 on the SS *Lake Manitoba,* bound for what is now Lloydminster on the Saskatchewan-Alberta border. They brought along 150 pet dogs, that freely roamed the ship, barking, fighting, and befouling the decks without restraint. Having driven the crew beyond endurance, a good number of them seemed to have found their way overboard.

Liners often had comfortable accommodations for travelling pets. Let us remember the £2 fee ($207 today) for dogs on the *Titanic,* one fourth of the cost of a steerage passage. Kennels are still available on the *Queen Mary 2,* at a cost varying between $800 and $1,000 for dogs, and $1,600 for cats, including a litter box. Cruise ships make no provisions for pets, but they have suitable facilities for service dogs. These usually share their owner's cabin and are sometimes offered a choice of facilities to suit their individual preferences—grass or dirt.

Animals still commonly travel, often in large numbers and, while no longer intended for consumption on the voyage, they serve the same purpose. The *Danny F II,* for instance, a livestock carrier from Uruguay on her way to Tripoli, is only noteworthy for sinking a few miles off the coast of Lebanon in 2009 with a crew of 83, and carrying 10,224 sheep and 17,932 cows intended as meat for the Middle East.

ON THE MENU

Steamship passengers often mentioned that their food was appealing, plentiful, and tasty. There were variations from line to line, and from ship to ship on the same line, and tropical heat or seasickness did not boost appetite, but food was usually a part of the pleasure of sailing.

Before considering the food offered round the clock on cruise ships, it is sobering to remember how basic was that served on early crossings, as described by Don Eugenio. "I would see the ships' boys emerge from the half-deck with a bundle of what they called table cloths; but alas, not white or handsomely embroidered. They spread out these damp and dirty lengths of canvas in the waist of the ship, and on them piled little mounds of broken biscuit, as white and clean as the cloths, so that the general effect was that of a culti-vated field covered with little heaps of manure." The niceties being observed and the table thus being set, the partakers were called and the meal was served. It consisted of "three or four wooden platters full of beef bones without their marrow, with bits of parboiled sinew clinging to them… On Fridays and vigils, they have beans cooked in salt water, on fast days salt cod." We will consult him again on the matter of table manners.

The food served to Don Eugenio and his fellow passengers was clearly inadequate. Ours is plentiful and tasty, but the new problem is providing food that appeals to international passengers, even if the cultural variations among them are more illusory than real. The tendency is for Europeans to travel together, and for Americans (including Canadians and Australians) to do likewise, but the food is inspired by the dominant cuisines familiar to everyone. The crews, often Asian, have their own cooks and provisions.

While the passengers' culinary preferences are generally compat-ible, much consideration has undoubtedly been given to ensure that the selection of foods is acceptable to everyone. People of similar culture follow the same dietary rules and are easy to accommodate, but there are several nationalities and cultures with different food traditions present on board. Nevertheless, those who sit together for dinner have no problem ordering their individual menu from a kitchen used to accommodating many health and religious restrictions such as vegan, low-sodium, low-sugar, gluten-free, and kosher diets, all of which can be served simultaneously at the same table.

There is substantial meeting ground when people eat their meals in common, yet differences do exist. Strangers do not sit to dinner together without having metaphorically travelled along the history of food and variously participated in its evolution. Their culinary origins are far more distant than their mothers' kitchens and they are not solely guided by their national traditions and personal histories and tastes when choosing from their menus. The old duality of nature and culture (translated into raw vs. cooked, when food is concerned) forms the basis for many of their decisions. Here is not the place to discuss it, but we should be aware of the deep cultural complexity of our choices and of the daunting task of ship chefs when feeding two or three thousand people of various origins.

French structural anthropologist Claude Lévi-Strauss has examined the continuum of our food preferences in their various states. They range from raw to cooked (the transformation of raw), and to rotten (its ultimate transformation), and are all present in one form or another in most diets. A propos of the latter choice, he provides a startling anecdote that shows how our sensory perceptions are linked to our culture and our life experience. "Certain incidents which occurred after the Allied landing in 1944 show that American soldiers had a broader conception of the category of the rotten than the French; under the impression that the Normandy cheese dairies stank of corpses, they sometimes destroyed the buildings." The odour cannot be denied; it is simply interpreted differently in France, where the stench of strong cheeses (overcome for the sake of eating them) seems more reminiscent of unwashed feet macerating in their filth than of corpses. Since the American soldiers knew little about cheese and cheese-making, their only reference for such a stench was that of the battlefield. As an aside, we should note that cheese trays on board are remarkably bland.

No doubt facilitating the task of cruise chefs, former barriers have often broken down as the flavours of many cuisines have been combined. In earlier times, it was often a matter of overcoming one's natural repugnance to experiment with foreign foods. Today, it is usually a matter of fashion, and many cruisers have long abandoned any strict observance of their inherited diets.

Culinary tastes have evolved significantly in Europe and North America through travel and, even more fundamentally, through immigration. The food eaten by low-salaried Chinese immigrants in North America was cheap and filling and was prepared with whatever ingredients were available there. The new dishes seemed exotic and were appreciated in the host countries, and the mongrel *chow mein* and *chopsuey* became standard Chinese dishes for them.

Origins were eventually blurred and many of these dishes became incorporated into the cuisine of their countries of adoption. The French, for instance, consider *couscous royal* their meal of predilection, pizza and pasta are the fallback food in North America, and it is the rare Canadian party where finger food does not include sushi.

Immigration, while popularizing certain cuisines, usually betrays their integrity, not only using new ingredients, but also through the vagaries of emigration itself. It is often the case, particularly with the early Chinese and Italian immigrants to North America, that they were of peasant stock and the basic food preparations they brought with them lacked the variety of ingredients and the sophistication of the cuisine served to their elites. Moreover, they were often regional cuisines, with their own preferences and biases. However, this was the food first eaten in the host countries and from which they derived their taste for the immigrants' cookery. For instance, it was once believed in British Columbia that Italians only cooked in olive oil. In reality, their choice only reflected the tastes and cooking of the south, from which they came, and Canadians of a previous generation were unaware of the preference for butter in the northern part of Italy.

The introduction of a particular foreign cuisine does not always signal an increase in the ethnic population from which it is issued.

Thus, the popularity of Japanese restaurants in many parts of the world does not reflect a massive immigration from Japan, but merely a new preference for fresher meals and lighter dishes. On board Holland America ships (and no doubt others), a section of the cafeteria is devoted to Asian food, including sushi, yet I do not recall having seen more than a handful of East Asians on any of our cruises.

This recent popularity may even appear to have gone against an earlier grain, at least as far as Anglo-Saxon palates are concerned. Victorian travellers to Japan could not abide the local food. "Nothing short of actual starvation would induce a European to face the forbidding native food," wrote major Henry Knollys in 1887, bemoaning the absence of meat, bread, milk, or coffee. "Japanese tea is exceedingly insipid and even distasteful to English people." No well-equipped Englishman would have thought of travelling to Japan without the following stores in his baggage: "Liebig's Extract of Beef, German Pea-soup Sausage, Chicago Corned Beef, Tinned Milk, Biscuits, Jam, Cheese, Salt and Mustard, Worcestershire Sauce, Bacon, Tea and Sugar."

Ignorance runs both ways. In 1867, Ernest Satow, stopping for a meal in Kusatsu, described the stupefaction of the attending Japanese upon hearing their order. "The people of the inn were astonished to find that we could eat rice, having been taught to believe that the food of Europeans consisted exclusively of beef and pork." Given the isolation of Japan at the time, these people's surprise is understandable; they were ready to believe any rumour about the white travellers' unique culinary tastes because they knew so little about them. Actually, their belief was an echo of earlier times and the enormous amounts of meat eaten by Europeans during the Renaissance. The rich ate meat four times a day and even the poor, resorting to poultry and venison, ate it several times a week. By the middle of the sixteenth century, the consumption of meat had started declining in favour of cereals, so the Japanese's belief during Satow's visit was merely outdated. By contrast, without the excuse of isolation, the often well-travelled Victorian Britons' astonishment at finding so little suitable food locally seems simply symptomatic of a powerful imperialistic tradition. Cruisers, even if their shore dining experience is often limited, have nevertheless tasted enough different cuisines to be a little more broadminded in their acceptance of ethnic dishes.

While food is merely sustenance, taste mostly follows fashion, often with snobbery close on its heels. There was considerable effort made in 1850 Canada to get rid of those nasty bony-plated sturgeons, only worth ten cents apiece, that sliced open or weighed down the fishermen's nets. They were a nuisance, particularly the gravid females laden with up to twenty-five pounds of eggs which, when released, had a terrible smell. Today, the same eggs arrive, carefully refrigerated, from Russia and Iran and are worth a king's ransom. Their consumption on special occasions is subject to fussy rituals; caviar is served on a bed of ice and requires a spoon made of horn, mother-of-pearl, ivory, or gold. Undoubtedly, the 12 lbs of caviar loaded on one of our ships were served with appropriate decorum to the special few allowed to enjoy it.

Tastes change not only with time but also with geography. Take offals, for instance (I'm tempted to add "please" in a cheap comic's fashion, so distasteful do they appear to many). In North America, their consumption is generally limited to steak and kidney pies and to liver usually served with onions and bacon. We do not appreciate braised hearts, sautéd brains, tripes (much enjoyed in France *à la mode the Caen*), or sweetbreads, the *ris-de-veau* of French tables, a costly glandular dish consisting of the thymus or pancreas of young calves. On board, only liver occasionally figures on the menu, yet the more objectionable snails are offered at least once on most cruises, served as unrecognizable brownish and rubbery bits deliciously drowning in butter and garlic.

Given the numbers and varieties of dishes served on cruise ships, it is remarkable that none of us need fear finding anything objectionable on the menu. The international (basically European) dishes are described with the usual restaurant terminology and in a manner intended to appeal to the palate through imagination. They all evoke international haute cuisine and the professional pampering of cognoscenti and fine palates. More to the point, they reassure us that the food put in front of us meets all the usually expected requirements of familiar taste.

Thinking of some foods as being potentially objectionable means that we have not been culturally trained to eat them and do not even categorize them as edible. As omnivorous animals, there is no biological reason why we should reject harmless comestibles. Indeed, Cook and his crew, who were not used to considering dogs as food, resorted to eating them when the need arose, and many were reduced to eating rats. Geography and penury render some sources of protein palatable and even desirable for some, while still disgusting others. In theory, travel should be a great means of broadening our outlook and our repertoire of tastes, as we see other humans eating what would make us cringe, being a type of food so foreign to our customs that we judge them repellent rather than merely foreign. However, eating on board does not offer such opportunities and there is little adventure in it, beyond a timid foray into the better-known international culinary traditions. As we cruise, we eat the same food in Helsinki, Papeete, or Auckland, since our kitchens and our cooks move along with us.

In the past, when nutrition simply meant basic sustenance with a few treats thrown in, the problem consisted mostly in avoiding illness and ensuring an adequate supply of food until the end of the voyage. Today, when meals are the highlights of our cruising day and passengers' satisfaction means the success or failure of a cruise line, the difficulties of feeding hundreds and even thousands of passengers have no doubt grown exponentially. That it is done successfully is truly a remarkable feat. It is also done discreetly. Some of our extreme distastes are linked to the sight of the living animal eventually served on our plates, even for meat we might otherwise enjoy eating. We prefer to remain ignorant, and more than a few would balk today at seeing livestock awaiting their fate on deck, as was commonplace until meat could be stored unobtrusively in frozen lockers.

The consumption of the enormous quantity of food on board is a source of time-filling entertainment. This overabundance is not new and, in fact, was the earmark of first-class sailing from the earliest days. Over a century ago, travellers had already commented on it. Ernst Haeckel, on the *Helios* (1881): "The absorption... of superfluous quantities of food and drink absolutely unnecessary for the maintenance of a healthy frame." P.T. Etherton, on the *Kalgoorlie* (1898): "Meals of six or eight courses for the full number [even though most of the passengers were seasick at the time] were always prepared, and the waste of food would have kept two or three hundred people daily in plenty." Annie Beauchamp, on the *Ruahine* (1898): "We feed really magnificently, the dinners every night are a circumstance."

When considering comments made about the quality of food by steerage or third class passengers, we should naturally remember their usual fare at home. Some found ship food an improvement over their regular diets, but many reports were negative. For instance, neither the quantity nor the quality of the food seemed to have satisfied anyone in steerage on the SS *Lake Manitoba* on their way to Canada. Ivan Crossley, a young farmer, explained, "We had a horrible concoction called 'lingfish.' It was yellow smoked cod and it smelled to high heaven. That and hard-boiled eggs... Some of those eggs were half-hatched. No bread, just ship's biscuits, big as a saucer and about half an inch thick. No butter; they did give us some margarine near the end. We did not die but we damned near starved to death."

9 AT THE DINNER TABLE

As social animals, we consider a meal taken with strangers to be a social event. It is in fact the most social encounter cruisers have on board, even if they participate in all the other organized activities. While they share the occasion through sitting and eating together, conversing, and exchanging small customary courtesies, it is not like a meal shared at a dinner party, where almost everyone is known and all eat the same food. Instead, they eat with strangers and from different menus, and it is akin to the unlikely circumstance of partaking of a pre-paid, no-host meal at a restaurant with previously unknown people. For some, it is a new experience. Although meals are also taken in common and according to certain rules of conduct in boarding schools and prisons, eating together with strangers is essentially peculiar to travel, an old tradition from the early days of country inns where travellers or pilgrims met, ate, drank, and chatted to while away the hours before bedtime.

Captain Baillie, commodore of the P. & O. Line, was aware of the importance of these meals. "Mealtimes for passengers are usually something they look forward to with pleasurable anticipation; for the lonely, they provide a welcome chance of company, for the greedy, the highlights of their daily routine." We saw previously what the greedy found on their menus, and should now consider the company promised to the lonely.

As they dine together, cruisers engage in a sort of contract, a tacit understanding that, having committed to sit with others to share a meal, they will obey the physical and mental rules of polite society. Indeed, the two most important ingredients for making this affair

109

of dining together a civilized one are the participants' agreeable table manners and their ability to exchange lighthearted views—a seemingly easy task. However, these new companions at dinner are strangers, and only assume that they share the same understanding of how to behave in polite society.

The table (meaning the people around it and the nightly ambience they create) can be a source of pleasurable companionship. By the end of the voyage, those people have become more than mere acquaintances. At the end of our Baltic cruise, for instance, an American presented us, his Canadian and Australian dining companions, with a nicely crafted small stamp box, a result of his new woodworking hobby. The Australians gave us a symbolic Australian quarter "for a phone call," should we ever get to the other side of the world. Another time, all those around our table managed a reunion on land, with promises to repeat the event. Such connections are not unusual on longer cruises.

TABLE MANNERS

When drilled as young children into the niceties of table manners, we usually shrug them off as unimportant. Even as adults, we may not always appreciate how much our opinion of other people may be affected by their manners. In Dickens, for instance, the despicable Mr. Quilp is described purely in terms of his revolting behaviour at the table. "He ate hard eggs, shell and all, devoured gigantic prawns with the heads and tails on, chewed tobacco and watercresses at the same time and with extraordinary greediness, drank boiling tea without winking, bit his fork and spoon till they bent again, and in short performed so many horrifying acts that the women were nearly frightened out of their wits and began to doubt if he were really a human creature." With his disregard of other people's feelings, the objectionable Mr. Quilp would not have lasted long on a cruise ship.

Naturally, the way we behave towards strangers has much to do with circumstances. When food is scarce and must be pounced upon to eat at all, table manners are soon forgotten. Such was the situation during Don Eugenio's voyage, where crew and passengers gathered around a dirty canvas stretched out on the deck as the boys announced the meal: "Table, table, Sir Captain and master and all the company, the table is set, the water is drawn."

> In a twinkling out come pouring all the ship's company saying 'amen,' and sit on the deck round the 'table,' the bo'sun at the head and the gunner on his right, some crosslegged, some with legs stretched out, others squatting or reclining...; and without pausing for grace these knights of the round table whip out their knives and daggers... and fall upon those poor bones... stripping off nerves and muscles... and before you can say a credo, they leave them as clean and smooth as ivory.

Would that this were the only exception to the most basic rules of genteel behaviour. Don Eugenio ironically continued with his description. "And if the food and drink are so exquisite, what of the social life?... Men and women, young and old, clean and dirty, are all mixed up together, packed tight, cheek by jowl. The people around you will belch, or vomit, or break wind, or empty their bowels, while you are having your breakfast. You can't complain or accuse your neighbour of bad manners because it is allowed by the laws of the [place]." Indeed, the laws of the place being as don Eugenio describes them, and the laws of nature unavoidably being what they are, what else could passengers have expected on board a sixteenth-century vessel? It is only Don Eugenio's sophisticated background that permits him to see the roughness of his more common fellow passengers' behaviour. His acerbic comments also reassure us that people of his status (which we assimilate to ours) normally behaved with more appropriate decorum.

Etiquette—the obedience to rules whose origins may sometimes be forgotten—and courtesy that, we are told, comes from the heart, are different, even if both are perceived as "manners" intended to make life more agreeable. Generally, we do not look kindly upon the way people of other cultures eat their food if their manners affront some of our most strongly held conventions. For instance, the more silent the consumption of food, the more Westerners deem it to be civilized. We dislike some Asians' habit of noisily slurping their soup and think the Arabs' appreciative post-prandial belches abysmally rude, even if they only hurt the delicacy of our feelings. Actually, our rules merely contradict theirs. Japanese etiquette for eating noodle soup decrees that it must be noisily sucked and slurped to demonstrate true enjoyment. Who is to say which set of rules should prevail? It could even be argued that such audible signs of appreciation as slurping and belching are a courtesy our own cooks might envy.

While keen to demonstrate our manners, we do not wish to be seen as etiquette bullies—a label we would deserve if showing disapproval of some manners familiar to another culture or another class of our own society. We all know the apocryphal story of the hostess who drank from her finger bowl to avoid embarrassing a socially awkward guest who had mistakenly done so. That she found it necessary to repeat his gesture indicates that others at the same meal—obliged to do likewise out of respect for her—might not have been so elegantly charitable on their own. Such an etiquette lesson could not be imagined on board, where the spirit of egalitarianism reigns. All cruisers are equal, all reasonable manners of eating are acceptable, and no one could rightly be perceived as a potential arbiter of taste and of the "proper" way of doing anything.

There is nothing innate about etiquette; all of it is acquired, as the ethnographer Malinowski explains when commenting on his fieldwork in the Trobriand Islands. "Over and over again, I committed breaches of etiquette, which the natives, familiar enough with me, were not slow in pointing out. I had to learn to behave, and to a certain extent, I acquired the 'feeling' for native good and bad manners." But cruisers do not constitute a cohesive society and, given their various origins, who could possibly decide which set of rules ought to prevail? If Malinowski had visited France and shared a meal with his hosts, he would have been told to keep his hands lightly on the table, the wrists barely resting on either side of his plate. In England, he would have been advised to lay them on his lap. Doing otherwise would have been inappropriate in both countries. There are, however, more serious breaches. Bee Wilson, writing on the history of food, mentions a rule based on a concern for hygiene, yet the repercussions for ignoring it seem today out of proportion. She writes, "In 1836, it was thought that to pick up sugar using fingers rather than sugar tongs was such a terrible faux-pas, it might lead a gentleman losing his good reputation." We may think such a minor slip of attention did not merit the loss of reputation, yet it was perhaps more revealing of the man's mentality than we assume today.

At the end of the fourteenth century, Chaucer described the prioress's refinement. "She never lay any meat fall from her lips, and she did not dip her hands too deeply into the sauce; not a drop of it fell upon... her breasts. She wiped her lips so carefully that not one smudge of grease was to be found in the rim of her cup, after she had drunk from it, and she was careful never to grab at the food on the table." Merely good table manners, we think. Yet, Chaucer (who no doubt also mocks her aspirations at gentility) concludes with this telling observation, which should reawaken in us a greater concern for what we deem forgivable lapses in modern behaviour, "She knew that the manners of the table reflect the manner of a life."

But manners do evolve. Thomas Coryate, an Elizabethan traveller who visited Italy in the 1610s, noticed a new implement used there for holding down the meat while it was being cut. Seduced by the novelty, he soon started using one himself to pin down food morsels. Some of the sixteenth- and seventeenth-century elite (Montaigne, Anne of Austria, Louis XIV, and the Princess Palatine) preferred to eat with their fingers, although individual forks were already used in a few elegant households. Those who adopted these refinements were often scornful of those who did not, and vice-versa, since the use of eating implements was deemed affected and pretentious by those who still mostly used their fingers. New rules were introduced concerning the use of knives at the dinner table. From individual and multi-purpose implements carried on the person (the "knives and daggers" of Don Eugenio's company), a shift in ownership occurred when knives became solely intended for cutting the meat served at the table. From then on, just like any of the other eating implements (spoons, forks, plates, bowls, and goblets), they became the property of the host rather than his guests, and lost much of their sharpness—in fact, special (steak) knives are now required to cut meat.

Other civilizing influences also came into play. As today, it was a time of transition, an era of travel for reasons other than trade and religion. People became interested in each other's customs, which they often started imitating. The Franco-Hungarian Baron de Tott described in his *Mémoires* how, at a dinner party in a country house near Istanbul, he saw people sitting on chairs around a circular table, where spoons and forks were displayed, and where "nothing was missing except the habit of using them." He added, "They did not wish to omit any of our [French] manners, which were just becoming as fashionable among the Greeks as English manners are among ourselves."

International meeting places, such as cruise ships today, have a potential for displaying a vast repertoire of manners. Yet, in our case (I now write as a cruiser), since most of the passengers broadly share a similar culture (the vast North American melting pot), nothing appears unusual or shocking in our conduct around the dining room table, often a source of greater discrepancies. Whereas some dishes might require different handling or implements (such as escargots in their shells) and thus give a clue to the etiquette familiar at home, such food is only offered on board in a way that leaves no equivocation about how it should be eaten.

A quick glance around the dining room shows similar looking people, many of a certain age, equally attempting to dress smartly for the occasion, and sitting with straight backs in front of a table covered in crisp white linen. Much of a muchness, we would be tempted to assume, and we would be right, were it not for one obvious difference in the way we cut our meat.

When American soldiers landed in Europe during WWII, people discovered their different table manners. They were of various ethnic and social origins, yet all seemed to be eating and cutting their meat the same way, which was not the European way. The latter is described by Bee Wilson as follows: "The knife is never laid down until the course is finished. Knife and fork push against each other rhythmically on the plate, like oars on a boat. The fork impales; the knife cuts. The knife pushes; the fork carries. It is a stately dance, whose aim is to slow down the unseemly business of mastication." Instead of performing a stately dance, the young GIs jitterbugged their way through the meal, switching hands incessantly to the sound of the knife being put down with every mouthful. Being different, their manners were judged as wrong.

Some would cut all their meat into small pieces, as is done for small children, then put down their knives, switch their forks to the right hand, and eat all these pieces. Others would put down their knives after cutting each piece of meat and transfer their forks to their right hands to eat, then back to their left, repeating the process with every mouthful. This custom had originated in Europe after the use of the fork became widespread. However, the English, in a quest for further refinement, later devised a new approach and abandoned this method. The new English custom, generally followed on the Continent, is the one described by Bee Wilson, that Canadians and Europeans alike still use. Lest we think this difference a matter of minor importance, it has instead created a sense among Americans and British that the others are actually quite "vulgar" and their own sense of propriety is reinforced by their differences. "The British think they are polite because they never put down their knives; the Americans think they are polite because they do," confirms Wilson. Being British, but also able to back her pronouncement through her study of the evolution of the knife's function, Wilson believes that the right and polite way of holding the knife is the one habitual in Europe, consisting in having "the index finger poised delicately along the top of the... spine with the palm of the hand wrapped around the handle." The knife does not change hands and is not put down.

Naturally, these are merely two slightly different conventions for the manipulation of eating implements. It could also be argued that when the Americans cut all their meat at once, their manners reflect their reputation for practicality: cutting the meat quickly and efficiently, putting down the knife, and getting on with the business of eating, while eschewing the prissy and repetitive process of cutting, eating, cutting, eating, cutting, eating. It is only when they complicate matters by cutting and eating each piece individually (cutting, switching, eating, switching back, cutting, switching, eating, switching back, etc.) that they compromise their reputation.

In a short story ("A Real Life"), Alice Munro confirms the class distinction revealed through the manner of handling eating implements. "It was the way that Dorrie used her knife and fork that had captivated the man... Dorrie kept her fork in her left hand and used the right one for cutting. She did not shift her fork continually to the right hand to pick up her food. That was because she had been to Whitby Ladies College when she was young." The man was naturally able to appreciate this refinement, for he "used his knife and fork the same way. He was from England." The touch is subtle and the impression positive, since Mr. Spiers shares Dorrie's table manners, but it is not always the case that such remarks are kindly meant. It is more likely that any notice of someone else's table manners serves to distance the observer from the performer.

Dining on board often forces a return to stricter manners. At home, fast food consumption, general laxity in behaviour, conflicting schedules often preventing sitting down together at the family dinner table, eating in front of television sets, teenagers' greater independence, and cross-cultural influences have all contributed to weakening the rules governing the way we eat together. On board, the formality of the ship's dining rooms, reflected in the elegant china pattern, the proper table setting, and the well-trained attendants promotes a return of more formal manners than those exhibited in everyday life. At the same table, for instance, it is customary to wait until everybody is served before starting to eat. Those who initially neglect this courtesy may be encouraged to start without waiting—upon which they usually stop eating and wait. We tend to put our best foot forward, not necessarily to impress but simply to display appropriate public behaviour, and are guided by the assumption that everyone will understand and appreciate our conduct. At a deeper level, this behaviour exemplifies a trend observed by the sociologist Norbert Elias in groups constrained to live in close proximity, where they find themselves becoming more attuned to the sensitivities of others. This gradual process is accompanied by an increasing desire not to offend or shock anyone.

In general, we attempt to behave according to rules we believe will accommodate most people around us. At the same time, we remain aware of our differences and often disapprove of the manners of others. This is not new. In 1560, a Frenchman described these differences and the displeasure they caused. "The Germans eat with their mouths closed and think it is unseemly to do otherwise. The French, on the contrary, half open their mouths and find the German practice rather disgusting. The Italians eat delicately, the French vigorously, so that they find the Italian practice too refined and precious... Each nation has something peculiar to it and different from others. This is why a child learns to eat according to the place where it happens to be and the customs of that place."

We may follow rules that make social contact smoother and less perilous because we have the common good in mind and theorize that civilization requires rules to ensure the smooth running of society. But what of other, less "civilized" cultures, whose rules are often stricter than ours, and punished by taboo, exclusion, and other harsh penalties when challenged or ignored? Lévi-Strauss has an interesting conception of the differences of manners and thought between our civilized society and traditional cultures. As an anthropologist, he sees their opposition being due less to geography or time than to different perceptions of the deep-seated cultural notions of purity and of impurity, from which individuals must protect themselves.

In our societies, self-protection is the ultimate goal. We use hats and gloves as protection from the elements, forks to keep unsoiled while eating, straws to avoid drinking unpleasantly cold beverages, and we preserve food to prevent being contaminated by anything raw, rotten, and dangerous to our health. Hats, gloves, forks, and so on are meant to protect us against external factors. Yet, argues Lévi-Strauss, "whereas we think of good manners as a way of protecting the internal purity of the subject against the external impurity of beings and things, in savage societies, they are a means of protecting the purity of beings and things against the impurity of the subject." He further comments on our being accustomed from childhood to seeing impurity as being external to ourselves, and reminds us that the familiar formula "hell is other people" is less a philosophical proposition than an ethnographical statement about our civilization. "When they assert, on the contrary, that 'hell is ourselves,' savage peoples give us a lesson in humility which… we may still be capable of understanding."

Walt Kelly's Pogo, a North American cultural icon, put it a little differently: "I've seen the enemy and he is us." More simplistically, we can all agree that manners, while protecting us from others, also protect them from us.

INTERACTION

A recent book describes the composition of a particular table and the conversations around it. The passengers are on the *Oronsay*, a ship of the Orient Line sailing in the 1950s from Ceylon to England. Table 76, the Cat's Table of Michael Ondaatje's 2012 eponymous book, is described as "the *least* privileged place," but who would not wish to have sat around it? Including the eleven-year old narrator and his two young friends, those around that table form a little separate universe. During twenty-one days at sea together, they have plenty of time to discover their unique, idiosyncratic personalities.

There is the half-Sicilian pianist, Mr. Mazappa, who goes by the professional and ill-suited name of Sunny Meadows. A great admirer of Sidney Bechet, *"le grand Bechet,"* he relates at will the famous duel with McHendrick in the Paris of 1928, after the latter had accused Bechet of playing a false note. There is also a Mr. Nevil, a retired ship dismantler who had helped to take apart *Normandie,* "the most beautiful ship ever built," burnt and half-submerged in the Hudson River. He has a detailed knowledge of everything related to ships, and is happy to share it. Doing safety research for the Orient Line, he has access to every nook and cranny on the *Oronsay,* and carries with him the blueprint of the ship.

Larry Daniel, an "intelligent and curious man," is a botanist who has spent most of his life studying the forests of Sumatra and Borneo. He is growing an artificially lit garden in the entrails of their ship, which the three boys visit with him. Two other people grace the table with their presence. Mr. Gunesekera, a tailor from Kandy, "gracious and courteous," speaks not a word but laughs at all jokes, understood or not. The mysterious Perinetta Lasqueti, slim, blonde, and a sleepwalker, has "a laugh that hinted it had rolled around once or twice in the mud." Their conversations range from Italian art and Madonnas to hiking naked in the English countryside, and they speculate about the suspected murderer of an English judge imprisoned on board and the wealthy Sir Hector de Silva, travelling with his retinue and suffering from hydrophobia.

Not being characters in a book, John and I have never had the good fortune of having such varied passengers sharing our tables. It does not mean that our fellow cruisers had not often led interesting and adventurous lives (there have been veterans of several wars and immigrants of various origins among them, people with interesting former careers, and the majority had travelled extensively), but these facts were not necessarily revealed or discussed.

The *Oronsay* was not a cruise ship. Unlike us, her passengers were not self-selected for leisure and part of a homogeneous social or cultural grouping. Many decades and purposes also separate our voyages, as well as different age groups, social classes, and ethnic backgrounds. No doubt we are the poorer for it, but our own homo-geneity, while dulling any potential excitement, ensures compatible grounds for safe, if uneventful developments. Cruisers' behaviour at the table is codified in a manner that would have surprised the passengers at the Cat's Table, but even on the *Oronsay*, there were differences, and Ondaatje's description of those sitting at the head table is a familiar one. "Nothing much of lasting value ever happens at the head table, held together by a familiar rhetoric. Those who already have power continue to glide along the familiar rut they have made for themselves." This might indeed apply to many retired cruisers of comfortable means, gliding along the familiar ruts of conventional good manners and discretion, with little of much sig-nificance usually revealed in conversation.

At sea, the conversations we hold often depend on the seating choice we make, either the "fixed seating" with the same people meeting around the same table every night for the length of the voyage or the "open seating" where every meal is the occasion for new encounters. In the latter option, particularly on small ships and long crossings, there is the odd chance of sitting more than once with the same people, but the expectation is that new table com-panions will be met every night. But even if the same people should meet again, the others at the table would be new, so the composition of the table and the nature of the conversation would be different.

In the fixed format, a form of routine settles in after a while. At the first meal, we learn each person's first name and residence—and whether our personalities will be mutually acceptable on the cruise. Gradually, hobbies are revealed, a rich field of superficial conver-sation, and in some cases, it is even discovered that some people share the same sense of the ludicrous. After each shore visit, a little more is unveiled, revealing personal sensitivities. For instance, while encouraged to bring useful gifts to Fanning Island (clothing, school supplies, etc.) we were advised not to bring candies for the children, as there is no dentist on the island and there is no way to dispose of the garbage caused by the wrappings. Two women at our table saved the nightly chocolates on their pillows and added them to the wrapped candies they also brought. Had they committed a serious offence, I would not have been more (mutely) censorious. I had so far enjoyed their company, but this small slip made me reconsider my opinion. Because we are contained and have so little that actually needs doing, life on board is reduced to its essentials—the good is very good and the bad is very bad. We can be jovial, irritable, suspicious, boastful, discreet, vain, friendly, and judgmental, as I was, according to our usual manner, but on board it seems to matter more because there is little to distract us from ourselves.

The situation is different when we opt for open seating, since we cannot re-evaluate our first impressions. For extroverts who may only seek superficial encounters, this option is an opportunity to meet a large number of passengers, to shine in conversation, and perhaps to relish assuming and maintaining a certain persona. More reserved people may find having to introduce themselves and establish their status every night a difficult pace to sustain.

We may wonder at our decision to eat dinner with strangers, since there is always a little stress involved in this exercise, and let us remember that some cruisers chose to share different tables at all three meals. Instead, we could eat alone in the dining room, or in the informal Lido at separate tables, or even dine in our cabins. Rather, succumbing to the lure of the unknown, we take the trouble to adopt the dress code suggested for the evening and engage in the ritualistic and mannerly process of dining with others. Some of us may simply look forward to the possibility of forming friendly relations with a greater variety of people than can be met at home. Else, we may find the opportunity of parading for a while an optimal version of ourselves (unchallenged by those who know us well) to be one of cruising's unavowed attractions.

The only element of surprise as we are led to our dining room table is who will be sitting beside us. Since our dinner partners will help determine the nature of the exchanges and contribute to setting the mood, this unknown element is important. Sociologists who observe private performances in public places suggest that establishing and then maintaining status is of prime importance when we share the stage with others. The practice offers a "drama-turgical" perspective combining individual performances and the interaction of all participants. Each performance varies, depend-ing on each cast of characters and each specific circumstance, as we move nightly from table to table in the open seating format. Moreover, each participant is responsible for the development of the play, either by influencing it directly through active participa-tion or by providing an inert or static presence against which the others' playacting will bounce, first challengingly, later dismissively if the lack of participation continues.

What about initial timing? Arriving first on the first night may give us a passing feeling of owning the table, while coming later may mean that we are joining those who already form a group through prior arrival, even by a few minutes. It would be foolish to say, "May we join you?" as we are ushered to a table according to seating arrangements established by some distant office, but the temptation is there. If our companions arrive at the same time as ourselves, we are equal partners on still neutral ground. Naturally, some people have such strong self-esteem that whenever they arrive and wherever they sit, they act as the dominant participants at the table, while others may need coaxing to position themselves. It is also immedi-ately evident that round tables are better equalizers than rectangu-lar ones that often privilege the centre seats.

Whether we are alone or part of a couple (married people or friends travelling together, as most of us seem to be), our approach to self-presentation may be different, but we are all aware that every-one is equally unknown to the rest of the table. Connections are sometimes discovered later through living in the same city or having unknowingly been on the same previous cruise. Since most of us come as couples, we may have to help each other in confirming our self-presentation to the group and sustain our *fictio* or image over time. One partner's tacit acceptance of the other's self-pre-sentation seems to confirm its validity. Partners can offer support in many ways, for instance by introducing a new dimension to the other's self-presentation. While modesty may prevent some from proclaiming their own accomplishments, the partner may step in to boost the couple's status by establishing the X factor that makes the other person outstanding in some manner. When done in a gently teasing way, it reinforces the modesty of the person who did not mention the achievement, particularly if the latter is substantial. I can't think of any occasion when a husband might say, to illustrate good-humouredly his wife's clumsiness (already noticed by everyone), "Elsie made a complete ass of herself when she tripped over her dress while getting the Nobel last year." We would all understand the sly objective of the remark, since how else can one introduce in polite society the topic of outstanding merit unless easing it with light-hearted disparagement?

These accomplishments, which we may seek to introduce as general information about ourselves, are actually an essential part of our self-image, to the same extent as any other distinctive characteristic (abilities, social connections, accomplishments, profession, ancestry, possessions, political beliefs, interests, self-appreciation, etc.) and an intrinsic part of who we are. We must decide how much we need to impart to strangers; in other words, how important is any of it to the functioning of our table and how should it be doled out? It would be untoward for one person to hold the stage for too long. On the other hand, it seems fair to divulge delicately such information at permanent-seating tables, for how would we feel learning Elsie's unusual accomplishments at the end of the cruise if we had tended to think her a little dull and dowdy and shown her much less attention than we did another woman of far lesser merit?

In our case, John and I have acquired a new peculiarity that has contributed to altering the image we projected on our first three cruises. Following an accident, I sometimes use a walker, definitely an image-altering contraption. Both my slow progress (a negative trait) and John's attentiveness (a positive one) are no doubt noted and weighed as silent factors in the general impression we make as a unit.

Finally, before leaving the topic of couples, we may wonder about today's relevance of a fact mentioned by sociologist Erving

Goffman, namely that wives (whatever their independent behaviour at home or in front of the couple's old friends) tend to show a "respectful subordination to the will and opinion of her husband," thus permitting him to assume a more dominant public position in the partnership. Goffman wrote about middle-class people of sixty years ago, and today's young couples would not recognize their public behaviour in this obsolete description. Yet, around our table, we are older and remember those days well. So influential were they in determining respective public positioning within the couple that we sometimes see them reappearing. Women still tend to speak to women and men to men, usually on topics deemed appropriate to their gender. However, on longer cruises, true characters tend to emerge more readily.

On board, what often determines female-male roles in the conversation is how the second couple chooses to sit at the table, be it wife beside wife, or alternating husbands and wives. The decision could be triggered either by class or ethnic origins. People used to attending dinner parties may automatically adopt the alternating pattern, while those issued from societies deemed to be more "macho" could prefer same-sex associations. However, the order may change occasionally during the voyage to give everyone more opportunity to speak directly to others. This change is often initiated by the women, not surprisingly so since our sex is deemed more sensitive to establishing moods of companionship and compatibility.

Do jokes have a role to play at the table, whether to ease a particular situation or to promote a certain ambiance for the voyage? Some may come naturally, as a follow-up on a shared experience, such as a shore visit or exceptionally bad weather, or in response to a person's self-mockery. One of our dinner companions' discomfiture with his expensive camera became well known, and as he had been the first to give examples of his incompetence in handling it, this gave us licence to enquire of his progress with a levity we would not have indulged in, had he not initiated it.

In some cultures, a system of joking relationships exists to defuse tense situations. There is no such thing on board, but we are aware that jokes may have negative connotations and should be handled carefully. Thus, whatever jokes may be occasionally heard between strangers are determinedly mild. A man who had noticed me sitting every morning working on my computer, lightly asked, as he walked by, "Writing the Great American Novel?" Just as lightly, I responded, "I wish!" It is the appropriate level of attention, tone of communication, and degree of familiarity permissible between strangers sharing the same relatively small space and presumably a similar relaxed holiday mood.

The reason jokes around the dinner table always remain tentative is that we never reach the status that would make their more relaxed use acceptable. The table is a microcosm of our world; all takes place on its stage, and because this shared stage is limited by time and space, it is not conducive to greater intimacy, and we are always careful not to offend. The more unusual our circumstances, the more sensitive we are to the impulses of others, and the less latitude we allow ourselves in order not to offend. Moreover, our short acquaintance does not make it worth taking the risk of testing the strength of the relationship. Were we to retire more or less permanently on board and attempt to recreate at sea our own society and culture, we would probably be more daring in testing the limits we deem appropriate for living in superficial harmony.

IV
ENTERTAINMENT

10 WHILING AWAY THE DAYS

At sea, we are surrounded by water, and water on its own and in calm weather does not provide much entertainment. There is usually little to be seen; sea birds only appear close to shore and only occasionally are large fish or mammals seen swimming by or flying fish leaping over the surface.

On her way to Australia, Margaret Meredith was luckier than most. She saw Mother Carey pigeons, mutton birds, and the odd albatross, and someone caught and skinned a Cae pigeon that measured three feet across. On another day, she wrote, "Captain called us early to see penguins. I was dressed in time to see them before they disappeared swimming under water with heads out, looking like rats with wings. They made a curious sound, like an old man saying 'Ah' and some, further off, sounded like a child crying spasmodically." Even today, any sighting of marine animals will have passengers flock to the railings to watch their performance.

The ways of allaying the monotony of the voyage have remained the same: organizing some entertainment on the ship or finding it on shore. Romance, naturally, can also add a little spice to what might otherwise seem like the slow unfolding and grey emptiness of time wasted.

OCEAN GAZING

Anyone who has unhappily spent days gazing at the ocean's grey-green immensity can empathize with Don Eugenio.

> What pleasure can a man have on board a solitary
> ship at sea? No land in sight, nothing but lowering sky
> and heaving water; he travels in a blue-green world,
> the ground deep and far below, without seeming to
> move, without seeing even the wake of another ship,
> always surrounded by the same horizon, the same at
> night as in the morning, the same today as yesterday,
> no change, no incident. What interest can such a
> journey bode? How can he escape the boredom and
> misery of such a journey and such a lodging?

Unlike us, Don Eugenio did not have the choice: he had to go by sea. Three centuries later, many passengers continued to find little attraction to sea travel. Among them was Ralph Waldo Emerson, not "a good traveller" by his own account, who had nevertheless accepted an invitation to visit England to present a series of lectures. In 1847, he boarded a Boston packet-ship, the *Washington Irving*, on her way to Liverpool. He considered sea life an "acquired taste" and was not in favour of it, given the "confinement, cold, motion, noise, and odour." His outlook was grim as he concluded, "Nobody likes to be treated ignominiously, upset, shoved against the side of the house, rolled over, suffocated with bilge, mephitis, and stewing oil. We get used to these annoyances at last, but the dread of the sea remains longer." As much as the unpleasant conditions on board, he disliked the cost of such voyages and feared the dangers related by the captain and mate, concluding, "The wonder is always new that any sane man can be a sailor."

By 1907, the mood had not improved. Harry Clark on the *Cassandra* wrote of the boredom of sailing "with nothing to do and all day to do it in." He added, "Only one week at sea should satisfy everyone but I confess I have had enough of it. The monotonous daily round, nothing to do, nothing to see except water, water everywhere."

For others, this monotony becomes an unbearable burden. Julian Huxley, sailing to East Africa in 1929, wrote, "Those people who assert the real autonomy of the human soul ought to take a long sea journey. Robbed of the usual variety of outer stimulus, the spirit gradually flags and sinks... after days confined to the same ship, the same few people, the same eternal sea, the same games, the same food, a horrible sluggishness and apathy descends on one's life... and all because of the increasing monotony." It is puzzling that Huxley should have experienced such monotony on board, since it is during this voyage, and while travelling with his wife, that he fell in love with an eighteen-year old American woman. One would have thought this complication capable of sweeping away the cobwebs of boredom and making the voyage extremely challenging.

The nineteenth century saw a vast improvement in transatlantic passages. After the previously long and miserable voyages, passengers on Thomas Cook's tours could now enjoy rapid crossings, hot baths, gas lighting, deck games, musical entertainment, and good food with champagne. With their dedication to passengers' comfort, these crossings were the precursors of our cruises, with food and entertainment already the two main attractions. It is with this new pampering that the feeling of boredom started to recede and many began to recognize the romance of being at sea.

Passengers even reported finding pleasure in the slow unfolding of the ocean. Frederic Treves waxed eloquently on the pleasures of forging ahead at sea with something new to see every day. "There was always the 'stark-barrelled swell' of the sea... a misty cape... a ship on its way homewards. There were the porpoises who tumbled in the vessel's course... the timid fringe of phosphorescent light... the pathways made by the moon across the indigo plain of waters at night." Even when nothing else happened, "there was still the swish of the sea along the side, the ship's bell marking the hour, the deep pulse of the engines, and the mysterious creaking of innumerable bulkheads." Art historian Simon Schama also enjoyed watching the rolling waves and commented on "an eyeful and a day full or nothing other than the rhythm of the sea and silvery curving rim of the world" being the best thing about crossing the Atlantic. However, he was sailing on the *Queen Mary 2* and no doubt enjoying many more distractions than the peaceful contemplation of the grey expanse.

For Treves, Schama, and others, much of the allure of sailing comes from the sea itself, the delight in the motion of the swell, and the play of light on the water. Some even relished the monotony of sailing. "One day is very like another; it is a lazy life, sitting on deck and walking and occasionally sleeping... Everybody is occupied in killing time–when not eating.... The voyage has been an uninterrupted delight," wrote Lewis Upcott on his way to Bombay on the *Arabia* in 1913.

However, it is true that, depending on our experience at sea, or even on a particular day, we could side with either opinion and mixed feelings are probably the rule with most passengers, who need the added gratification of organized entertainment, shore excursions, or ship romances to fully enjoy their voyage. The *Illustrated London News* of November 23, 1872, wondered how passengers "were enabled to support existence under a burning hot sunshine, during their voyage down the Red Sea on board the Peninsular and Oriental Company's mail steamship." The answer was not unexpected: Games of card, chess, backgammon, draughts, and a long forgotten "Aunt Sally" were soon organized, while "lotteries of wagers upon the day's run of the ship, or the hour of arrival at each port, are resorted to by many of the passengers." As well, "novel-reading goes on without intermission," while "children are running about, and playing with their dolls." For those afflicted with seasickness and only able "to recline listlessly," there were China chairs, or "seats made of cane and admirably adapted, by their shape, for ease and comfort." Finally, "scandal may also become one of the means of passing time; and flirtation is almost certain to give material for scandal to work upon."

CREWS' EARLY ENTERTAINMENT

The tedium of gazing at the endless sea that befalls passengers is not usually shared by busy crews. Seamen have concerns of their own, but boredom is not usually one of them. Records show that from early days their amusements were mostly limited to drinking, gambling, and carousing—often on shore, as ship duty required stricter discipline. Even captains, whose responsibilities were onerous, apparently did not escape from the occasional need to pass time in idle ways. Sir Francis Drake was said to have coloured in the illustrations of his copy of the *Book of Martyrs,* John Foxe's recently published book.

On Dutch Indiamen, life was just as tedious and the passengers and crew's favourite pastimes were gossip and games. Crews also entertained themselves with songs and theatricals, with illegal gambling with dice, draughts, and a form of backgammon. Reading was restricted to the few books available on board, usually of a religious nature. The few women passengers knitted or tatted, and occasionally lent a hand in the kitchen to improve the diet, which would become tedious after many months at sea.

There was also on some Dutch ships what could be construed as a game (as bear baiting and cock, rat, or dog fights are also deemed to be). Seamen had always caught sharks, universally thought to be man-eaters, and used some of their parts as tools or health remedies. At times, delving into their deep fear of the sea and the monstrous creatures within, and reflecting their harsh society and their brutal environment, they indulged in capturing them—gratuitously, it would seem, thus putting the exercise into the game category. No doubt, they enjoyed avenging sailors fallen overboard and prey to the beasts, but the greatest pleasure was torturing the enemy. They gouged out their eyes and cut off their fins. Finally, they tied a barrel to the tail of the mutilated sharks and tossed them back into the sea. Blinded and unable to swim or dive, losing blood, the exhausted animals kept smashing into the sides of the ship, until they died, often eaten by other sharks, which the spectators must have deemed an appropriate retribution. Such exercises were seen as suitable outlets for the seamen's pent up violence. Passengers were no doubt treated to the show, but we can assume that their sensibilities were not as heightened as would ours be today if faced with the same spectacle.

On British ships, crews often showed off their athletic abilities by engaging in physical contests, fighting and boxing being favourite sports among them. Moreover, they were not averse to taking part in brawls whenever the occasion arose. We will see later the comic relief and entertainment value of the Crossing the Line rituals, with neophytes repeatedly dunked into sea water and manhandled to the delight of the onlookers, themselves previously victims of such established shenanigans.

According to Patrick O'Brian's novels, recognized for their historical accuracy, officers on board eighteenth-century Navy ships agreeably spent the evenings recollecting events of naval importance or curiosity, following the careers of colleagues, playing music, reciting poetry, and exchanging droll remarks at dinner.

Other entertainment was also available, such as one offered the Prince de Nassau-Siegen, a paying passenger on Bougainville's ship, who occasionally went botanizing with Commesson, the naturalist of the French expedition. On at least one occasion, the elegant aristocrat found more ashore than he had bargained for. In Tahiti, a naked young girl was obligingly offered to him; the prince demurred when observing fifty curious onlookers gathered to see him perform. Ordinary sailors visiting Polynesia, starting in 1768, would have eagerly accepted the same entertainment.

SONG AND DANCE

Music seems to have been the entertainment of choice in third class or steerage on emigrants' ships. We saw such scenes in the movie *Titanic,* but the more contemporary description of Robert Louis Stevenson, sailing to America in 1879, confirms the predilection for this form of distraction. Despite minimal amenities on board, there were many compensations to be drawn from the emigrants' fellowship. "We were indeed a musical ship's company," he wrote, "and cheered our way into exile with the fiddle, the accordion, and the songs of all nations. Good, bad, or indifferent—Scottish, English, Irish, Russian, German, or Norse—the songs were received with generous applause. Once or twice a recitation, very spiritedly rendered in a powerful Scottish accent, varied the proceedings." Dancing was another matter, however. "The performers were all humorous, frisky fellows... but as soon as they were arranged for the dance, they conducted themselves like so many mutes at a funeral. I have never seen decorum pushed so far... The quadrille was soon whistled down, and the dancers departed under a cloud."

These scenes took place in the nether regions of second class and steerage. In the elegant first-class quarters, bands played, concerts were given, and talks provided an educational slant ("In the evening, at 9 o'clock Colonel McDonald gave a lecture on the Maori war... Not very interesting."). In first class, passengers also provided some entertainment often of excellent quality. John Fergusson, on the *China* in 1901, noted, "Most of the passengers were musical, and as there were some very good voices among them, and we had three pianos, we were well off."

However, the favourites were dances and, particularly fancy dress balls. Annie Beauchamps, on the *Ruahine* in 1897, describes the fancy dress she would wear for the Crossing of the Line ceremony; her costume was that of "a New Woman" and she wore her *"bloomers,* waistcoat shirt front and blue serge jacket and Percy's sailor hat." She thoroughly enjoyed her trip. "It's really wonderful the way we have been entertained on this boat. Dances, Tableaux, Fancy dress Ball, concerts, games of all sorts... and catered for in every way possible and the attention one gets from stewards, officers etc is admirable."

Dancing has certainly remained an attraction on cruise ships, even on the sedate Holland America Line. It is rather old-fashioned in some of the salons, and more energetic into the night in the Crow's Nest frequented by a younger set. For unaccompanied ladies there are gentlemen of a certain age recruited by cruise lines to serve as dancing partners. They keep a modest profile off the dance floor and show perfect manners. Their performance shows them to be adequate to the task.

SEDATE PURSUITS

Turning once more to Stevenson's descriptions, irresistible for their good humour and the genuine pleasure he takes in sharing his experience, we learn that "there was a single chess-board and a single pack of cards. Sometimes as many as twenty of us would be playing dominoes for love. Feats of dexterity, puzzles for the intelligence… Puss in Corner, which was rebaptised, in more manly style, Devil and Four Corners, was my own favourite game, but there were many who preferred another, the humour of which was to box a person's ears until he found out who had cuffed him." More refined games were played by Margaret Meredith and her companions, including bridge, checkers, quoits, other games called Consequences, Grab, General Post, and so on.

Reading is also a major pastime on board and the library is one of the consistently busy places. The monotony of life at sea seems conducive to reading. The library also offers board games, puzzles, and some computers with costly access to the internet, but reading is definitely a favourite occupation, perhaps owing to the easy pace, the lack of ordinary tasks, the soft rolling of the waves, and the peaceful and immense vista of the sea. The library holdings are usually varied and seem sufficient to hold the interest of most passengers. On many ships, there is also a book club and, as with most such clubs, the participants are usually women.

The joys of reading at sea are best described by Maurice Baring on a P&O liner in 1912. "A ship is the pleasantest place to read in the world. Firstly, you have the advantage of being indoors and out-of-doors at the same time, if you sit on deckchair, or in a smoking room near an open door, secondly… you can pause and watch the passengers, overhear scraps of talk, [and] engage yourself in desultory conversation."

Ralph Waldo Emerson also enjoyed reading, along with the pleasure of intelligent conversation. "We found on board the usual cabin library; Basil Hall, Dumas, Dickens, Bulwer, Balzac, and Sand, were our seagods. Among the passengers, there was some variety of talent and profession; we exchanged our convenience at sea, and sometimes a memorable fact turns up, which have long had a vacant niche for, and seize with the joy of a collector." However, he concluded, "But under the best conditions, a voyage is one of the severest tests to try man."

Similarly, Margaret Meredith and her companions exchanged books and ideas. They read some of the favorites of the day (Henry Drummond, William Clark Russell, Rudyard Kipling, Anthony Hope, Benjamin Kidd), and when the weather was too rough to sit on deck, there was always someone to show photographs of Sicily, Australia, Sark, or Bromley. They would also assemble in the saloon to play whist or piquet, play the piano and sing, and attend Sunday services. On the return crossing, where gentlemen numbered thirteen, there were sporting contests against apprentices. She and her companions often participated in "theatrics" or concerts for the enjoyment of all on board. They wrote and performed plays like "A Pair of Lunatics," for which Miss Meredith made wigs of tow, "My Lady Help," "A Checkered Career," "Done on Both Sides," "Burglar & Judge," or "Never too Late to Mend."

Meredith also describes some of the gentlemen passengers in their routine tasks like helping the crew put up awnings to protect the ladies against the sun, stretching weather-canvasses to shelter them from the frequent squalls, or even assisting the crew and apprentices in taking the life boats out to sea to verify their seaworthiness. They used this opportunity to take photographs of the ship from the sea.

Whether they played the piano and sang in the upper-class salons or danced energetically below deck on immigrant ships, passengers had to rely on their own resources. Well-educated women such as Miss Meredith, who had studied philosophy at Lady Margaret Hall, the Ladies' College at Oxford, and who had many social skills, were a welcome asset. Her talents included play-writing, acting, sketching, card-playing, the art of conversation, and accompanying singers on the piano, particularly male passengers sought after for duets with lady performers.

Self-generated entertainment is rare on modern ships, where passengers are kept busy and amused by professional entertainers and speakers. They can try their luck at the casino, go to the cinema, attend lectures or cooking demonstrations, or take dancing or gymnastics classes. However, there is still a modest attempt at involving passengers in their own amusement, including treasure hunts, Trivial Pursuit contests, games inspired by television shows, or the odd afternoon devoted to passengers' talents. There also seems to be a growing trend for cruises to offer conferences on the countries of destination, introducing their geography and history, and revealing local usages and mores. On Polynesian cruises, for instance, passengers can learn to play the ukulele and the toere drum, dance the hula, make grass skirts and leis, and learn a few Hawaiian words. The initiates hold their own show after some practice and companions and friends attend, clapping heartily and taking photographs of the wahines in their makeshift grass skirts.

On Holland America ships, in particular, with the obvious desire to be thought of as a "family" of sorts, two nights are devoted to displaying the crew's talents at the end of the performers' regular duties, with one showcasing the Filipinos, the other the Indonesians. Despite the late hour, passengers are encouraged to attend and show their appreciation to the crew who, in turn, are said to perform to show their appreciation of the passengers. The turnout is usually good, and the following day, passengers congratulate on their performances the steward or dining room attendant they recognized. The lack of professionalism is touching, and we are reminded throughout that rehearsals were done on the staff's free time. Yet, it is always the same show, as if Filippinos and Indonesians only knew two or three dances. There is nothing new in this marshalling the crew for the passengers' entertainment. In 1898, Annie Beauchamps wrote, "Tomorrow we are looking forward to an Entertainment in our saloon by the Stewards of the ship. I think it will be very good, they are such a nice lot of fellows and some so nice looking."

THE PROFESSIONALS

Every night, there is a performance by a singer, a comedian, the odd ventriloquist, a magician, some musicians, and perhaps the ship's troupe of dancers and singers, and all are well attended. Their quality depends on the cruise line's willingness to pay for the acts, and we may not always see performers at the peak of their career. However, this is not true of every line, and some hire outstanding performers, making a selling point of the quality of the entertainment they offer.

If we travel often enough, we probably see the same performers more than once.

"Oldsters' jokes" used to be in fashion. One particular stand-up comedian affected astonishment upon entering the stage and taking his first glimpse of the audience: Had he just woken up and found himself transported into an old folks' home? Roars of laughter greeted this rude remark, produced by an audience unpleasantly apologetic for being indeed the butt of those routine jokes: the elderly. The sole really amusing allusions to our age came from a magician/comic, accompanied by his little dog gamboling joyously on stage, a charming Coton de Tulear said to have been put to work in order to help pay for its veterinary bills. The magician's only ageist joke, skipped over very lightly while performing a Houdini trick, was to ask whether we had seen Tony Curtis in the film role of Houdini, adding under his breath, "Actually, some of you may even have seen Houdini do it." Three years later, the joke was no longer an aside but firmly entrenched in his routine, and definitely less subtle. Perhaps my bias is showing since, in truth, there is only one old-folks joke I like. An ancient roué walks into a bar and spots an attractive woman sitting alone. Debonair as ever, he leans over and asks, "Tell me, my dear, do I come here often?"

A cruise director, fond of the *bêtisier* format—a collection of inanities pronounced by passengers over several cruises—once gave us some choice samples. Hilarious as they may have seemed to some, who could then distance themselves from the authors of the naïve lines, they were in fact meant to be offensive. The audience, characteristically, laughed at them.

- A woman passenger asked, "Does the crew sleep on board?"
- After having explained to passengers that even numbers were port side and uneven were starboard, a woman asked, "What do I do, I have both?" [the cabins have four numbers]
- Seeing him looking at the ocean, a woman passenger asked whether he was watching for wild life. "Yes," he said, "whales, dolphins." She then asked, "At what time do they come out?"

Naturally, all were women, seemingly enhancing the comic nature of the joke.

SHORE EXCURSIONS

At first, ports were simply visited to load or unload cargo or take on fresh provisions. Even then, some care was taken that passengers be able to explore. When the *Hesperus* landed in 1895 on Saint Helena, passengers toured Jamestown, the island's main town. A few visited Longwood, Napoleon's residence in exile. The three lady passengers were invited to take tea with the exiled Zulu King, Dinni Zulu, in his cottage. There seems to have been genuine and mutual pleasure taken by the king, his wives, and these ladies, who drank tea while listening to him play old English favourites on the piano and sing for their entertainment. Margaret Meredith related their visit in a ladies' magazine, giving us a good idea of the type of excursions only possible when small groups of passengers were involved, and when such visits were not yet commercialized.

Today's cruise ships must devise interesting events, tours, and shore excursions to break the monotony of sailing. The excursions must have intrinsic artistic, architectural, natural, historical, or folkloric value to justify the choice of the cruise, and all compete in ingenuity to provide out of the way experiences for passengers. Cruisers expect tours to Pompeii, Herculaneum, and Capri when anchored in Naples, and visits to the Vatican while in Civitavecchia

(Rome), but the real quest is for those unusual places that few other cruise ships have visited before.

Visitors venture on their own while on shore but, through lack of information, ignorance of the language and customs, being used to be taken care of, and mostly lack of time, most resort to being herded into buses on organized tours. When several ships are in port, the sheer number of tourists seems overwhelming. These numbers, as well as some occasional careless dress or behaviour that disregard local sensitivities, can make them an objectionable presence. It may not take much to raise local hackles. The following note was circulated to the passengers of the S.S. *Ormonde* of the Orient Line upon their arrival in Lisbon in 1933. "Without wishing to restrict their liberty, the Captain desires to impress upon passengers the desirability of normal attire on shore in Lisbon. Last year, as result of criticism by the inhabitants of Lisbon, some unpleasantness and inconvenience was caused to tourists which eventually led to police intervention. The Captain has received a Circular letter from the Chief of Police at Lisbon, on this subject." No further light is shed on the 1932 incident.

Since the 1930s, many countries have realized that tourism is the lifeblood of their economy and, while still privately resenting tourists, they are spreading out the welcome mats farther and wider than ever before. Furthermore, poorer countries or those struck by natural disaster sometimes receive directly significant contributions from cruise companies, individual ships, and the passengers themselves.

Having considered formal and informal entertainment, the joys of reading and observing nature, and seen passengers deployed ashore, one element to the attraction of sailing has obviously been left aside: romance...

11 ROMANCE

Love, exciting and new...

Come aboard. We're waiting for you.

We all remember the 1977-1987 television series *The Love Boat* and its theme song full of promise, or are at least familiar with its concept. Who knows how many decisions to go cruising the show has prompted, with its evocation of fun-filled voyages, full of excitement and romance.

Keeping a number of people mostly intent on diverting themselves in a close space, with no other requirements than eating and sleeping, certainly sounds conducive to creating connections and making the most of chance encounters. The same relaxed environment also serves to strengthen existing relationships, and it is not unusual to find that many people are on their first, second, or third honeymoon—not always with the same partner. Even if not new, love always seems exciting and coming on board, as the song invites us to do, implies that it will intensify. Let us consider what amorous opportunities being at sea can afford.

WOMEN

We should remember that most sailors are young. On Cook's *Endeavour,* for instance, where the admiralty had authorized a crew of seventy, later raised to eighty-five with the addition of marines, the average age was twenty-five, and we can safely assume that sex was on the mind of many.

Women, loose or otherwise, were deemed to have no place on eighteenth-century ships and, even if some were on board, their name or presence was not mentioned on the lists. The exceptions were usually older women, often acting as nurses, but sometimes with a more active role. For example, at the Battle of the Nile in 1798, several were said to have served as ammunition-handlers. Until women became passengers in their own right, the only woman officially on board was the captain's wife,

The occasional presence of others on board came out indirectly. Thus, the transcripts of the *Narcissus* court-martial (1782) show one of the mutineers' alibi that he had been lying at the time beside a "Mrs Collins." Another case occurred on the *Etoile,* one of Bougainville's ships, when it was suspected, and later confirmed, that Jean Baret, the servant of the naturalist Commerson was actually Jeanne Baret, his long-time housekeeper and mistress. She had worked arduously at collecting specimens and sorting them, done her best to pass herself off as a man, kept discreetly out of the way, but Bougainville was enormously relieved when Commerson and his assistant decided to stop in New France (Reunion) and continue collecting botanical specimens locally. It solved the dicey situation of knowingly having a woman on board, which was against the rules and deemed bad luck by the sailors.

On the other hand, while in port, the presence on board of women was sometimes implicitly encouraged, with captains closing their eyes to obvious debauchery. John Mansfield, researching maritime life in the days of Nelson, wrote, "It was not unusual for a monstrous regiment of women to march right across England so that they might join their mates on the other side." When wives were not available, other women were easily found. "In England, a boatload of women would come alongside an anchored ship of the line, and sailors would climb down the gangway, make their choice, and carry the women back on board." Since captains did not begrudge the temporary presence of wives on board, many women outside the blissful state of wedlock were nevertheless passed off as the legitimate things, at least as far as captains were concerned. This probably created the saying that a sailor had a wife in every port (although that may have also been true).

Sailors also found the same comfort from prostitutes in the numerous brothels in every port or young native women involved in perhaps more innocent idylls, such as in the Polynesian islands, celebrated by British and French sailors in the eighteenth century. There, they discovered a generous culture that permitted free love, in return for which the young vahines received iron nails and trinkets, discovered prostitution, and experienced the first symptoms of venereal diseases.

Later, passengers of both sexes had other opportunities, such as shipboard romances, on which gossip could feast unabashed. Much flirtation seems to have occurred on board ships, where the out-of-reality atmosphere of sailing and the limited time during which moves could be effected often made light of the usual restrictions and customary reserve found in ordinary life at the beginning of the last century. Even Margaret Meredith mentioned one such flirtation between Laura, the young woman she was escorting to the colonies, and a Mr. Percival Soames. The progress of the affair was revealed through the mentions of his name in Meredith's logbook—first "Mr. Soames," then "Mr. S." and, eventually, "Percival." There were briefly engaged, but nothing lasting came out of it. It is clear evidence that long, monotonous sailing in close quarters causes young people's hearts to inflame and feeds their matrimonial hopes.

While most amorous encounters were benign and left to chance, luxury liners were not short of the odd adventuress among their passengers, often working in tandem with a blackmailer. Regular ones were known and officers made every attempt to discourage them, protecting wealthy but remorseful philanderers caught in the scam.

ARTICLE 28

Sailors whose interests led them in another direction faced enormous opprobrium.

While it was a simple matter to find sex with women ashore, the alternative was deemed unacceptable and Article 28 of the Royal Navy's *Articles of War* (1757) made sodomy a hanging offence. "If any person in the fleet shall commit the unnatural and detestable sin of buggery and sodomy with man or beast, he shall be punished with death by the sentence of the court martial."

Some officers, when confronted with the evidence of such an offence, turned a blind eye and sometimes punished the guilty parties for the crime of "uncleanliness" that did not carry such a heavy price, although a few were sentenced to receive up to five hundred lashes. At other times, men were hanged in accordance with Article 28. Officers were not necessarily spared and, when found out and sentenced, would also suffer the fate decreed by the *Articles of War.* Two such officers were Captain Henry Allen of the *Rattler,* executed for sodomy in 1797, and Lieutenant William Berry, hanged in 1807 for sodomizing a young tar. There were others, but these two show that there was no discrimination among the ranks in these matters.

Jane Austen was well aware of these practices through her family connections to the Navy. In 1798, on her brother Frank's ship, the *London,* men were flogged "for insolence, mutiny, and an unnatural crime of sodomy." That such affairs were known can be deduced from the remark made by one of Austen's heroines (Miss Crawford in *Mansfield Park*) about "Rears" and "Vices" when speaking of admirals. Lest we suspect her of innocence, we should note that she added, "Now do not be suspecting me of a pun, I entreat."

Other navies were equally adamant that homosexuality be severely punished. Leendert Hasenbosch, sailing on a Dutch ship, avoided hanging for the crime of sodomy but was set ashore on May 5, 1725 on the tropical Ascension Island in the Atlantic Ocean. With only a tent, a survival kit, and water for about four weeks, it was his bad luck that no ship called at the island before he died of thirst six months later. His diary, later found by British sailors, showed that he ate seabirds and sea turtles, and drank turtle blood and his own urine. The diary also showed the moral torment he endured. It read, "I must inevitably perish. I hope this my punishment in this world may suffice for my most heinous crime of making use of my fellow-creature to satisfy my desire, whom the Almighty Creator had ordained another sex for. I only desire to live to make an atonement for my sins, which I believe my comrade is damned for."

In France, sodomy was also a capital crime, even if few were actually executed. In 1791, however, the National Constituent Assembly set out to revise the criminal law and abolished the penalty against sodomy. The change was formalized in the *Penal Code* of 1810, which dealt with sexual crimes, becoming an offence "against public decency" that could still be used for cases deemed outrageous.

The Napoleonic Code influenced a certain relaxation of the penalty in other European countries, but the Royal Navy was not inclined to follow this trend. Sodomy or buggery remained a capital crime and hanging offense until 1861, with the last British naval execution taking place in 1829.

We see today a major leap in the acceptance of the once forbidden love in such alluring attractions as "Cruise Planners Court Same-Sex Couples With 'Sea of Love' Cruises," advertised in 2013 by American Express Travel on board the *Norwegian Getaway* with the support of the International Gay and Lesbian Travel Association. These cruises attract homosexual couples with the offer of "commitment ceremonies" on board. On Holland America's ships, there is a routine rubric in the program of daily events for the time and place of a "LGBT Gathering." Naturally, the cruising industry only responds to the shifting demands of society, and one can only marvel at the progress made in accepting homosexual partnerships—from hanging in European navies to exchanging vows during a "Sea of Love" cruising ceremony.

12 CROSSING THE LINE

POLLIWOGS AND SHELLBACKS

John and I crossed the equator six times on Holland America ships and received on three occasions our "Equator Crossing Certificates." Printed on pale green paper, devoid of any decoration, they read:

A Proclamation

To all ye officers and members of the crews of all ships plying the waters of my kingdom; ye mermaids, mermen, and sea urchins; ye whales and porpoises; ye fish both great and small; and to ye crustaceans and lowly barnacles, greetings.

Know ye that on this date, there appeared within the limits of our Royal Domain, Holland America Line's ship [name of ship] *and that this vessel; along with it's* [sic] *passengers, officers, and crew, have been inspected and judged worthy by Ourselves and Our Royal Staffs; and let it further be known that* [passenger's name]

having been found to be seaworthy has been duly initiated into Our Royal and Ancient Order of Shellbacks; which exalted status confers upon its freedom evermore to cross our Equator.

This notification supposedly guaranteed that we had satisfied some mysterious criteria that turned us into seasoned shellbacks. In reality, our seaworthiness had not been tested, nor had we been initiated through any ceremony, yet we seemed to have lost our *pollywog* status to become *shellbacks,* as part of a long naval tradition.

149

The passage of a line is always a symbolic event, variously celebrated at sea. In antiquity, human sacrifices sometimes ensured the protection of sea deities and secured safe passage. By the early sixteenth century, crossing the equator was marked with a ritual evolved from the earlier propitiatory tossing of a victim overboard to his death to merely, if roughly, dunking reluctant sailors into the sea. By then, the Europeans had crossed the Equator many times. The first were the Portuguese, as early as the 1470s, rounding the tip of Africa and also discovering Brazil in their search for a sea route to the riches of the Orient; among them were Pedro de Cavilha, Pedro Alvares Cabral, Bartolemeu Dias, Vasco de Gama, and Magellan. Several lesser-known navigators sponsored by the powerful merchant Fernão Gomes had also made their slow progress along the Western African coast, eventually crossing the line. An English vessel first crossed the equator in 1526, at a time when the Dutch were regularly doing it on their way to the Indies.

In these early days, there was little horseplay to mark the passage of the line and such pagan antics were not always deemed suitable on Christian ships. However, it soon became a source of celebration, sometimes known as the "sailors' baptism," even if the ceremony did not have the purifying connotations of the sprinkling and dunking of Christian baptisms or the cleansing rituals of other religions. By the seventeenth century, it was an established routine. Among the tersest log entries must be that of Captain Pennycook (1698) "This morning we passed the Tropick of Cancer. I caused perform the usuall Ceremonies by ducking. Such as had not past it before, and would not pay the usuall Forfeit viz a Bowl of Punch."

The ritual was by then well established. Of perhaps more concern was the occasional parallel ceremony on the eve of the crossing where the roles were reversed, the hierarchy went topsy-turvy, and utter chaos and confusion briefly ensued. Such goings-on were isolated and were usually frowned upon by the captains, as they seemed to threaten discipline. On the other hand, there is little doubt they brought in great comic relief for the crew.

Over time, other crossings also became causes for celebration and were often marked with a special tattoo, made fashionable after the sailors' visit to Polynesia, including one showing King Neptune that was traditional for the crossing of the Equator (a shellback turtle, in modern navies). A golden dragon tattoo attested to the crossing of the International Dateline on the way to Asia, and a full-rigged ship was a proof of having sailed around the Horn.

NATURE OF THE RITUAL

By the early sixteenth century, there were reports of shenanigans taking place upon crossing the Equator. A century later, the celebration had become a rowdy and commonplace event on the Dutch and English ships plying their trade to the Indies. Over time, more elaborate ceremonies evolved and followed a set format with a full cast of characters, each with a specific function. They were noisy affairs, full of dreadful surprises for the initiates, but causing much merriment for the spectators who had previously undergone the same treatment themselves.

The ceremony consisted of having the novice seamen (*pollywogs*) called upon to answer for their sins or misdemeanours, then shaved and made to swallow some awful concoction, and finally dunked into seawater, the event witnessed by the old tars on board (*shellbacks*). It often resulted in rough handling and cruel abuses, and today, most navies see it as potentially harmful hazing.

Seamen could have avoided the rituals by paying a liquid forfeit, yet few appear to have done so. Money was short and drink highly prized; sailors were used to hardships and, in spite of their usual fear of water, probably thought they could handle the discomfort and keep their precious rations of grog.

As well as sailors, there was also consideration given to a ship on her first crossing, and she too had to be "baptized." A captain would not be immune, and neither would be some pet animals. Later, when passengers started crossing the line in ever-growing numbers, they too were subjected to some form of ceremony. The important point was to acknowledge the first crossing from the northern hemisphere to the southern one. For Europeans, it also marked the passage from the familiar to the unknown.

Special characters were needed to produce a full traditional performance, and the court of the sea god attended *en masse*. Neptune, wearing a golden crown and brandishing a trident, presided over a retinue that included his queen (Neptunia or Amphitrite, coiffed in long curls and often well endowed), the astronomer (to read the skies and know when the line was crossed), the bishop (to preside at the "baptism"), the doctor or barber (carrying a large wooden comb and scissors, his tunic always covered in "blood"), the herald (or messenger, often dressed as a pirate) and at least two guards. There were variants with more modern personages, such as the royal baby (whose belly must be kissed), the royal scribe (also named Davy Jones, to whose undersea locker drowned sailors are said to go), a prosecutor, and sometimes a bear. All attendants had distinctive attributes, props, or insignia to denote their rank and function.

The ceremony used to require lengthy preparations for the various events planned to torment the often unsuspecting pollywogs. The certificates they were afterwards issued, although not official documents, were precious records of an important evolution of their status and also proof they had already been tested and need not go through it all again.

PERFORMANCE

By the eighteenth century, the quest for scientific knowledge had become a new element in European explorations, and many navy ships soon had naturalists on board. This included Joseph Banks on Cook's *Endeavour*, Philibert Commerson on Bougainville's *Etoile*, Charles Darwin on FitzRoy's *Beagle*, as well as artists, astronomers, and cartographers. The most detailed descriptions came from the pens of the naturalists, who were trained observers and free to be entertained by the scene of the various penalties imposed by those who had already crossed the line upon those who had not. Not being navy men, they were not expected to undergo the full ritual, which intrigued and amused them. They sometimes chose to participate, but they were spared the humiliations to which real seamen were subjected. Many bought their way out with drinks for everyone.

An earlier description sets the norms for the unpleasant ritual undergone by sailors who could not, or would not, pay the price of their exemption.

> The manner of ducking is this; there is a block made fast to the main yard arm, through which is reeved a long rope, one end whereof comes down on the Quarter Deck, the other to the water, at which end is made fast a stick about a foot and half long thwartways, on which the person sits across, holding fast with his hands the rope as it goes up having a running knot about him; when being ready he is hoisted up close to the yard arm, by the people on the Quarter Deck, the other to the water, at which end is made; His own weight from that height plunges him under the water as low as the ship's keel; then, they run him up again as fast as they can and so serve him three times, then he is free and may drink with the others that paid.

A terrifying sketch of "The Ceremony of Ducking Under the Tropic," drawn by Woodes Rogers in 1711, illustrates this description and shows three seamen hanging precariously high up from the yardarm before being dunked in the roiling waves.

The ceremony was practiced by all nations, and the same patterns and intentions are evident in both English and French relations. On his first voyage, Cook himself was on the black list of those to be ducked, as were Dr. Solander, the Swedish naturalist, and Banks with his servants and his dogs. Banks paid the exemption fee for himself, his people, and animals, but mentioned that many ordinary sailors "chose to be ducked rather than give up four days allowance of wine which was the price fixed upon and as for the boys they were always ducked of course." The performance he then described seems to have changed little from the earlier ones, including the three successive dunkings. Banks then commented that it had lasted until almost night, noting the different expressions on the sailors' faces, "some grinning and exulting in their hardiness whilst others were almost suffocated."

The French and English ceremonies varied slightly (the French seeming a little more theatrical), but the principle remained the same. Commerson described the arrival of Father Tropic (rather than King Neptune), in front of whom were paraded the uninitiated candidates, tied together by a line around both thumbs. Comparing Father Equator's acolytes to devils, he described the fearsome sight presented to the terrified novices, surrounded by their tormentors, "covered in sheepskin, decorated with horns, with tails and claws, some walking on all fours, others dancing about like bears, the boys swinging like monkeys in the rigging, others making convulsive gestures and all of them neighing, growling, meowing, barking to the accompaniment of twenty goat horns and all the pots and pans from the kitchens."

Much frolicking seems to follow for the lucky ones who could negotiate the extent of their participation, but others had to undergo the full force of the initiation, being submerged and then covered with soot. Commerson concluded, "After this, the boys were whipped on the forecastle and everyone holding a bucket ran back and forth until the bumps and bruises given and received during this friendly exercise had wearied the actors." To our modern eyes, the treatment seems extremely rough, particularly when inflicted on young boys. Such was the custom, and Commerson noted that the scene he had described was followed by "much nightly rejoicing, with numerous bacchic libations." Yet he was still surprised that, in spite of the jollity exhibited afterwards, such "depressing ceremony" at the expense of the neophytes should have been widely adopted by every nation, and that no ship ever failed to carry it out.

Among the naturalists who underwent part of the trial in earnest was Darwin, who crossed on February 1832 on the *Beagle* and wrote that he was "placed on a plank, which could be easily tilted up into a large bath of water. They lathered my face & mouth with pitch and paint, & scraped some of it off with a piece of roughened iron hoop—a signal being given I was tilted head over heels into the water, where two men received me & ducked me—at last, glad enough, I escaped." The other unfortunate novices or griffins "were treated much worse, dirty mixtures being put into their mouths, & rubbed on their faces."

Mouth washing must have been great sport, at least for onlookers. John Bechervaise related in 1825 that it consisted of "all the cleanings of the hen coops, pig-stys, & with it a due proportion of tar had been mixed." A large paintbrush was dipped in "this villainous compound" and slapped across the mouth of the unfortunate sailor, whose best option was to keep it firmly shut, in spite of being pressingly questioned by Neptune. The formula did not improve over time. Hans-Jörg Pust, on the *Anna Katrin Fritzen* on her way from the Caribbean to Australia in 1970, described the "medicine" he was made to drink in order to cure him from his ailment, diagnosed by Neptune's Doctor as "stomach ill-humour with extreme bad breath." The "vile brew" was made up of "left-over soup left three days in the warm sun, decayed fish, and waste water, seasoned with Tabasco and Maggi." Pust added that he would never forget that day.

Half a century after the ceremonies described by the naturalists, the model had not changed, but the violence had abated. Bechervaise, playing Neptune, gave the following account of the ceremony on HMS *Blossom* in 1825. His "legs and arms well blacked, his cheeks vermillion," he had "a long grey horse hair wig, a venerable beard of the same colour, a tin crown, a trident, and… a hoarse churchyard cough." Sails were used as a sort of hammock, entirely filled with water, to which were led the poor novices, blindfolded and their heads shaved, then slapped across the face with the disgusting slop. Perhaps their only consolation was knowing that on future crossings, they would be in the audience, having a good laugh at the expense of new victims.

With the substantial increase of passenger ships crossing the equator, the ceremony has now become entertainment for people never expected to pay their dues. Many navies also started preventing the excesses of former rituals, and the ceremony became much tamer.

The new shellbacks on ships of every type and from every nation were issued beautifully decorated certificates of crossing. They were, and still are, usually couched as an entreaty to ocean dwellers to offer the new shellback safe passage, and list all the real and imaginary denizens of the sea to be informed of the sailors' and passengers' new seafaring status.

Even today, whether crossing on a German freighter, a Royal Navy aircraft carrier, or an American tanker, a sailor's accomplishment remains the same in that he has crossed the line and proven his mettle. There are small differences across ships and nationalities in the details of the ceremonies, but we recognize the familiar elements even as late as 1970 on the German freighter *Anna Katrin Fritsen*.

There, the "candidates" were forbidden to smoke or drink alcohol before the ceremony. If the board police caught them with a bottle of beer, they had to throw it overboard, calling "Auf Wiedersehen" for at least ten minutes. Then, chained together, they were examined by the "doctor," and made to drink the vile brew already described. Finally, having been declared cured, the barber washed his hair with shaving cream and lasting yellow dye. Today, he still finds the treatment barbaric. "I was held in place under water in the swimming pool so long that I had almost no air left. As a signal that I couldn't take it any longer, I held up my hand... The Bathmaster... let me out, and gave me one can of beer. That was decreed not enough! After a short time to take air, I was again gracelessly resubmerged. This was repeated until I had at least six cans of beer."

What we have read so far seems to have been the standard practice over time and across European nations. Other descriptions of this widespread ritual only offer only slight variations. But why put people through such trials, even if spectators have fun watching them?

Seamen arc notoriously superstitious and it is not surprising that a ritual intended to placate the hostile forces of the deep should have existed across the fleets. Crews were not segregated by nationalities and seamen moved around. The only restriction was that seafaring was strictly a male affair and normally performed by the poor and the young. Otherwise, race and colour mattered little, and crews were international, most notoriously so on pirate ships. Captains of British-owned vessels hired other European sailors, particularly from maritime countries, such as France, the Netherlands, Portugal, or Scandinavia. With such a pattern of mobility, it is natural that traditions travelled along with these men.

But why this particular tradition and why should it continue to be acted out? One reason could be the need for a break in the harsh routine of life at sea; another, the need to propitiate those unseen and often mythical powers that control the potentially tragic fate of sailors; and a third the necessity to test the novices' mettle and ensure that they will be adequate and reliable partners in whatever hardships the sea and the elements throw at a crew. All three might well occur at the same time, since such an enduring ritual is more complex that may first appear.

An intrinsic part of being at sea, crossings also appear in fiction. Patrick O'Brian briefly relates one that had the singularity of being held on a Sunday, hence limiting the usual "obscene merriment" because of the presence of the attending parson and, second, of taking place soon after the deck had been painted, hence the frequent shouts of "Mind the paintwork!" when things threatened to get rowdy. For these reasons, the ceremony seems to have fallen rather flat, though it followed the established pattern. "Badger-Bag [the usual name for the gaily garbed members of Father Neptune's court] came on board... exchanging the customary greetings and witticisms with the Captain and calling for those who had not crossed the equator before to redeem themselves or be shaved...

The youngsters paid their forfeit and the others... were brought to the tub, but there was not much zeal in their shaving."

A COMIC BREAK IN THE ROUTINE

On October 26, 1768, Captain Cook's enters the passage of the line in his logbook and comments that, the weather being "favourable for that purpose, this Ceremony was performed on about 20 or 30, to the no small Diversion of the Rest." The word "diversion" reveals that the exercise served as comic relief for the rest of the crew, and the ritual certainly served that purpose.

We know the severely restricted space on early voyages, the violence of the elements, the unknown destinations, the becalming, the harsh discipline and floggings, the accidents and diseases, the diminishing rations and the looming prospect of scurvy, the constant shifts allowing for limited sleep and rest, and the high mortality rate at sea. All contributed to a difficult life on board, defined by what Marcus Rediker calls "the uncontrollable vicissitudes and the extreme vulnerability of sailors." Any sanctioned horseplay and comic break in this harsh routine could only be welcome relief, considering that sailors' common amusement on long voyages only consisted of gambling, boxing bouts, some music, and religious services for the salvation of their souls.

Many believed that this was the sole purpose of the ritual. Bernardin de Saint-Pierre, observed on his way to Mauritius in 1768 that "these are rituals invented to dispel melancholy in the crew. Our sailors are very sad. Scurvy gains ground bit by bit and we have not yet covered one third of the journey." Whether these unfortunate sailors actually found solace in these rough pranks is another matter, as hijinks were not likely to alleviate the symptoms of scurvy. More likely perhaps, the established rituals were expected to be performed, whatever the circumstances. The cancellation of such an event would have added to the gloom and misery. However, the point is valid that by the time sailors reached the equator, many were already experiencing the early symptoms of scurvy, which must have magnified the harshness of the rituals.

When he crossed the equator in 1823, Otto von Kotzebue, apparently also subscribed to the notion that sailors needed a break from their continuous work. Mentioning "the usual ceremonies," he added that, "In the evening, the sailors represented, amidst general applause, a comedy of their own composition." He also believed in the health benefits of the ritual. "These sports, while they serve to keep up the spirits of the men, and make them forget the difficulties they have to go through, produce also the most beneficial influence upon their health; a cheerful man being much more capable of resisting a fit of sickness than a melancholy one... Diversion is often the best medicine, and, used as a preservative, seldom fails of its effect."

We see this element of entertainment on modern cruise ships. Banks and Commerson, as jovial spectators and semi-participants in the 1760s ceremonies, prefigure the modern passenger audiences. It is doubtful that their "initiation" was much more meaningful than our receiving automatically the title of honorary shellbacks three times in a row. The certificates given to cruise ship passengers are only a patronizing nod in the direction of their having been luxury human cargo transported across the line by real sailors, a courtesy gesture of little import and the pale imitation of a meaningful seafaring tradition. Clearly, for Mrs Beauchamps (the *Ruahine*, 1898), the crossing was reduced to the entertainment planned for the occasion. "There are to be some Tableaux to our show evening on the Deck, and a Fancy Dress Ball next Friday."

The growing presence of civilians must have led the captains to wonder what to do with them when it came time for the crew to engage in the long-established ritual of testing the sailors' fortitude and formalizing their reliance on Neptune's protection. There was nothing there that applied to the passengers. Apart from coping with seasickness (both Commerson and Darwin suffered terribly from it) and undergoing the discomforts of life on board, there was little merit to their experience at sea. So, it was probably thought best to leave it up to them to decide to what extent they would participate in the entertainment.

Crossings on packet-ships usually offered few frills. When Margaret Meredith crossed the equator on the *Macquarie* on September 28, 1894, her logbook only had two entries. One reads, "Collection made for Athletic Sports, £5.5.0 to be held on Friday afternoon when we cross the line," and, "Crossed the line about 9:30. Crew, holiday. Athletic Sports began 2.0 till 5.0. Crew gave concert after prayers on after-hatch." We are far from the frothy excitement created on modern cruise ships. The *Macquarie* was a working ship and even the Australian "apprentices" were not pollywogs, having already crossed the line on their way to England. The crew was friendly but went about their business. Their small break to celebrate the passage merely consisted in a sporting context with a purse offered by the passengers and a concert given as a way of thanks. During four months at sea on each voyage, the passengers had entertained themselves, and one might think that the crossings' tradition would have appealed to them. But there is no mention of any extra effort made to mark it as a special occasion among themselves.

Today, even on cruise ships, the crossing rituals for the crews roughly follow the known routine. However, because of the modern passenger's more delicate temperament, the harsh treatments previously meted out has become good-humoured antics that amuse everybody. Mass tourism has taken over a once meaningful tradition, transforming it into a mere simulacrum of the event it once was. An eighteenth-century sailor would be hard put to recognize his own ordeal in what passes nowadays for a crossing of the line ceremony.

PROPITIATION TO THE POWERS OF THE DEEP

The fear of the unleashed elements and the dread of the unknown monsters from the deep is probably universal. Since their appearance in Genesis (1:21), where God "created the great sea monsters and every living creature that moves," man has feared the mysterious beasts of the sea, the "twisted serpents," "the fleeing serpents," the "dragon who lives in the sea," found in Isaiah (27.1). The sea monster called Leviathan (Psalms 104:25) is so dreaded that, says the Book of Job, "the mere sight of him is overpowering (9)." Job describes him as follows: "firebrands stream from his mouth; sparks of fire shoot out (19), smoke pours from his nostrils as from a boiling pot over a fire of reeds (20), his breath sets coals ablaze, and flames dart from his mouth (21), Nothing on earth is his equal–a creature without fear (33)." The most fanciful depiction of the dreaded Sea Serpent is found in Revelations 13.1, where he is seen "coming up out of the sea, having ten horns and seven heads, and on his horns were ten diadems, and on his heads were blasphemous names."

The Odyssey describes the powerful wrath of the sea displayed against the hero, combined with the mysterious dangers that lie beneath. "A towering thunderhead mounted over our small ship… / All of a sudden killer squalls attacked us, screaming out to the west, / and a murderous blast toppled the most backward. / The mast went crashing into the stern, it struck the helmsman's head and crushed his skull to pulp." Below were Scylla, a hideous tentacled beast, and Charybdis, a monster that would suck down entire ships.

Forty days after the Irish monk Saint Brendan and his companions set sail, "there appeared to them a beast of immense size following them at a distance. He spouted foam from his nostrils and ploughed through the waves at a great speed, as if he was about to devour them." The beast caused the waves to rise to horrifying heights, as if ready to engulf them. Terrified, the monks asked God to subdue the beast. Eventually, "a mighty monster passed near them from the west to encounter the beast. He immediately attacked him, emitting fire from his mouth." The monster then sliced the beast into three parts before the monks' eyes and disappeared from sight.

Almost from the start, sailors have imagined the presence at the crossing ceremony of Poseidon/Neptune and his attendants, who held power over the sea and its denizens. Sailors' folklore and worldview were broad enough to include Christian and pre-Christian beliefs, classical mythological figures, biblical stories, and the traditional yarns of the sea. A hodgepodge of themes and characters almost routinely appeared in the sailors' tales, such as Castor and Pollux (connected with St. Elmo's fire) or Charon (said to appear to dying seamen to receive his coin to ferry them safely over the River Styx), so the appearance of Neptune and his retinue should not surprise us. Seamen's beliefs were not particularly attached to traditional religions, but gambling with luck played a great part in their lives and superstition was often their guide.

It is easy to see why the irrational would occupy an important part in lives so frequently subjected to the fanciful play of the elements and victimized by an avenging nature. In July 1819, a resident of Nantucket reported a large comet with an "uncommonly long tail"; he considered this vision the "most extraordinary event" in the history of his island. So shaken were people with the apparition of "these eccentric visitors" that they could only see it as an omen of something even more unnatural. Indeed, during that spring and summer, an "extraordinary sea animal" was seen along the coast of New England, "a serpent with black, horse-like eyes and a fifty-foot body resembling a string of barrels floating on the water." Is it then surprising that one of the most horrific ordeals at sea occurred soon afterwards, the ferocious attack on the whaleship *Essex* by a sperm whale, the only survivors reduced to eating their dead companions as they drifted across the South Pacific?

We also know that seamen feared falling into the sea. Few could swim, and there were tangible dangers from sharks and other creatures, but there was also something more threateningly obscure in their fear of the deep, dark, and so often hostile sea. In *Making It Up*, Penelope Lively imagines the World War II voyage of members of the English community who fled Cairo for South Africa as Rommel approached. Naturally, as they crossed the line, selected passengers had to appear before the court of Neptune, a selection clearly made based on some of the female passengers' willingness to flirt with the young officers. First, they were made to drink "some horrible mixture," then were shaved with "wooden razors," and finally were soaked with water. Two men stood for Neptune and his daughter, and the cortege included "heralds and trumpeters, and some bears to do the ducking in the children's canvas pool... Neptune's long flowing hair was made up of frayed rope, the crowns were done with silver foil from cigarette packets, with jujubes for jewels, the bears wore sacking suits and navy socks on their hair."

The real dangers of wartime and the presence of many women and children on board were no doubt reasons for attempting to lighten up the ritual and render it as playful as possible. However, the underlying basis for its taking place at all is more than symbolic of an initiatory passage from one status to another, from one hemisphere to the other, from a potential war zone to a peaceful station. The ship's medical orderly explained, "It's something that's always done, the sailors told me. Because the sea's a dangerous place and you've got to keep it sweet. You've got to give a person to Neptune so he'll leave you alone."

While ancient mapmakers did their best to show land masses and coast lines as accurately as they could, their seas were filled with marvellous and terrifying creatures drawn from mythology and bound to Neptune's will. Here were mermaids and mermen, sea snakes, sea horses, tritons, krakens, remoras, sirens, and the dreaded Charybdis and Scylla, and many were featured on certificates of crossing. In the face of such fearsome beings, we cannot doubt the need to placate Neptune's mood and save the ship and crew, even if the Phoenicians' real human sacrifice had only become the mock drowning of polliwogs.

Only the mermaids and mermen have a mythical connection; the others are real sea or river creatures, even when whimsically figuring on the list. Many of the sea monsters that emerged from the sailors' imagination were probably based on real animals. The fearsome sea serpent, for instance, featured in many illustrations, was probably inspired by the mysterious oarfish, seldom seen but known to exist. With its luminous red crest, or "mane," and reaching up to thirty-five feet in length, it is present in all the seas and oceans. Known as "the King of the Herring" (usually seen where herrings are found) but more properly named *regalecus glesne* (in cold waters) and *regalecus russellii* (in warm waters), the harmless oarfish is only one of those real sea dwellers promoted to monster status in the sailors' mythology. Similarly, the dreaded kraken may have been based on the occasional sighting of giant squid. Malacologists agree that some specimens can reach between forty and fifty feet in length, including the tentacles.

There is no shortage of such sea monsters in older literature. In the *Arabian Nights* appears the dandan, a dweller of the deep said to be "larger than any animal you have on land and were it to come across a camel or an elephant, it would swallow it up." Much is also made of the curative ability of its liver, a potent secretion apparently greatly favoured by mermen. It seems reasonable that one of the larger whales served as model for the mythical dandan. Such creatures persist in literature and modern popular culture (Moby Dick, Jules Verne's giant sea monsters, the *Creature of the Black Lagoon*, video games, etc.).

The sea has always held real and hidden dangers, and humankind is wont to give a physical shape to what is most feared. Few prospects would feel more dreadful than being eaten by killer sharks, gigantic fish, sea serpents, or other beings of the depths, and these fears need to be allayed by important rituals. Sailors naturally wished to be on the safe side and seek many protectors against both obvious and hidden perils. Their whimsical list of underwater denizens and the ceremony's horseplay would only have been ways of disguising the real importance of the protection they sought.

A TRADITIONAL RITE OF PASSAGE

The crossing's humiliating and frightening rituals converted novices into seasoned seamen, worthy of sailing under Neptune's protection. How could a mouthwash, a shave, and a dunking lead to such an important change of status?

At the time the ritual started appearing routinely in the English Navy's records, an increasing number of men were mobilized for sea duty, often with no experience of working on ships. It was thus essential to create a seafaring identity among them and reinforce a sense of community; they needed to trust the men working next to them. The rituals were merely a series of connected events designed to serve this purpose.

The French ethnographer Arnold van Gennep elaborated a theory of socialization that followed a person's social progression through distinct rituals, which he called "rites of passages" (1909). These are particularly formalized in traditional societies in which various stages are carefully monitored and recognized through achieving a new position in the social hierarchy. They surround us even today. Judeo-Christian cultures have a number of ceremonies combining social and religious elements, particularly those celebrating a child's birth and coming of age, such as circumcision, baptism, bar and bat mitzvah, quinceañera, and so on. More extreme and alien to our western minds are the African scarifications, the vision quests of some North American cultures, or the walkabouts of the Australian Aborigines, but we recognize them as rituals to achieve a new status as people progress through life.

Van Gennep describes the three stages of the rites of passage: separation (withdrawal from the previous societal status, severance from former ties), transition (the intermediate stage, suspended in temporary limbo), and reincorporation (integration into the new group). The sequence of symbolic disappearance and reappearance corresponds to a notion of rebirth into a new phase of life. Some rites are real ordeals and the ultimate reward of the new status must justify the initiates' sometimes painful process.

The scheme clearly applies to the crossing of the line. The first stage (separation) is often symbolically accompanied by overt signs of detachment, of "cutting away" a part of the old identity. In the polliwogs' case, there was either real cutting of the hair or a symbolic "shaving" using a large wooden razor and comb. Fasting was often part of the ritual during that stage, which we recognize in the

German ship's explicit requirement to abstain from alcohol and tobacco. To be worthwhile, the rituals celebrating the polliwogs' change of status needed to be onerous. Mouthwashes and shaves, even if roughly administered, held no danger, but dunkings must have been frightening for men who always feared falling overboard. Even if every precaution was taken to protect them and if the water in which they fell was only a deep canvas pool, not the ocean, the sensation must have caused them a great deal of anxiety and discomfort, particularly if they were roped together.

For the second stage of the rite of passage (transition), we see this ambiguous process played out in Hans-Jörg Putz's description. As a polliwog, he was forbidden to drink beer (a severance from a usual source of enjoyment in his previous life) and was even made to throw it into the ocean. Later, not yet a shellback but reaching the last stage of his trial, he was permitted to have some beer, the mixed signal of a changing identity.

The last and irrevocable stage of a polliwog' s higher status was being integrated into the group of experienced "sons of Neptune" shellbacks, able to handle with them the relentless perils of the sea, the harsh physical conditions on board, and the trials of long voyages. Those comical or cruel pranks now make sense when we see them as rituals of an initiation into a cohesive community.

Whether a break to help with sagging morale and re-energize the crew, an offering to propitiate those hostile powers making their voyage unsafe, or a means of testing the mettle of new sailors, we have been told that the practice was always similar across European navies. We also know that it continues to be practiced—albeit with milder versions.

A charming story illustrates the slightly magical aspect of crossing the Equator. It was sometimes told in Buenos Aires, whose parks have been designed by Charles Thays, a Frenchman and former apprentice of Edouard André, the noted Parisian landscape designer. Sent to Buenos Aires to design the Parque de Palermo, Thays remained in Argentina for the rest of his life and, named director of parks in 1891, created all the public and private gardens of any significance in the country. He was particularly inspired by the famous rose gardens of Bagatelle, and his Buenos Aires parks reflect the regular and formal outlines of a French garden, including the greenhouses and the abundant use of roses, which are not native to South America and had to be brought in from France. Once, he ordered a large shipment of rose bushes, and it is said that when the ship crossed the equator, all the roses came into bloom at once.

V
ILLNESS AND MISERY

Medics on Board

The Elements

Mal de Mer

13 MEDICS ON BOARD

"And don't forget the three service dogs!" said my neighbour at the table. I had commented on the unusual number of old and handicapped people on board. Nearly half the passengers seemed to be sitting in wheelchairs, pushing walkers, or walking with canes. There had already been two medical evacuations, one in Astoria where an ambulance waited discreetly by the gangway; the other when we anchored in front of Christmas Island and waited the whole day for a plane to arrive with a medical team. Two years later, the scenario was repeated, with a similar evacuation from Rarotonga.

EARLY MEDICAL CARE

Earlier ship surgeons did not have the luxury of evacuating problematic patients from the middle of the ocean, and had to deal with every disease and wound that befell the crew and occasional passengers. These complaints were seldom minor, for seamen were expected to be tough. Edward Barlow wrote in 1696 that those who "were not used to hardship and had not known the lack of drink" were the first to collapse and die. Sailors were exposed to scurvy, rheumatism, yellow fever, ulcers, wounds, and skin diseases, and their daily work included heavy lifting and dangerous practices. They often suffered from "the bursted belly" [hernia] and it was common for them to lose a finger while shifting cargo or to be burned while tarring ropes. Finally, many drowned and "took their habitation among the haddocks."

Epidemics on land naturally had their echoes at sea, and the inability to deal with the spread of diseases had terrible consequences. During the 1545-46 plague, both French and English sailors started falling sick with "swelling in their heads and faces and in their legs, and diverse of them with the bloody flux." On September 11, 1545, eleven English vessels were infected, and 1,882 men had already succumbed or were at risk of doing so. Two weeks later, a roll call of the fleet anchored in Portsmouth showed that the number of healthy men had decreased from 12,000 to a mere 4,888. Such catastrophic losses continued to grow in the coastal garrisons.

Ship surgeons were somewhat ahead of military medics, but neither had any notion of using quarantines to quell epidemic infections. This inaction is difficult to understand, since there were precedents for isolating potentially contagious patients. Lepers' hospitals had existed in some English ports for the previous two centuries; in Venice, ships were routinely isolated for chronic dysentery; in Marseilles, plague victims had been kept out of bounds for forty days (*quarantaine,* or quarantine) since the fourteenth century. However, in 1545 the authorities decided to demobilize the English fleet rather than putting it in isolation; with the seamen's return home, the disease spread even further among the general population.

We know the devastation brought on by scurvy, and the lack of medical assistance for it—apart from cutting out the rotten part and rubbing the spot with urea, a treatment as bad as the disease itself. Until the role of vitamins was eventually discovered, once seamen entered the "scurvy belt" (from the Tropic of Capricorn to the Cape on the African route and mid-ocean on voyages to the New World and Oceania), they could only hope to find some hospitable islands. Eventually, some captains and surgeons' intuition and experimentation would allay the problem.

The Dutch, with one of the largest shipping fleets trading with the Indies, suffered all the contemporary woes of sailing, including scurvy, fractures, dislocations, shot-wounds, concussions, burns, gangrene, knife wounds, amputations, dysentery, and, particularly on that route, fevers of all kinds. On land, Dutch physicians were scarce (in 1628 there were only nine in Haarlem for a population of 40,000), and much of contemporary medicine relied on the apothecaries' knowledge of herbal remedies. At sea, Dutch surgeons faced dreadful living and working conditions and their own mortality rate was higher than if they had practised on land; they were consequently hard to recruit.

A seventeenth-century Dutch sea surgeon reveals their daily routines.

> First thing in the morning, we must prepare the medicines that have to be taken internally and give each patient his dose. Next, we must scarify, clean, and dress the filthy, stinking wounds, and bandage them and the ulcerations. Then we must bandage the stiff and benumbed limbs of the scorbutic patients. At midday we must fetch and dish out the food for sometimes 40, 50, or even 60 people, and the same again in the evening; and what is more, we are kept up half the night as in attending to patients who suffer a relapse, and so forth.

Dutch surgeons had to master the art of the apothecary, as well as be adept at reducing fractures and amputating limbs they could not save. Their chests contained some two hundred different preparations, barely sufficient to treat the variety of ills commonly suffered on board. Their task was made easier when they had barbers with them; unfortunately, both often perished, and untutored seamen took over their surgical duties. Unable to bleed patients and amputate shattered limbs, they were simply expected to do the best they could.

European captains and ship surgeons had a daunting task. They lacked a basic understanding of the prevention, spreading, and treatment of diseases, yet bore the responsibility for bringing back seamen alive, even though they knew they would probably lose half of them. In spite of their best efforts, some situations could not be controlled. For instance, the *Endeavour* had started out for Tahiti in 1768 with provisions to feed ninety-four people for eighteen months. They had pigs, poultry, a milking goat, and the resources of every port of call to replenish the hold. Cook had not lost a single man to scurvy or any other disease. However, on the return journey, the *Endeavour* needed repairs in dry dock after a mishap on the Great Barrier Reef and stopped in Batavia (Jakarta). Batavia, built on canals after the Dutch manner, unsuited to the Indonesian climate, was then famous for its miasmic air and known as "the cemetery of the Europeans." Most of those who had stopped there on their return from Tahiti (Wallis, Carteret, Bougainville) suffered extensive human losses, and so did Cook when most of the *Endeavour*'s crew were taken ill with dysentery, food poisoning, and malaria from the mosquitoes breeding in Batavia's canals. Thinking that polluted water had made them ill, Cook ordered it to be purified with lime juice, but to no avail. By March 1771, their repairs finished, Cook had lost one third of his men. Among them were Tupaia, the Tahitian guide who had contributed to his mapping of the South Pacific islands; the young artist Sidney Parkinson; the astronomer Charles Green, a witness to the transfer of Venus; the Swedish naturalist Herman Spöring; William Monkhouse, the ship surgeon, and his brother Jonathan. They were enormous losses for Cook, who had been proud of his outstanding survival record.

Medicine could do little to prevent diseases or alleviate their symptoms. On the other hand, there was progress made in the normal conditions on board. At the end of the eighteenth century, the Royal Navy instituted a number of reforms dealing with staffing and victual stocking procedures, some specifically aimed at dealing with scurvy. In 1795, Dr. Sir Gilbert Blane, Royal Navy Commissioner for the Sick and Wounded Board, was the first to introduce limes as part of the sailors' diet (causing them to be known as "limeys"). The results were extraordinary. In 1795, the ratio of scurvy sufferers among sick seamen was one in three; in 1804, it became one in eight; and in 1811, one in eleven.

As well, the belief in the antagonistic effects of sea air, previously deemed a possible cause of scurvy, vanished entirely, now replaced with the discovery of its beneficial influence. Jane Austen ironically praised the new fad, writing, "The Sea air and Sea Bathing together were nearly infallible, one or other of them being a match for every Disorder, of the Stomach, the Lungs or the Blood: They were anti-spasmodic, anti-pulmonary, anti-septic, anti-bilious and anti-rheumatic." Sea bathing became fashionable on English beaches. Everyone wanted to do it, particularly if they could use the "bathing machines" that ensured modesty by taking bathers directly into the sea. However, ship surgeons held no such faith in the curative powers of the sea breeze, and it would have taken a lot of coaxing to overcome most sailors' fear of water.

The medical conditions the surgeons handled were usually classified as having "predisposing causes," such as pneumonia, colic, diarrhea, dysentery; or they were brought on by "antecedent causes," including all the air-borne varieties of fever; or they were "disturbances" related to drink, diet, sleep, exercise, mental states, etc. The medicine they practised was still based on the knowledge of Ancient Greek physicians, who had explained their patients' symptoms in terms of "humours" (blood, phlegm, yellow and black bile). These included varying states of heat or cold on the one hand, wetness and dryness on the other, and their combination; for instance, phlegm related to moisture and cold, and black bile to cold and dryness. They considered that the imbalance of these humours was the cause of most diseases.

Respiratory ailments (severe colds, or catarrhs; consumption or tuberculosis; pneumonia) constituted about half the cases diagnosed in European and American navies. Upon hearing of the cases of tuberculosis among Cook's men, novelist Fanny Burney—whose knowledge of the Navy came through her brother James, one of Cook's officers—wrote, "'Tis strange that all the circumnavigators, though they seemed well at first, are all now apparently broken in their constitution." She mentioned three officers by name and added, "There are eight others failing into the same premature decay."

There was also an assortment of conditions such as malaria, jaundice, and liver dysfunction ("bilious fevers"), as well as those attacking the intestinal tract, such as diarrhea and dysentery. Influenza, generally a mild condition for sailors, had catastrophic consequences when introduced to unimmunized native populations. Typhus (known as ship fever or gaol fever) and yellow fever (associated with the West Indies) also struck frequently.

Finally, routinely found on ships were ordinary rheumatism, lower back pain, and sciatica. Surgeons manipulated hernias and contained them with a truss. Other conditions were more frequent among sailors than in the general population; for instance, mental illness struck seven times more often on ships. Flogging often resulted in wounds and blisters that had to be dressed, and, given the attachment of sailors to their grog, drunkenness and its aftermath frequently caused concern. After shore leave, many surgeons anticipated dealing with new injuries caused by drunken brawls and an increase in venereal diseases.

Gonorrhea ("gleet") and syphilis ("pox"), also known variously as "Cupid's itch" and "the curse of Venus," were the sailors' frequent companions, shared with the women they contaminated all over the world. The number of infected sailors made doubtful Captain Wallis's accusation that venereal diseases had been introduced to Tahiti by Bougainville's French crew, rather than his own. All European ships had their contingent of infected sailors, and so pervasive was the condition that captains and surgeons tried to ensure that sailors diagnosed with it did not go ashore, or that they did so only under supervision. We see proof of the serious attempts to curtail the spread of infection in Cook's log entry for January 25, 1779 on *Resolution*. "W. Bradley, Seaman, was given 24 lashes for having connections with a native women knowing himself to have the venereal disorder." This was twice as many lashes as commonly inflicted for usual misdeeds. Unfortunately, contemporary lack of knowledge of the dormant stage of syphilis could not prevent it from spreading to indigenous populations with disastrous effect.

Exceptionally, venereal diseases contributed to the surgeons' income because they were deemed self-inflicted. The fee was £5 for every hundred cases, treated mostly with mercury salts. Ship surgeons' salary was about £5 a month, so this extra income was not negligible, particularly after shore leave. The payments were financed from the fines imposed upon sailors suffering from gonorrhea and syphilis. The long-range effects of syphilis were mostly unknown, and their fine may have seemed to sailors the worst consequence of their indiscretion; perhaps they even thought it money well spent after the long crossings.

Among the usual treatments for various ailments were blisters or epispastics—"Spanish flies" reduced to powder and used in solutions, which raised large blisters when applied to the skin, draining away the foul humours contained inside the blisters. Similarly, patients were bled to remove the "unbalanced" blood at the origin of the symptoms. Twelve ounces were usually drawn at a time, except for the seriously ill patients when the amount might be doubled. Finally, olive oil was used to clean and dress burns. When teeth needed extracting, they were pulled out with a turnkey—a claw-like device that provided maximum leverage.

In addition to these common conditions and the fractures resulting from falls or accidents on deck, surgeons had to deal with the wounds received in battle. Most were caused by swords, bayonets, bullets, and large splinters from backfiring cannons, often requiring surgery. The nature of injuries naturally evolved with the weaponry used in naval warfare–starting with catapults firing arrows and stones, javelins flung at the moment of ships' impacts, and pot fires swung from long poles and splashing blazing material–known generally as "Greek Fire." The latter were particularly dreaded because the petroleum-based mixture they contained caused fire, a death sentence for wooden ships at sea. Cannons and guns came later in the available war panoply and produced different types of wounds.

Surgeons preferred to operate on deck in calm weather and without the stress of battle, and advances in surgical techniques meant they sometimes achieved good results. During battle, however, surgeons had to work in the cockpit. The wounded would be carried down for triage and treatment. It often became slippery with blood, so the deck was usually spread with sand before fighting started. The scene must have been terrifying and the surgeons' task daunting. William Beattie, who tended to Nelson's injuries at Trafalgar in 1805, had 145 other severely wounded men to treat, and the Reverend Alexander Scott, who stayed by the dying Nelson's side, suffered recurrent nightmares for the rest of his life after what he had witnessed there.

We should also remember that general anesthesia was not introduced until 1846. Instead, patients were strapped or held down during surgery, and were often given rum or opium to reduce their pain and relax their muscles. Hemorrhages were one of the greatest immediate hazards of battle wounds and operations and, where possible, were contained with canvas tourniquets. Gangrene, which was usually fatal, often followed amputations. On the other hand, surgeons had become adept at reducing their operating time. By 1800, some were known to be able to cut through the muscles of the thigh with a knife and then saw through the femur in as few as two minutes. The pain must have been excruciating, but the speed reduced the trauma considerably.

Robert Young, surgeon on the 64-gun H.M.S. *Ardent,* describes his operations during a fiery engagement against the Dutch at Camperdown (October 11, 1797). "I was employed in operating and dressing till 4.0 in the morning. So great was my fatigue that I began several amputations under a dread of sinking before I should have secured the blood vessels. Ninety wounded were brought down during the action. The whole cockpit, deck, cabins… together with my [operating] platform were covered with them. So that for a while they were laid down on each other at the foot of the ladder." He was forced to stop his operations to seek help in shifting the wounded and making room in the cockpit.

Sixteen men died soon after they were brought down, but Young seemed particularly affected by the dreadful wounds suffered by a certain Joseph Bonheur. "He lived nearly two hours, perfectly sensible and incessantly calling out in a strong voice for me to assist him... All the service I could render this unfortunate man was to put dressing over the wounds and give him a drink." In spite of such unfortunate cases, Young found great satisfaction in some of the results he obtained. "Those who survived to undergo amputation or be dressed, all were found the next morning... in as comfortable a state as possible, and on the third day were conveyed on shore in good spirits."

We might assume that naval battles would account for the majority of casualtie, particularly when in a single battle (Trafalgar, 1805) the Royal Navy lost 1,483 men, with a further 4,266 wounded. However, they only amounted to six percent of the Navy's total loss during that period. The great killers of man were diseases and injuries (82%), followed by major accidents, including shipwrecks (12%).

How effective was the ordinary ship surgeon's treatment, given these many negative conditions? Patrick O'Brian's excellent, if fictional, ship-surgeon Stephen Maturin reveals his limitations: "Medicine can do very little; surgery less. I can purge you, bleed you, worm you, and at a pinch set your leg or take it off, and that is very nearly all." Nevertheless, as a matter of routine, he bled all men when they crossed the Tropic of Cancer or Capricorn sailing to the Equator "as a protection against 'calentures' [fevers] and the effect of eating too much meat and drinking far too much grog under the almost perpendicular sun."

Ship surgeons availed themselves of well-tried remedies, often intended to restore the balance of the body's humours and usually found on board. These included tonics (red wine, and even cold water) to speed up the body's recovery; cinchona or Peruvian bark for malaria, often successful and thus used for other fevers; opiates (opium, laudanum, or Thebaic tincture) for sedation; tar-water, a mixture of Scotch pine extract and water, deemed to be an effective panacea in the 1740s; emetic drugs (tartar and ipecac);

cathartic drugs (calomel, jalap, medicinal rhubarb, castor roil, cream of tartar); diaphoretic drugs (antimony or James's Powder); and antispasmodics.

Apart from caring for the sick and wounded, surgeons were responsible for maintaining cleanliness and hygiene on board, fumigating the sickbay and decks with sulfur, and overseeing the ventilating machines supplying fresh air to the lower decks.

In 1814, at the end of the Napoleonic wars, there were 14 physicians, 850 surgeons, 500 assistant surgeons or mates, and a large number of apothecaries caring for the 130,000 men in the Royal Navy. In the face of such responsibilities, one may wonder about the training these medical practitioners received, which, together with their social status, determined their rank.

At the top were the physicians, usually holders of medical degrees, mostly from the Scottish universities of Edinburgh, Glasgow, and Aberdeen. University training carried weight, although it was sometimes possible to graduate by paying a fee rather than attending classes. Physicians were therefore deemed gentlemen, did not take the usual tests to serve in the Royal Navy, and were better paid than surgeons, whom they sometimes supervised. They were usually appointed by the Navy Board to serve with large squadrons and at naval hospitals.

Ranking below them came the surgeons (having only recently distanced themselves from barbers), their mates, and the apothecaries, who did the bulk of the treatments and operations. While experienced in surgery, particularly amputations, they lacked the physicians' medical knowledge, and thus unexpected medical conditions were mostly beyond their experience. To be accepted in the Royal Navy, surgeons had to pass an oral test in front of the Barber-Surgeons' Company, often lacking rigour and almost perfunctory. They had sometimes started as apprentices, furthering their knowledge by attending lectures and assisting in hospital wards. They were hired as medical officers by individual captains until 1806, when the admiralty started appointing them. After 1806, they had the same status as commissioned officers and were assisted by surgeons' mates, then known as assistant-surgeons. We can gather that the quality of medical and surgical care on board depended at least as much on the surgeon's character as on his training.

The ship surgeons' task seemed awesome, particularly when we remember the limitations of contemporary medicine and Dr. Maturin's philosophical acceptance of them: "Medicine can do very little; surgery less." His feelings must have been shared by many ship-surgeons, even with the many successes they were able to achieve.

The descriptions apply to disciplined navies, but others may have followed lesser rules. One physician, Georg Heinrich von Langsdorff, related his adventures on the Russian ship *Maria* in 1805. Not keen on returning to his previous post on the "pox-ridden" *Nadezhda*, he accepted Captain Rezanov's offer. What he found on the *Maria* was a crew consisting of "adventurers, drunkards, bankrupt traders and mechanics or branded convicts in search of a fortune" who were all suffering from scurvy, the result of a diet of "dry and frozen fish, the fat of whales and sea dogs [seals] as their principal nutrient," and also "sported an impressive variety of venereal diseases." His was not a happy passage along the Aleutian coast, as the fastidious doctor was kept "in a constant fever of disgust and horror" at the sight of the carpet of dead lice, ticks, and fleas on deck of which the sailors ("these dirty disgusting men") were constantly divesting themselves.

1894: ON THE *MACQUARIE*

Margaret Meredith reports an incident that would seem unusual today. On the *Macquarie*'s list were a physician and a "stewardess," whose duties probably included assisting the physician. However, this is not how it turned out on their way to Australia. Several entries in Meredith's log refer to the stewardess's nursing care. The first reads, "Helped Doctor with Stewardess operation." Nothing is said of the nature of the operation, but ten days after the first entry comes another, "A good deal of time taken up every day nursing Stewardess." Nearly four weeks later, "On deck most of the day when not engaged with Stewardess." Three days afterwards, "Up and down all day to Stewardess, not so well." In the ensuing month, until they arrive in Sydney, nothing more is said about the stewardess's care (or fate).

These entries, terse as they are, raise an interesting question: Why had a passenger been selected to nurse the stewardess? Nowhere in her diary does she mention having particular experience with such activities, nor inclination for their performance. Her ambiguous situation was probably the reason for this *ad hoc* enlisting into nursing service. The other three female passengers, one of them her charge, were clearly ladies, whereas her own status as a paid companion may have destined her to attend to such duties as assisting the doctor in his medical care, a duty otherwise performed by the stewardess herself. Miss Meredith, a clergyman's daughter, may have been a gentlewoman by breeding but she clearly was not one by status as a mere governess and companion. On the other hand, her common sense, poise, and excellent education would have made her the perfect choice for such assignments. But this is mere speculation on my part.

MEDICAL CARE TODAY

Miss Meredith's assistance in the stewardess's surgery and medical care seems quite extraordinary today because it could not be envisaged in normal circumstances on modern ships. Without even thinking of potential lawsuits, there would be no need for it. Passenger ships have a sick bay with appropriate medical staff and equipment, and it is always possible to seek medical evacuation should it prove necessary.

Any hint of sickness is kept carefully hidden from today's passengers unless general safety requires it to be acknowledged. Passengers are meant to be entertained and disconnected from the reality of old age, accidents, and illness, and they only hear about the odd fracture sustained from people present during the accident. Similarly, medical evacuations are only mentioned when they

182

delay departure or alter the ship's course. Far more probably goes unmentioned and unnoticed than cruisers imagine.

The guidelines adopted by the International Council of Cruise Lines are designed to ensure appropriate emergency medical care for passengers and crew, either by stabilizing patients and initiating reasonable diagnostic and therapeutic interventions or by evacuating seriously ill or injured patients to shore hospitals when deemed necessary. On board, the medical stations are staffed by physicians and nurses trained to handle emergencies. They mostly treat respiratory infections, fractures following falls, strokes, and heart attacks. Chronic conditions can also be accommodated, and a Canadian medical officer told me she even had a patient on dialysis on one her cruises.

The medical reviews of health problems occurring on ships show that the incidence of infectious diseases (notably acute gastroenteritis) and fractures along with injuries sustained in falls increase with ageing passengers. These findings are consistent with those in a similar population in retirement residences.

Cruisers' testimonials are available online and range from satisfied to enthusiastic. "Ruth C." surely beats them all for the variety of problems she presented. "Many's the time I've had to visit the ship's infirmary. Never a good thing to have to do, but always a good visit. I was treated for a possible heart attack off the coast of Bora Bora, a bad scalp infection in the Caribbean, and a very bad fall sailing off Cape Horn. I've always been very pleased with the care and follow-up received." The problems encountered by those former patients varied and required anything from a few pills to evacuation to a land hospital. Most go on cruising after their experience, which is certainly an endorsement of the treatment they received.

However, the *Cruise Critic* (written by cruisers for cruisers) warns that one should avoid getting sick on board, meaning "*really* sick, like a heart attack or a stroke or a serious injury." If hospital care is required, ship doctors will "have you whisked off the ship at the next port of call and taken to the nearest hospital." However, the article continues, "it might not be the best hospital, and you might not be able to speak the local language, but if you're quite ill or hurt enough for immediate surgery, you will be booted off quicker than you can say 'liability.'"

The self-contained nature of these ships, while facilitating control of anything going awry, can also have negative consequences, made worse by the age and frailty of many passengers. Infection could spread and reminders are posted widely on board urging passengers to take the necessary precautions: "Fight disease. Wash your hands." Dispensers of hand disinfectants are everywhere, particularly at the entrance of dining areas. Since self-service trays can also spread germs, they have now vanished from cafeterias.

Ships sailing for reputable cruise lines are under constant scrutiny to uncover any health problems on board and to address immediately any issues. Efforts to control outbreaks included basic food and water sanitation, disinfecting the ships during the cruise, and isolating sick people for seventy-two hours. Much is at stake, obviously, and it makes sense for the cruise lines to follow these rules scrupulously. Two of our Holland America ships, the *Statendam* and the *Westerdam*, scored a perfect 100 on a snap inspection by the Centre for Disease Control in 2014, and the latter ship also scored 100 from the Public Health Agency in 2013.

Medical care dispensed on board can deal with most emergencies until the patient is evacuated and transferred to land hospitals. However, if all else fails, there is always a large freezer acting as a morgue—proving that, like so many other sea traditions, the ritual of entrusting bodies to the deep has long disappeared from modern vessels. However, cremated remains can be scattered at sea in restricted areas.

14 THE ELEMENTS

Sailing, sailing over the bounding main,
Where many a stormy wind shall blow
'Ere Jack comes home again.

(Children's song. Godfrey Marks, 1880)

"The wind commands me away!"

(Sir Francis Drake, off to fight the Spanish Armada)

Whether they used oars or sails, ships of all nations, sizes, and destinations once depended on the weather for their progress and their safety. Safe passage was never a certainty, and seamen had good reasons to fear bad weather and adapt their sailing to the seasons. "If you are afflicted with the desire for uncomfortable travelling over the sea, then remember that the blasts of all the winds rage when the Pleiades flee before the mighty strength of Orion and set in the misty deep... The right season for mortals to sail is... after the solstice, when the burdensome days of summer come to an end. All that time you will not wreck your ship, nor will the sea destroy the men, unless the Earth-shaker Poseidon desires it or Zeus, king of the immortals, wishes to destroy them," wisely advised the Greek Hesiod, c. 700 BCE.

Indeed, knowing when to sail was of primordial importance. Sailing in winter was deemed so dangerous that a law of ancient Rhodes forbade marine insurance in the Mediterranean during that season. Even in the sixteenth century, records show that sea travel,

185

for any purpose, was always more desirable in the summer months. Whether they were transporting grain or pilgrims, ships mostly sailed in good weather, and when they were forced to leave in autumn, the voyage was said to take almost twice as long because of difficulties. Ships on long voyages with changing latitudes, such as those bound for the Indies, left several times a year, and often in the autumn, but they were soon within warmer temperatures as they proceeded towards the equator on their way to rounding Africa. The dangers of the climate, for them, resided as much in facing sweltering heat and being becalmed along the African coast as in being subjected to disabling storms.

Today, we are free from the exigencies of trade winds and currents, the fear of being becalmed in doldrums, or from many of the other weather-related headaches experienced by earlier navigators. The key innovations creating modern safety, particularly on long voyages, are all the result of technological advances and the human genius for tampering with nature, including inventing the chronometer to calculate longitudes (1760s), replacing wind-powered ships with steam-powered ones (roughly 1870-80s), inaugurating the Suez Canal (1869), and opening the Panama Canal (1914) after protracted and exhausting efforts.

To appreciate their impact on navigation, let us embark on an imaginary journey in the mid-1840s, stepping on board a clipper in a western European port for a voyage to the East Indies. Our captain would likely be duplicating the route once established by merchant ships from the Dutch Republic, sometimes impatiently waiting for days at anchor for favourable winds. To save time, these captains had abandoned the earlier stops in Madeira, the Cape Verde Islands, and Saint Helena, and headed straight for the Cape. Substantial bonuses were offered for prompt passage: 600 guineas for taking only six months, 300 guineas for arriving after seven months, and 150 guineas for completing the passage in less than nine months. Two ships achieved exceptional records: the *Gouden Leeuw*, taking 127 days in 1621, and the *Amsterdam*, making it to the Indies in only 119 days in 1639. Such speed could only be achieved at the cost of tremendous physical exertion, but most of all, they required favourable weather.

On this new voyage in the 1840s, our ship would first take us down the west coast of Africa, where we would experience the extreme heat of the tropics and the equator, and no doubt suffer from sunburn. Without air conditioning, we would be going on deck for some air, however stifling the heat might be. When we eventually reached the Cape of Good Hope, we would have the opportunity to remember that it was originally named Cabo das Tormentas by its first European navigator, Bartolomeu Dias, in 1488—a name that needs no translation and is illustrated by the hundreds of wrecks littering the South African coast. This route was well established, reflecting the experience drawn from earlier voyages. Too far to the east, ships could be becalmed in the Gulf of Guinea and, too far to the west, the same stillness would engulf them off the coast of Brazil. Having reached the Cape of Good Hope, our 1840s captain would sail in an easterly route until the point where the two great oceans meet at Cape Agulhas. There, he would use the headwinds of the Roaring Forties (the strong westerly winds usually found between 40 and 50 degrees of latitude) to guide our ship across the Indian Ocean to our destination, the East Indies.

From Cape Agulhas, an earlier route, preferred by the Portuguese, had been to sail north to Madagascar and follow a northeastern course across to the Indies. There were numerous problems associated with this route, including extreme heat, unidentified shoals and shallows, and constant contrary winds. The latter, in particular, could make the voyage last as long as sixteen months, and hurricanes had been fatal to many ships. However, a Dutch captain found in 1610 the alternate route much farther south. This new route shortened the passage by 2,000 miles and up to ten months. With less time at sea and an easier route, the men arrived in better condition. However, there was a deadly proviso: this new passage risked coming close enough to shore to wreck the ships on what is now Australia. While Europeans would not discover the new continent for another century and a half, the reefs were only too real.

Whatever the route taken by the captain of our 1840s ship, he would have avoided coming too close to Australia, which was by then adequately charted, and he would have no problem calculating longitudes, since chronometers had been available for a hundred years. For our return voyage, we would continue eastward across the Pacific, sailing around Cape Horn and heading home, first along the eastern American coast, then across the Atlantic.

There were other routes bypassing the tedious rounding of Africa, and India-bound passenger ships of the Peninsula and Oriental Steam Navigation Company sailed instead across the Mediterranean. In this case, our 1840s voyage would take place on the *Tagus* or the *Braganza* (wooden vessels relying on both engine and sail) leaving Southampton once a month. At an average speed of ten knots, they reached Malta ten days later, weather permitting. Rather than outside cabins (today's preference), we would occupy accommodations in the middle of the ship to lessen the rolling motion and avoid the rushing sound of water along the vessel's sides. After disembarking in Malta, we would transfer to the smaller *Iberia* for Alexandria. There, the problem was conveying us to the Red Sea, 280 miles up the Nile and across the desert to Suez. From sea to sea, the uncomfortable journey took about 88 hours in the Middle-Eastern heat. The first leg consisted in sailing from Alexandria to Cairo on a small Nile steamer. For the next onerous 159 miles, across the desert from Cairo to Suez, we would ride a horse, a donkey, a camel, or use a slightly more civilized horse drawn carriage—sitting with five other passengers "on knife-board seats, knees touching knees, and backs bowed to fit the curve of the arched canvas cover." The thirty-six hours of that journey included seven stops for rest, refreshment, and change of horses. Our own and our neighbours' extravagant luggage would be carried (with the coal for the ship) by some of the almost 4,000 camels required for each P & O crossing. The ships refueled in Aden, with a further ten days of hard steaming towards Ceylon. There was more refueling in Ceylon and, again, four days later in Madras, before the final four days' sailing to the final destination, Calcutta.

Today, cruise ships passengers heading for the Far East are spared these long detours and sail directly through the Strait of Gibraltar and the Suez Canal in air-conditioned cabins, enjoying the sea breeze and dropping into some Mediterranean ports along the way. After emerging from the Suez Canal, what would distinguish our 2016 cruising from our former imaginary 1840s would be the appeal of visiting tourist stops along the way, whether the winds were propitious or not. They include Dubai, Colombo, Phuket, Singapore, Komodo Island, and so on, before arriving to Jakarta, Java, and Bali—the sole guiding principle in this extraordinary journey being visiting places whose names make people dream.

While all sailing ships depended on the weather to favour or impede their progress, other weather conditions brought their specific problems and consequences.

DOLDRUMS

"Day after day, day after day / We stuck, no breath, no motion / As idle as a painted ship / Upon a painted ocean," wrote Coleridge in *The Rime of the Ancient Mariner.* When he wrote "Water, water, everywhere, / And all the boards did shrink, / Water, water, everywhere, / Nor any drop to drink," he only reflected the frightening experience of those who were becalmed in the heat of the equator.

The "equatorial calms," the doldrums' other name, are found in low pressure areas around the equator where the prevailing winds are calm and, consequently, where ships propelled by wind and sail were "becalmed." These intertropical convergence zones, where winds and rising air encircle the earth near the equator, are found in the Atlantic and Pacific Oceans. Early European sailors only discovered these meteorological conditions when they first reached tropical or equatorial regions. There, powerless and bereft of wind for days and even weeks, they could do nothing but wait anxiously, watching their rations and water reserve diminish.

Don Eugenio's constant worry was water. "The worst longing is for something to drink; you are in the middle of the sea, surrounded by water, but they dole out the water for drinking by ounces... and all the time you are dying of thirst from eating dried beef and food pickled in brine." He was fearful of sailing into the doldrums. "If you are becalmed in the midst of the sea, the victuals running out and no water left to drink, then indeed you have need for comfort."

Having to conserve water in these circumstances often translated into drastic moves. Thus, the zones located between the Trade Winds and the Westerlies and prone to prolonged calms were known as the Horse Latitudes, because water shortages sometimes forced crews to push overboard the horses they carried.

MONSOONS AND STORMS

Keen observers of winds and currents, seamen always tried to use them to their advantage. When the Romans looked to the east to establish trading posts along the shores of the Red Sea, East Africa, and India, they studied the monsoons. These were naturally familiar to Indian sailors, but not to the Romans. They discovered around 150 CE that in June the southwest monsoon blew across the Indian Ocean in one direction, with the seas becoming heavy and dangerous. Yet, the wind was so strong that sturdy ships could catch it coming out of the Red Sea and quickly sail across to India. In November, after these winds had died down, the northeast monsoon would blow the ships back the other way. They put this knowledge to good use, and after learning from the Arabs how to build ships that could withstand these special winds, they established a succession of trading posts along the coasts to India.

Unpleasant and even deadly as the doldrums were, they did not bring the same terror as violent storms, whose fatal power was described in Longfellow's *Hesperus*: "Colder and louder blew the wind,/A gale from the Northeast,/The snow fell hissing in the brine,/And the billows frothed like yeast./Down came the storm, and smote a main/The vessel in its strength...Her rattling shrouds, all sheathed in ice,/With the mast went by the board;/Like a vessel of glass, she stove and sank."

The sinking of Francisco de Bobadilla's fleet in 1502, after it was caught in a hurricane, is among the first recorded. There are many descriptions of horrendous storms at sea and what they did to ships, their crews, and their passengers. Let us allow those who lived through them relate what occurred and how they experienced it: Vasco da Gama, rounding the Cape of Good Hope on his first voyage (1498); Colonel Norwood, crossing from England to Virginia on *The Virginia Merchant* (1646); the return voyage from Jamaica of the *Terra Nova* (1688); and the wreck of the *Serica* (1868) on her way from Liverpool to Aden, as told by her master and owner, Thomas Cubbin. All were nightmarish affairs and it is surprising that anyone survived to tell the horrific tales.

Da Gama, who established the sea route to India and, in so doing, laid the foundations of the Portuguese empire, set out on his first voyage from Lisbon in July 1497, with four ships, whose often-mutinous crews included convicts for the harsher duties. His return voyage was disastrous, plagued with unfavourable winds and scurvy and suffering great loss of lives. Here, he describes the rough passage around the Cape, with the crew "in despair," the ship "in great peril," and the danger twice as great as the storm renewed its attack.

> Suddenly the wind died out, so that the ships lay dead between the waves, lurching so heavily that they took in water on both sides; and the men made themselves fast not to fall from one side to the other; and everything in the ships was breaking up so all cried to God for mercy. Before long, the sea came in with more violence, which increased their misfortune, with the great difficulty of working the pumps; for they were taking in much water, which entered both above and below; so they had no repose for either soul or body, and the crews began to sicken and die of their great hardships.

Next, the adventures of Colonel Norwood seem so extraordinary as to almost defy belief, yet many of the calamities that befell *The Virginia Merchant* were not exceptional for the times. From the beginning, the difficulties of their passage (notably their insufficient provisions) had been evident, but they were not prepared for the dreadful weather that all but wrecked their ship soon after they left port. They were caught in a violent and fast moving storm. The winds increased and the waves grew in magnitude. "The mountainous towering north-west seas… were so unruly, that the seamen knew not how to work the ship about." The noise, "like the report of a great gun" filled them with terror. So far, only the seamen's efforts at fighting the storm had been mentioned. Only later do we realize that passengers, including children, were also involved. Facing a desperate situation, "We took a short leave of each other, men, women, and children. All assaulted with the fresh terror of death, made a most dolorous outcry throughout the ship." Norwood then described how their main topmast was on the point of crashing down, and the shrouds and rigging seemed to fight against them. The exhausted seamen had not had proper food for several days.

Their torments grew as the voyage continued. Finally, seeing an island with the prospect of water and some provisions, a few set ashore, led by the mate who took twelve sickly passengers with him in the hope the land air would cure them. Astonishingly, the ship sailed away, abandoning them on a small desert island that only provided fresh water, the odd fowl, and a bed of oysters. A few perished and the rest resorted to cannibalism. Eventually, a group of Indians rescued them, and they discovered they were only a few miles off the coast of Virginia.

Another disastrous voyage, already mentioned in another context, is that of the *Terra Nova*, returning home to England from Port Royal (Jamaica) in August 1688, taking on the Duchess of Albemarle and her retinue. Much of Captain Charles May's description of this voyage deals with the technical matters of repairing a severely damaged ship while at sea, but he also shows how seamen and passengers coped under the direst circumstances.

The voyage almost seemed doomed from the start. The crew faced horrendous weather conditions, with gigantic waves smashing into the ship. The great cabin "was like the rest, full of water; and the chest of drawers, cabin table, chairs, and what else lay to windward fell all upon the captain, keeping him striving for life under water. The passengers far'd no better; for being in close low cabins, they were almost smother'd before they could get out." The crew pumped out the water and repaired the extensive damage as best they could. To lighten the ship, they threw overboard the unnecessary cargo, including the guns, the Duchess's expensive furnishings, and several casks of priceless indigo. After inspecting the damage and considering the amounts of food and water, they proceeded to share fairly what was left. Later, they met a Portuguese ship homeward bound, which offered the possibility for the passengers and some of the crew to sail with her. The captain even offered to send them away with their food allowance, but all resolved to stay with him. They finally reached Plymouth three and a half months after leaving Jamaica.

The case of the *Serica* was even more painful for the captain because his wife and two young sons were sailing with him. Three months after leaving Liverpool, "a fearful gust came down" upon them. The main topsail was blown to pieces, forcing them to rig up tarpaulins and hammocks in the mizzen in an attempt to keep the ship's head to the wind. The captain was lashed on the poop to avoid being washed overboard. When his wife came up from the cabin where their two young children waited, paralyzed with fear, and asked him what the weather was like, he said, "It looks like the mouth of hell," and told her to attend to her prayers. "The sea looked like great avalanches coming out of the clouds; [it] was like a boiling caldron, and sometimes the ship looked as if in a deep vortex... all other storms dwindle into insignificance compared to this awful one."

By the fourth day of the gale, the ship was a "miserable derelict" and most of their boats were destroyed, yet they kept the pumps going. There was dissension among the crew about whether to abandon ship or keep her afloat. The captain's authority was questioned, even as some of the crew—particularly the mate—continued to perform admirably. The nearest lands were the islands of Mauritius and Bourbon [Reunion], at least 250 miles away. Against the captain's advice, the crew repaired a small boat, hastily built a small craft, and abandoned ship. The captain put his distraught wife and children in the boat, with some water, bread, and cheese. "I kissed them, thinking it might be the last time. They wished me to be in the boat with them. I said no, I must be the last to abandon the ship. We lowered and got the boat safely afloat." Finally, everyone got into the boat or on a raft, but they were later separated. Unable to reach Isle Bourbon, they headed for Madagascar, soon suffering both thirst and shark attacks. Before they reached shore, the two children had drowned. The anguished captain, the last to get into the boat, accused the men in charge of looking after them of having thought only of saving themselves. One answered, "At such a time as that, it was every man for himself."

FOG AND ICE

Being engulfed in fog has sometimes caused grief to ships, either through collisions with other ships or by making reefs and icebergs invisible from the crow's nest. No one knows how many narrow misses have occurred, but a couple of collisions are still present in our minds. We know the one involving the *Andrea Doria* and the *Stockholm* (1956), in spite of the radar that should have warned them of their proximity. An earlier and far more tragic collision in the fog happened in 1914 between the Canadian passenger ship *Empress of Ireland* and a Norwegian coal ship, the *Storstad*, in the St. Lawrence. The *Empress* sank in ten minutes, taking more than a thousand people to their deaths.

When glacial ice, carried by its weight and momentum, reaches the sea, it often breaks and forms icebergs. Even small ones can be dangerous, as most of their mass sits unseen underwater. Naturally, we think immediately of the *Titanic* sailing in the path of an iceberg soon before midnight on April 14, 1912. Captain Edward John Smith, the *Titanic*'s commander, was mostly concerned with the fog hiding them, knowing that the big icebergs that come drifting into warmer water melt faster under water than on the surface. They then become far more treacherous as sharp, invisible reefs that could pierce through the bottom of a ship form below the water line. It is estimated that some three hundred icebergs, detached from the coast of Greenland, reached the North Atlantic that particular April.

The situation is different in the Arctic, where coping with the ice constitutes the *sine qua non* of navigation, and it is important for naval architects and sailors to know what type of ice their vessels will encounter. Much depends on the weather, since warmer conditions may cause cracks in the ice and open new sea lanes. On the other hand, weather changes can also trap vessels in the ice. This problem forced builders to rethink the shape of vessels intended for Arctic navigation, and they patterned the new ships after sealers built to cope with the ice they often encountered. While these craft were usually reinforced at the bow and stern for plowing through the ice, ships built to navigate the frozen ocean needed to be reinforced from side to side where the greater pressure would be exerted on the vessel if immobilized in the ice.

One such ship was the *Fram*, designed and built for the Norwegian explorer Fridtjof Nansen, whose expedition (1893-96) intended to prove the theory of the polar drift. It was inspired by the discovery of the wreckage of the American ship *Jeannette*, sunk in 1881 off the coast of Siberia and found three years later near Greenland. The wreckage being so far from where she sank gave rise to the theory of the polar drift, and Nansen sought to verify it by checking the progress of a ship frozen into the ice. The *Fram* was indeed moved westward by the ice and was tested again later by spending four years in the Canadian arctic. Nansen later gave her frame to Roald Amundsen, who used it to build the *Maud*.

TROPICAL HEAT

While heat did not directly affect sailing, it caused much discomfort before the advent of air conditioning. In May 1855, the *White Star Journal* described some passengers' misery. "The heat has been dreadful… Our ladies… have had headaches and fainting fits… Dinner time used to be our happiest time, but the tropics have rather taken the fun out if it." Indeed, the article describes meals taken in an atmosphere similar to that of "a brick kiln" and "the inside of a steam boiler." The nights were even worse, forcing passengers to bed down on deck in search of fresh air. Those fearing the dreadful temperatures and able to pay a higher price enjoyed the favoured status revealed by the acronym POSH: the ship's cooler sides, port on the way out and starboard coming home.

15 *MAL DE MER*

Seasickness, also known as motion sickness, could have featured in our chapter on illnesses at sea, but it is caused mainly by the ship's combined pitching and rolling, made worse in bad weather. Charles Dickens graphically described the motions of the ship taking him to America in such weather. "And so [the ship] goes on, staggering, heaving, wrestling, leaping, diving, jumping, pitching, throbbing, rolling, and rocking; and going through all these movements, sometimes by turns, and sometimes together; until one feels disposed to roar for mercy."

Motion sickness, known since the dawn of navigation, was surprisingly not studied scientifically until the early 1940s, when the Royal Canadian Navy set out to investigate it. Everyone knew about it, of course, even those who had not experienced it personally, but the steamship companies had done their utmost to avoid discussing the problem. While willingly installing bilge keels, stabilizers, and antiroll tanks to minimize it, they preferred to handle the matter with discretion.

Sailors were often conscripted from inland locations and many suffered from seasickness, but they usually did not have time to ponder upon their condition, even if some were ill from their first sailing day to their last. On the other hand, idle passengers had much opportunity to be devastated by the nausea. From his tiny cabin, Don Eugenio described their experience. "Packed in there, the movements of the sea upset our heads and stomachs so horribly that we turned white as ghosts and began to bring up our very souls. In plain words, we were seasick." Always keen on providing striking details, Don Eugenio continued, "We vomited, we gagged, we shot out of our mouths everything which had gone in during the last two days; we endured by turns cold depressing phlegm, bitter burning choler, thick and heavy melancholy. There we lay... we never opened our eyes, or changed our clothes or moved until the third day." Over the centuries, the descriptions have changed little.

Margaret Meredith soberly reported that several passengers suffered from seasickness, but probably would not have admitted to being affected herself. The condition does not elicit much sympathy. An old cartoon showed green-faced passengers heaving over the railing of a cheerfully festooned cruise ship, while the caption read, "Having fun yet?" Another showed a row of bilious passengers lining the side of a pitching vessel and was captioned, "Some of our shipmates made the crossing by rail." Rudyard Kipling injected a little humour at the expense of his sailing companions to Japan on the *Ancona.* "We are deathly sick, because there is a cross-sea beneath us and a wet sail above... The sail is to steady the ship who refuses to be steadied. She is full of Globe-Trotters who also refuse to be steadied. A Globe-Trotter is extreme cosmopolitan. He will be sick anywhere."

William Bastard, who probably had not been seasick while on the *Orient* in 1888, seemed to believe that "the disorder is largely controllable by will," and that all that is required to cure it is "first a little time and rest, then forced feeding and fresh air," which must come as news to those retching bodies unable to even face the thought of food. For those, he helpfully suggested sixteen "prominent drugs," among which cocaine, morphine, and strychnine, all common remedies at the time for many ailments. Another passenger recommended, "Just suck a lemon. And try to stand on your toes, as you would in an elevator... And don't forget to breathe in when the ship goes up, and out when the ship goes down."

Advice was freely offered to the ailing members of the sailing party, including jumping, standing still, lying down, using ear and nose plugs, staying below so as not to look at the sea, going out into the fresh air, or binding one's belly. They sound comical, but their contradictions prove that they were ineffective in treating the awful symptoms of seasickness. Many passengers comment on its devastating effects. "The ladies... lie on their deck chairs swathed in rugs and shawls like Egyptian mummies in their sarcophagi, and there they pass from ten to twelve hours a day motionless, hopeless, helpless, speechless," from one writer. From S. J. Perelman, "My stomach and the Arabian Sea arrived at a *modus vivendi*; it was agreed that the ocean would do its own heaving and my viscera the same." A lady in the deckchair next to his "exhaled a lugubrious groan that culminated in a graveyard knell and plucked weakly at my sleeve. The tortured, queasy face she turned towards me was Lovat green. 'I'm going to die,' she whimpered."

On the *Lake Manitoba,* built for 550 passengers but home to 1,962 British colonists (and their 150 dogs) sailing to Canada in 1903, seasickness contributed to the general misery. A passenger described the conditions in the bowels of the ship. "We lay on our bunks in our crowded quarters and suffered; those who had recovered would lean out of their bunks to read in the dim light. They soon learned, however, to pull their heads back in a hurry when a seasick mate in an upper bunk shouted 'Duck!'"

Finally, William Morris summed up the misery when he wrote during his 1874 Atlantic crossing, "You may recollect what Punch once said about seasickness. At first he was afraid he was going to die, and then he was afraid he was not."

Today, seasickness is only noticeable through the occasional absence from the dining table and the visible patches behind many passengers' ears. Dramamine and Gravol have discreetly replaced the various remedies of the past such as Mothersills Seasick Remedy in the 1920s, or drinking neat brandy or rum mixed with grapefruit juice every two hours.

There are several reasons why seasickness no longer ravages passengers, one being that most captains avoid whenever possible routes that will cause the swell to disturb the cruisers' peace of mind and stomachs. The guesswork in steering ships away from potential danger has been removed by the introduction of such aids to modern navigation as radar, the Globe Positioning System, the sonar/echo sounder that would have prevented so much founder-ing on shoals and wrecks on hidden rocks, and accurate compasses. Another huge improvement is the greater stability at sea resulting from advances in naval engineering, particularly the introduction of stabilizers that serve to reduce a ship's motion—not the pitching, which can hardly be allayed, but the annoying roll from side to side responsible for much seasickness. Finally, the massive construction projects that created the Panama and Suez canals rendered unneces-sary the rounding of the tempestuous Cape Horn and Cape of Good Hope. All these factors have naturally contributed to the success of cruising as a pleasant way of spending leisure time by largely elimi-nating the seasickness that commonly faced earlier navigation.

VI
THE DARK SIDE OF THE SEA

Crews

Mutineers

Pirates

Slaves

Convicts

Migrants

The Custom of the Sea

Sailing in suites and first-class cabins could be pleasant for society's elite, and fairly comfortable as well for second-class passengers, but there was a much darker side to being at sea than worrying about the accommodations on board or being afflicted with *mal de mer*.

Piracy, operating under the Jolly Roger's flag, is as old as navigation and the transport of goods by sea. Together with mutineering, piracy sometimes came as a consequence of the navies and merchants' unsavoury recruiting practices and the dreadful living conditions they provided for sailors.

Some ships also became dedicated to the displacement of people. Slaves (as either rowers or cargo), convicts, indentured workers, pilgrims, colonists, and waves of European emigrants in search of a better future in the New World have all been conveyed in ships, sometimes travelling in abominable conditions. Some hulks even had their own infamous names like "coffin ships," and "famine ships." In our century, a new type of migrants, sailing across the Mediterranean in unsafe conditions that sometimes prove fatal, replace those earlier seekers of a better life.

These darker topics are considered in this chapter, ending with cannibalism, which was seldom punished when known as the custom of the sea.

16 CREWS

Some people are responsible for catering to the passengers' needs—making beds, cleaning staterooms, cooking and serving meals, entertaining, smiling and greeting at every encounter, and generally ensuring comfort and pampering in a fashion usually alien to most cruisers' ordinary lives. Elsewhere, mostly unseen, sailors tend to the ship and ensure safe passage, seldom acknowledging cruisers and not bothering to ingratiate themselves. In emergencies, both groups have functions that will ensure passengers' safety or rescue, and have often shown equal courage and efficiency in the performance of these duties.

Seafarers have a long and often tortuous history, and they are often deemed to operate in a different realm, whatever their ranks and nationalities. They belong to an exceptional group, together with others—such as miners, loggers, or firefighters—involved in once exclusively male and high-risk professions that set them apart. Because of their dangerous lives, John Flavel, a seventeenth-century clergyman, believed they have a special status. "Seamen are, as it were, a third sort of persons, to be numbered neither with the living nor the dead; their lives hanging continually in suspense before them."

These words may have held more truth in the seventeenth century than today, but the distance to the bottom is still the same. Sitting in a lifeboat after the sinking of the *Soekaboemi* in 1942, when the radio officer asked where the nearest land was, a crewman answered, "Two miles away. Straight down." These were the murderous war years, but sailors still die at sea. The International Union of

Maritime Insurance stated that 2006 was a catastrophic year for hull claims; yet, the following year, the numbers were four times higher, and even today, more than two ships are lost every week. In July 2015, a *New York Times* article reported that, on average, a large ship sinks every four days and between two and six thousand seamen die annually, mostly through avoidable accidents and lax observance of safety practices, and because of the weather. When we consider the number of ships carrying cargo (four million fishing and small cargo vessels and one hundred thousand large merchant ships), the numbers should perhaps not surprise.

RECRUITING

A request to Holland America Line for information on their hiring practices and employment terms for their crew went unanswered. Without Holland America's confirmation and based on informal talks with crew and other passengers, I can only advance the following information. The line advertises in the Philippines and Indonesia, from where recruits are sent to various training centres, notably Jakarta, with standards said to be different from those of the European crew. Their promotion is based on their fluency in English and their personality. They are hired on a contractual basis and, depending on the work, these contracts vary between three and ten months, the latter being the norm for most jobs.

Most of the visible staff appear hard working and rely on tips automatically added to the cost of the cruise (divided equally among the cabin staff, the kitchen and restaurant staff, and the "unseen" staff like laundry workers, carpenters, etc.), and the ones privately given to particularly helpful crew members. Certain details, if true, seem to reflect a somewhat niggardly attitude on the part of the employers. On the other hand, if the competition for such jobs is as great as it seems, the advantages they offer must be substantial by homeland standards. We assume that the general regulations for employing maritime personnel and for establishing and monitoring their working conditions apply in the case of all reputable cruise lines, and we will dwell no further on today's practices, because the past is much murkier—even when officially regulated—and thus more interesting.

Many sailors did not arrive on board voluntarily; they may have been either pressed or shanghaied into service. From Saxon times, seamen had been procured through press gangs, and the custom became so established in Britain that the admiralty came to assume that every eligible man could be pressed into service in the Royal Navy. Impressment consisted in taking men by force and without notice, and it existed in several parts of the world. The size of the Royal Navy meant that it required many more men than did other Western nations. These measures were even more prevalent in wartime when the number of pressed men could be doubled or even tripled, notably in the eighteenth century. Unemployed men were particularly easy prey for the press gangs. The Vagabonds Act of 1597, which introduced penal transportation to the American settlements as an alternative to execution, also facilitated the drafting into service of men deemed to be of disrepute. A further act in 1703 excluded apprentices and gentlemen from impressment.

The Royal Navy resorted to several other devices to increase its intake of men, particularly during the Napoleonic wars (1803-1815), such as establishing a quota system for each county, sometimes bringing on board criminals, diseased men, or those totally unsuited for service. One of the reasons why the British (and colonial Americans) were more likely to be exposed to such recruiting abuses than continental Europeans is that conscription and the ample supply of men it provided did not exist in Britain, so other methods of supplying sailors for their large navy had to be found. Pressing normally resulted in getting on board males between the ages of fifteen and fifty-five with some experience of the sea, such as former merchant seamen, river boatmen, longshoremen, and fishermen, while there was no such guarantee with shanghaiing. There was no "career" to be had in the navy for pressed men and volunteers (the latter receiving a bounty upon joining and a higher salary), and they were free to leave after their particular term was over. Resistance to impressment was originally punishable by hanging, as was desertion; yet desertion was high in the Royal Navy, almost reaching twenty-five percent at times.

In both Britain and America, a similar recruitment method was practiced by "crimps," who rendered their victims unconscious, forged their signatures on the ship's articles, and pocketed what was known as "blood money." Later historical events, such as the California Gold Rush, occasionally depleted the stock of men willing to serve on U.S. ships, and the only practical way of recruiting seamen was then to shanghai them. Legislation on both sides of the Atlantic eventually put an end to these methods of recruitment.

Recruitment into piracy was different. Many found it to their advantage to abscond from legitimate vessels, and the shift was often a voluntary one. Almost all English-speaking pirates are believed to have come from the ranks of the Royal Navy or to have served as merchant seamen, which sometimes meant having been on a privateer. It was harder for them to survive as pirates because of the danger of pulling into port to get supplies or make repairs, the constant need to escape warships sent to destroy them, and their reliance on unchartered waters to keep a low profile. So, what was the attraction to this outlawed way of life?

The newly converted pirates left behind the strictest discipline, the most rigid and oppressive hierarchy and structure, the barest facilities, and a life ruled by officers who exacted total obedience, and who on merchant ships took the lion's share of prize money. What they found instead was an almost egalitarian and consensual environment where discussions were freely held and decisions reached collectively. As pirates, they enjoyed a form of freedom impossible to find on navy or merchant vessels, and almost unthinkable in their prior lives on shore.

A SEAMAN'S LIFE

An early saying described sailors' life as "Continual destruction in ye foretop, ye Pox above board, ye Plague between Decks, Hell in ye Forecastle and ye Devil in ye Helm." The combination of "a hot country, stinking Meat, and maggoty Bread, with the noisome and poisonous Scent of the Bilge Water, have made many a brave English sailor food for Crabs and sharks," quotes historian Redicker from contemporary sources. Another maritime historian, David Cordingly, described the sailors "living in cramped, damp quarters smelling of bilge-water, tar, and unwashed humanity in company with assorted collection of pigs, goats, cattle, and chickens."

Indeed, life on board offered them few comforts. Their routine was "hauling on wet ropes at all hours of the day and night, going aloft to haul heavy canvas sails, and often manning the pumps for hours on end." A small improvement came after Columbus dis-covered the hammock in the West Indies in 1493. It was adopted everywhere and became commonplace on English ships by 1597, replacing sleeping on deck. They were made, like the sailors' uncomfortable trousers, of rough brown canvas from damaged sails, a custom that survived to the nineteenth century.

The main features of their lives consisted in dreadful food, appalling weather, fear of drowning, and the constant prospect of injury. Facing a brutish way of life, many also died young. As late as 1880, the records show that 1 in 60 died violently at sea—in the next most dangerous occupation, mining, only 1 in 315 died accidentally.

Food

In the Royal Navy, the quality of food varied but the amounts remained more or unless unchanged during the eighteenth century. Many authors maintain that the food was not bad and its allocation was fair. Some captains, Cook, for example, made great efforts to improve their men's diet, and Nelson's standing order was that "all are to be equal in the point of victualling." To this effect, there was on most ships a kitchen implement named the "tormentor," a large fork used by the cook, who stood behind a curtain while picking pieces of boiled meat out of the cauldron and allocating them to the unseen men. It should also be noted that Royal Navy cooks were usually recruited from the ranks of disabled seamen.

Provisions were strictly controlled by the Victualling Board, and all efforts were made to prevent spoilage. Although vegetables were few and usually overcooked, rations were sufficient to ensure an adequate intake of calories, and food was regularly available—which was not always the case with men working the land. The expression "three square meals," which used to be served in the Royal Navy, comes from the square wooden plates used by ratings to eat their three daily meals. Their food was much like that hawked in port by street vendors, such as pease pudding or lobscouse, a favourite stew on Captain Aubrey's ships.

This was not necessarily the case with the merchant service, and far less scrupulous captains were known to buy food unfit for human consumption. Thus, Tom Dudley (the skipper of the ill-fated yacht *Mignonette* we will meet later), routinely ate "salt-horse," a "rank, unidentifiable meat pickled in brine" as a young sailor. His captain had followed some captains and ship owners' custom of buying barrels of salt meat from contractors who sold from the naval victualling yards food condemned as unfit by the Royal Navy.

Unlike men sailing on other eighteenth-century ships, whose diet was on the whole sufficient, French sailors went hungry. When taken prisoner on British ships, they were usually found to be suffering from scurvy. Food shortages were rife in France after the Revolution, owing to the conscription of farmers and the British blockage against Napoleon, and the French Navy suffered the consequences.

Discipline

Discipline on ships was harsh. The Articles of War, the naval code first written in 1661 under Charles II, were intended to uphold the principle "For the good of all, and to prevent unrest and confusion," which has endured to this day. They sought the common good, but often under the unflinching grip of an almighty captain and a handful of officers. In 1731, the King's Rules and Admiralty

Instructions regulated all matters of discipline administered in the Royal Navy, and the three most common types of punishment were flogging, keel-hauling, and hanging.

Flogging, by far the most common punishment, was imposed at the discretion of the captain for a variety of crimes. It was inflicted with a "cat-o'-nine-tails," at the gangway. Cats (nine waxed cords of equal length, each ending with a small knot, attached to wooden handles) were made by the prisoners themselves while they were kept in leg-irons awaiting their punishment, which was administered by the boatswain in front of the ship's company. Boatswain's mates would be replaced after each set of twelve lashes, renewed strength being required to administer the rest of the punishment. After the man was cut down from the mast to which he had been strapped, he was taken to the sick berth, and salt would be rubbed into his wounds to avoid infection. When tattoos became popular in the Royal Navy, some sailors opted to have a crucifix put on their backs, in the hope of preventing flogging, or at least receiving a less vigorous one. By 1750, twelve lashes were the maximum authorized, and in 1881, strong public opinion led to flogging being abolished in the Royal Navy. However, birching and caning continued until last century as a punishment for boys, cadets, and midshipmen.

A version of flogging as a punishment for theft was called running the gauntlet and upheld until the end of the eighteenth century. After receiving the usual dozen lashes, the thief had to run through two lines of the ship's company, being flogged by all with short lengths of rope, and was thereafter given another dozen lashes. Another version was "flogging around the fleet," where the offender was put in a ship's boat rowed from gangway to gangway and received a number of lashes from the boatswain of each ship.

"Keel-hauling" was intended for serious offences. The culprit was dragged under the keel of the ship, either across or from bow to stern. Razor-sharp barnacles from the keel tore the flesh away, and the punishment was usually fatal. Abandoned in the Royal Navy in 1720, it continued in Dutch and French navies until 1750. Finally, hanging at the yardarm was the punishment for mutiny, and death usually occurred by slow strangulation. The last hanging in the Royal Navy took place in 1860.

On American ships, flogging was banned in 1850 (although only seven out of the 241 senior officers consulted by the secretary of the navy said they wanted it discontinued), but seamen had to wait until 1951 to be protected from corporal punishment by the Seamen's Act. Until then, captains in the US merchant marine would punish their crew with an assortment of "fists, boots, pieces of rope, brass knuckles, pistols, and ship-board items such as belaying pins, marlin spikes, hand spikes, and other tools."

In Port

Many have described the dismal conditions of sailors' lives on shore. The times held little refinement for common people and even less for humble seagoing men. In Southampton, for instance, where many sailors were stationed between sailings, the area around the wharves and warehouses was a rat-infested "warren of cobblestreets, lanes and alleys... crowded with taverns and grog shops. Some had purpose-built pits in which dog-, cock-, and rat-fights were staged." For lighter amusement, "there were scores of brothels and the music and dance-halls were also thinly disguised as knocking-shops," with many of the prostitutes being little more than children. Moreover, unscrupulous people ("crimps" or landsharks, shady boarding house keepers or "gins," and others) conspired to rob seamen and left them so indebted that they could only go back to sea. In some cases, crimps even sold drunk and drugged sailors to captains ready to set out to sea, and even dead sailors were passed off as being merely dead drunk.

Wiser seamen chose to stay with tested boarding houses, often kept by retired sailors. Many also availed themselves of the services provided by popular charities established in the first half of the nineteenth century: Sailors Homes, the British and Foreign Sailors Society, the Royal National Institute for the Preservation of Life from Shipwreck, the Destitute Sailors Asylum. Some were more specialized, such as the Strangers' Rest Mission (catering to West Africans, Caribbeans, and Chinese until 1900) and the Home for Coloured Sailors. The Seamen's Church Institute of New York floated up and down the port of New York, as did The Floating Church of Our Savior for Seamen. Moreover, trustworthy chaplains resided in British ports of trades, such as Madras, Singapore, and Vancouver. The existence of these charities devoted to the sailors' welfare seems proof enough that their lives needed practical and spiritual succour.

THE SEAMEN'S FRIEND

The harsh conditions experienced by many seamen often existed in a context of greed and politics. A contributing factor to the heavy loss of life we noted earlier, at least on merchant ships, had been the actions of insurance companies. When they decided to pay for the shipment's full value, unscrupulous ship owners would overload their ships, eschewing the traditional three inches of hull clearance for every foot of cargo space, and thus putting them at risk. A profit could also be made from merely wrecking older vessels. Seamen had little recourse against those actions.

The *Epaminondas* (1855) is a case in point. Twice grounded and shipping water at the rate of over two inches an hour while being loaded, she was obviously unsafe. Refusing to sail, her crew were jailed for three months. On another ship, condemned by a Lloyd's surveyor as "utterly unfit to go to sea," the crew deserted and were immediately jailed; a replacement crew was then hired and went down with the ship in the Atlantic. Such excesses were eventually reported in the *Lifeboat,* the journal of the Royal National Lifeboat Institution.

The *Lifeboat* continued to monitor and report abuses, and revealed the national scandal of unprincipled ship owners or their agents being entitled to send any well-insured ship to sea, whatever her seaworthiness, her master's opinion, and her crew's willingness to sail. A politician rose to challenge the status quo. Samuel Plimsoll,

MP for Derby, pledged to force legislation that would protect merchant seamen. His book, *Our Seamen,* published in December 1872, denounced all the abuses he saw everywhere, including unseaworthiness, under-manning, over-insuring, overloading, faulty construction, and lack of repairs. The book also called upon all politicians to pass a truly protective bill.

Plimsoll succeeded in pushing through the Merchant Shipping Act of May 1873, remaining a single strong voice always raised in support of improving the seamen's condition and causing the popular press to dub him "The Seamen's Friend." As watchdog, he succeeded in curbing the worst excesses in spite of the opposition of some other politicians and most ship owners. A royal commission, consisting mostly of ship owners and builders and Board of Trade members—with no representation from seamen—consistently opposed his efforts.

In 1874, Gladstone and the Liberal government made way for Disraeli, and Plimsoll's chances of success in passing an efficient bill seemed even weaker. Indeed, the following July, Disraeli announced that the Merchant Shipping Bill would be abandoned. Infuriated, Plimsoll pleaded with other MPs, "in the name of our common humanity," to proceed immediately with the bill. "Failing this, I lay upon the head of the Prime Minister and his fellows the blood of all the men who shall perish next winter from preventable causes."

Surprised by the public support given Plimsoll, Disraeli shepherded The Unseaworthy Ships Bill that became law in August 1875. One of its terms was that ships were made to carry a conspicuous "Plimsoll Line" on their hulls, determining safe loading capacity. Nevertheless, the Board of Trade would not implement the Plimsoll Line until 1899. During that period, 1,153 ships went missing, with the loss of 11,000 lives.

17 MUTINEERS

Mutiny. *Bounty.* Those two words are indelibly linked in our minds, Hollywood no doubt playing its part in this equation. Yet, mutiny was once common and far bloodier examples exist. Magellan was plagued with it, Drake had to repress it, even Cook feared it, and Hudson died because of it. Whatever sanctions were taken—flogging, marooning, hanging—they were promptly executed.

Mutiny is broadly defined as resistance by force to recognized naval or military authority and it covers a great range of actions. In some cases, mutineers had nothing to lose and their revolts were tantamount to committing suicide, such as slaves' mutinies on America-bound ships. Other mutinies, often supporting legitimate requests for raises or for better conditions, were little more than versions of modern sit-ins. A few had far more duplicitous motives and could be very bloody. Let us review four cases: the Royal Navy's great mutinies of 1797; the *Bounty* of Captain Bligh; the *Batavia*'s nightmare in which civilians were involved; and the "soft" mutinies in the Royal Canadian Navy.

THE ROYAL NAVY

The admiralty experienced in 1797 the largest outbreak of discontent for nearly a century and a half. The country was at war—a dangerous time for social unrest—and the example of Revolutionary France was unsettling to the British authorities. The mutiny started at Spithead, near Portsmouth, followed by one in the North Sea Squadron and another at Nore, in the Thames estuary. The crews' demands focused mostly on raises (needed to offset the significant inflation in the last half of the eighteenth century), better living conditions, and the removal of some officers. The elected Spithead delegates tried to negotiate with the admiralty and, although the negotiations broke down, mutineers succeeded in obtaining some improvement. They had shown no real violence and were eventually pardoned.

At Nore, however, where the crew took control of the *Sandwich* and others attempted to do the same with their ships, the situation deteriorated, mostly through lack of organization. The mutineers' grievances and demands were deemed unacceptable; they were not supported by other crews and failed to impose themselves. They were court-martialled and flogged, hanged, or transported to Australia. The same year, violent mutinies occurred in the West Indies (the *Hermione,* the *Marie Antoinette)* and sporadically off the coasts of Ireland and Spain. The admiralty later recognized the merit of some of the crews' grievances.

THE *BOUNTY* (April 28, 1789)

Captain Bligh partly blamed the women of Tahiti and the "powerful inducement" and "allurements of dissipation" they offered his men for their decision to take over the *Bounty.* Naturally, there was more to it than the attraction of Tahitian life, notably the frequent clash of personalities between Bligh and Fletcher Christian, a master's mate. Only a handful of sailors, led by Christian, took an active part in the mutiny. Many sided with Bligh and seventeen went with him in the open launch in which they eventually reached Timor. There was not enough room for all and some (the "loyalists") were left on Tahiti, with Bligh's acknowledgement of their innocence. As Christian and the mutineers sought an isolated island to settle, some objected to the plan and were returned to Tahiti.

Thus, several groups were formed. First, Fletcher, the mutineers, and some Tahitian women and youths settled on Pitcairn Island after setting fire to the *Bounty.* Next, the loyalists who would have followed Bligh waited in Tahiti for a ship to be sent for them from England, and—keeping apart from them—were the mutineers who had been unwilling to follow Fletcher. Last, were the sailors who eventually reached England with Bligh.

When the *Pandora* arrived in Tahiti, a year after Bligh's return to England, her captain made no distinction between the loyalists who had eagerly welcomed his arrival and the mutineers who had fled inland and been recaptured. Both were put in irons. Christian and his men were never found, and the *Pandora* eventually headed home with her cargo of prisoners, treated with equal harshness and kept in fetters in their "Pandora's Box," a cage built to contain them on deck. Eventually caught in a terrible storm, many sailors and prisoners drowned. Some of the loyalists had been released to work the pumps alongside the crew, but others were kept in their cage. Notable among those drowned was the cooper, still in irons and unable to escape. In his report on the *Pandora*'s wreck and abandonment, Captain Edwards never mentioned the prisoners or their treatment. The ten prisoners who survived the wreck and the weeks spent in Batavia were eventually tried (September 12-18, 1792). Bligh could not attend the court-martial to support the loyalists. Nevertheless, four were acquitted and six were sentenced to hang, of whom three were later pardoned.

Since this is a book about ships, we should mention a little schooner, the *Resolution*, beautifully built on Tahiti from hibiscus and breadfruit tree by the mutineers. After their capture, one of Captain Edwards' young lieutenants had safely sailed her from Tahiti to Timor, where she was given to the governor in gratitude for his hospitality.

THE *BATAVIA* (Fall, 1628)

Three personages dominated the deadly incidents: Francisco Pelsaert, a senior *VOC* merchant, who fell seriously ill during the voyage and could not intervene in a timely manner; captain Adrian Jacobsz, often drunk and once publicly scolded by Pelsaert to his intense resentment; and a mysterious and perverse character, the merchant Jeronimus Cornelisz, a follower of the banned Torrentius sect, dedicated to satisfying the pleasures of the senses. To disrupt the voyage, Jacobsz and Cornelisz soon organized a series of attacks, particularly on a lady travelling to rejoin her husband in Batavia. She was violently assaulted by one of the captain's men. In the ensuing mayhem, the ship was wrecked on the coast of Western Australia. While 180 persons, including women and children, were ferried off the ship, some seventy men remained on board, including Cornelisz.

There was no fresh water on Beacon and Traitor islands on which the survivors landed, and the ship's provisions were not enough to sustain them. A group composed of Pelsaert, the senior officers, and some crew and passengers decided to sail to Batavia to seek help, leaving 268 people stranded on the waterless islands. Soon afterwards, the wreck of the *Batavia* broke up entirely, drowning forty men. The survivors rejoined the others on the islands, under Cornelisz's control. He intended to seize any rescue ship and carry off the *Batavia*'s rich cargo, and to do so unimpeded, he systematically undertook to get rid of the survivors. First, he sent a party of forty-five to Seal Island under the pretext of finding water and had them killed; then, he disarmed the soldiers and sent them off to explore nearby islands; next, he sent others on errands and had his accomplices push them overboard. Finally, he executed the ill, the infirm, the children, and some of the women. Other women were kept alive for obvious reasons. All these deeds were observed and later reported by a reliable witness.

Pelsaert eventually returned on the *Sardam* to rescue the survivors and was told of the mutineers' crimes, including the murders, the rapes, the seizure of the *Batavia*'s cargo. They were captured and tried on site. Their right hands were cut off and Cornelisz had both hands cut off before dying on the gallows. Men accused of lesser crimes were later tried in Batavia, where they were either flogged, keelhauled, or executed. The *Sardam* returned to Batavia on December 5, 1629, with the remaining survivors and what could be salvaged from the *Batavia*'s cargo. Some two hundred people had perished in the ordeal.

THE ROYAL CANADIAN NAVY
(February-March 1949)

On three separate incidents in different parts of the world (Mexico, China, and the Caribbean Sea), RCN sailors refused to obey simple orders. What characterized these mutinies (although most officers carefully avoided the word and its legal consequences) was the reasonable manner in which they were handled and the desire not to escalate matters. For instance, when the captain of the destroyer *Athabaskan* met with the men to hear them and discuss their grievances, he put his cap on the table, covering their written submission and affecting not to see it.

These mutinies—more akin to strikes—should be put in the context of the times and the fear of the so-called "Red Menace." There had been recent Communist-inspired strikes in the Canadian merchant marine, and the government was concerned with their influence, particularly since the protesting crew of the destroyer *Crescent* was in Nanking, where the Communists were then winning their war.

Rear-Admiral Rollo Mainguy headed a commission of enquiry that found no evidence of Communist influence or collusion by the three crews. While reassuring the government on this point, the *Mainguy Report* also alerted it to deeper concerns about the RCN's organization and management style. A previous *Morale Study* (1947) had been more or less ignored, although it outlined systemic problems in the RCN and pointed to an existing pattern of rebellious incidents *(Skeena,* 1936; *Assiniboine,* 1940; *Iroquois,* 1943; *Rivière-du-Loup,* 1945, and several others). None had been violent, but they indicated deep-seated discontent on a number of matters, notably a collapse of the personnel management system, frequent and unexplained changes in ships' names and routines, and a deterioration of the traditional relationships between officers and petty officers.

Two other strong points of concern—one practical, the other ideological—had contributed to the 1949 situation. The first was the lack of a welfare committee to which sailors could submit their grievances, forcing them to resort to a form of strike passing for mutiny. Perhaps more importantly was the lack of a true Canadian identity in the RCN. The latter was put in these terms: "An uncaring officer corps harbouring aristocratic British attitudes inappropriate to Canadian democratic sensitivities." Perhaps these were merely growing pains, but further developments tending to cut off British traditions (such as insignia and uniforms) attempted to answer some of the deeper concerns of the Canadian Navy.

The mutiny on the *Batavia* is the one that stands out, because of its violence and the fact that so many civilians were involved. It goes against the more usual pattern of submitting grievances and refusing to obey orders. The repercussions may vary, as we have seen at Spithead and Nome, but the response is always meant to be forceful. At sea, a few individuals hold authority over many whose only power lies in their numbers and their determination. Mutinies of the latter against the former are deemed unacceptable, whatever the circumstances. The spirit of the 1661 Articles of War ("For the good of all, and to prevent unrest and confusion") permeates all navies. Thus, while reprisals punish some, they also mean to serve as deterrent to others.

In some cases, our sympathies go to the mutineers, as in the case of the *Kniaz Potemkin Tavricheski* (June 1905), a Russian battleship of the Black Sea Fleet. It is difficult, even when merely reviewing the facts, not to be influenced by Eisenstein's 1925 powerful film, *Battleship Potemkin*, but the sailors' initial refusal to eat inedible meat does not seem to have warranted the violence that ensued. What followed was the shooting of one mutineer, followed by the mutineers' execution of the captain, the chaplain, and two officers; the frightful Cossack charge down the Richelieu Steps after the ship's return to Odessa; and five or six thousand people losing their lives during these events. The crew eventually scuttled the ship in shallow water, unable to find support in any of the Black Sea ports.

18 PIRATES

The motley lot we call pirates came from many nations, races, types, and levels of ability. They seldom engaged in piracy for more than ten years, and many only lasted two or three. While they plied their trade in much the same manner, they belonged to different groups and bore several names, from the lawless pirates and buccaneers who often ended up being hanged to the ambiguous privateers and corsairs who hoped for a more lenient fate. Generally, privateers and corsairs were an anomaly resulting from historical circumstances, while self-governed pirates have regularly operated wherever cargo ships could be preyed upon, from antiquity to our own century.

From China to the Mediterranean, pirates were a constant threat. Early mariners were easy targets because, often lacking compass and charts, they sailed close to the shore. In the Mediterranean, as early as the seventh century BCE, Phoenician ships were regularly attacked by pirates, as the Greeks and the Romans were later. The first Crusade in 1096 briefly secured the Mediterranean for European shipping. Nevertheless, the Barbary Coast pirates, notably the corsair brothers Barbarossa from Tunis, would later dominate that sea from Egypt to the Atlantic beyond Gibraltar, and once more terrorize Christian crews. Piracy continued, eventually reaching out from the west coast of Africa to the Caribbean, a hot bed of eighteenth-century illicit activity.

THE JOLLY ROGER

The white skull and crossbones, a common representation of death, likely became popular in the Caribbean in the early 1700s, and from there seems to have spread worldwide. Under the banner of King Death (the Jolly Roger) sailed disenfranchised sailors from many nations, apparently organized in a form of utopian society. Compared to other seafarers, the freedom they enjoyed was remarkable. The origins of this *confrèrie* are sometimes traced to a Captain Mission and his fellow pirates, full of idealistic notions—condemning dispossession, capitalism, slavery, and nationalism—who formed in Madagascar a society they called Libertalia. Whether Mission and Libertalia really existed is debatable. Nevertheless, given the conditions that shaped sailors' lives, why should they not dream up a reversal of the prevalent system? Even if Libertalia was fictional, the real pirates' lot was preferable to that of ordinary sailors often left to the mercies of criminally penny-pinching owners and harsh captains.

Much of what we know about the pirates' self-government comes from the tenth chapter of Captain G. Johnson's *A General History of the Robberies and Murders of the Most Notorious Pyrates* (1724), which was actually penned by Daniel Defoe, *Robinson Crusoe*'s author. Its articles cover all aspects of conduct, the most revolutionary of which were giving every man a vote in the affairs of the moment and equal title to provisions. Prizes were fairly distributed, based on shares valued at a thousand pieces of eight. The captain and quartermaster receiving two shares; the master, the boatswain, and gunner a share and a half; and the other officers one and a quarter. Desertion was punished by death or marooning. Quarrels were resolved on shore, the winner the first to draw blood. Musicians were allowed to take the Sabbath off. Morality was enforced by allowing no gambling for money, nor any boys or women on board.

Exception to the latter rule was made for two famous women pirates (who started their careers disguised as men), well known for their ferocity in battle, Mary Read and Ann Bonny, sailing on the *Revenge* with John Racham, alias Calico Jack. The crew was captured and made to stand trial in 1720, but the women, sentenced like the men to death by hanging, escaped their fate by "pleading their bellies," as the law did not allow pregnant women to be hanged. Mary Read died of fever in jail the following year, and Ann Bonny is thought to have escaped.

This 1720 trial presaged the end of what had been for Europeans the Golden Age of Piracy. The establishment of Colonial Admiralty Courts and the enactment of the Piracy Act of 1721 enabled vessels from the Royal Navy to destroy Indian Ocean pirate strongholds on Mauritius and Reunion, while French vessels concentrated on the Persian Gulf, and the Dutch patrolled the Red Sea.

The year 1722 was equally disastrous for pirates operating in Africa, ending with the trial at Cape Town Castle, the fortified base of operations and headquarters of the Royal Africa Company that had traded ivory and slaves since 1664. A total of 264 pirates from Bartholomew Roberts's ships, the *Great Ranger* and the *Royal Fortune,* were arrested. It was the largest pirate trial ever held. Nineteen died of their wounds before it started, and fifty-two were hanged "like dogs." Among those who were spared the death penalty, the largest group (seventy-four), including the musicians, were acquitted; twenty were sentenced to seven years of hard labour in the Gold Coast mines of the Royal African Company and did not survive their sentence; and seventeen were sent to prison in London (thirteen of them dying on their way to jail). Bartholomew Roberts, the last of the Golden Age captains, had for a motto, "A merry life and a short one."

BUCCANEERS

Buccaneers had the ambiguous status of pillaging for England and for themselves. It allowed them to steer their way through the political and economic strife of their times and benefit from the conflicts between England and Spain. Elizabeth I unofficially supported their raiding successes over Spanish ships routinely carrying precious cargo from the Caribbean to Spain. Of constant envy for England was the thriving Spanish trade (gold and silver from

Mexico and Peru and silk and spices from the East Indies), whose ships regrouped in the Caribbean before their long Atlantic crossings back to Spain. Eventually, much Spanish wealth was transferred to English coffers through piracy.

Thus, in 1743, Commodore George Anson, at the end of the disastrous circumnavigation during which he lost most of his ships, came across and captured on her return to Spain a galleon from Acapulco and Manila, *Nuestra Señora de Covadonça*. Yielding one million gold coins and thirty-five thousand ounces of silver, the capture redeemed Anson's lacklustre reputation and contributed handsomely to reducing England's war debt. Similarly, Francis Drake accumulated successes, his chase of the *Cacafuego* being particularly lucrative, bringing "great riches, as jewels and precious stones, thirteen chests full of riyals of plate fourscore pound weight of gold, and six and twenty ton of silver."

A group of buccaneers had started modestly as French hunters attracted to Haiti by the descendants of the cattle and pigs brought in from Spain and abandoned in 1605. They hunted and lived in the bush, learning from the native Arawaks how to smoke meat on a wooden grill they called *boucane* and hence were known as *boucaniers*. They traded their beef and pork jerky for gunpowder, liquor, and tobacco with sailors anchored nearby. Known for their rough habits, their poaching, and for generally being a nuisance, they were hated by the Spanish government, which ordered the slaughter of all the animals, thus depriving the *boucaniers* of their food and trade goods. In retaliation, the buccaneers plagued the Spaniards with constant forays from Tortuga, where they had settled around 1640, calling themselves the Brethren of the Coast. They continued to get their meat by raiding Spanish hog ranches to add to their fare of turtles and manatees and engaged in deadly encounters, torturing, raping, and murdering their Spanish prisoners.

Used to forming tight communities, they ruled themselves consensually. Their organization had the trademarks of pirate society, with an established scale to distribute the proceeds of their successful attacks and the recognition of every man's effort and contribution.

First, they dealt with the vessel, the captain's compensation, and the pay for the carpenter or shipwright who careened, mended, and rigged the vessel. Before funds could be individually allocated, they saw to the welfare of the group, including provisions for everyone and a suitable salary for the surgeon, which also covered the cost of his medicinal chest. Then, they provided for the injured according to a scale of compensations for injuries suffered at sea calculated in units of a hundred pieces of eight or one slave (of the same value). The amounts varied according to the resulting handicap—six units for the loss of the right arm, five for the left arm or right leg, four for the left leg, and one unit for the loss of an eye or a finger. What remained after these allocations was divided into shares. The share of the captain (duly elected to this post) was five or six times that of ordinary crewman, and the officers received an amount proportionate to their rank and functions; the lowest ranked boys were paid a half share.

Buccaneers operated on the honour system. No locks were allowed on board, and they swore never to steal from another. Punishment for infringing the rules was severe. Anyone caught stealing from a brother had his ears and nose sliced off, and a second offence was punished by marooning on a desolate shore with only a jug of water and a musket and shot. The punishment was the same for deserting their quarters in battle. While the discipline was strict, it was deemed necessary and was accepted by all, and they thought the organization of their groups to be equitable. There was intense competition for the elected position of leader and other choice posts.

However harsh the life and the discipline, they were a vast improvement over what most of these men had previously experienced. They came from many countries and most were derelicts when they joined the buccaneer fraternity. Some were convicted felons or vagrants sold by their respective countries and banned from returning. Others were religious or political dissidents, prisoners of war, and so on. The most pathetic were the indentured servants, often youths kidnapped from the street, such as the two hundred taken from France to Barbados in 1640 and sold for a term of five years at the cost of 408 kilos of cotton. Slaves, deemed a permanent investment, were treated better than those indentured Europeans.

The Brethren of the Coast were a maritime republic, made up mostly of French, English, Irish, Dutch, and Flemish seamen with no other allegiance than to themselves. From the beginning, they had roamed the Caribbean in search of plunder, their main targets being the treasures loaded on Spanish galleons. They often anchored in the new colony and buccaneering boomtown of Port Royal, Jamaica (the site of the present Kingston). Its governors had immediately welcomed the buccaneers with letters of marque to assist in harassing Spanish ships, and so much silver and gold flowed into the colony's coffers that in 1662 it even planned to create its own mint. These hopes were dashed when an earthquake and the ensuing tidal wave destroyed Port Royal in 1692.

PRIVATEERS AND CORSAIRS

Privateering constituted an ambiguous form of piracy, recognized and sanctioned with a letter of marque (*lettre de course,* for French corsairs), mostly prevalent during the second half of the seventeenth century. Put simplistically, some countries' solution to the problem of keeping only minimal navies in peacetime was to enlist private ship owners and captains to augment their ranks in wartime. Obtaining a privateer's licence was for these a ticket to legitimate piracy.

When countries constantly alternated between war and peace, as Spain and England did in the eighteenth century, with letters of marque issued on an ad hoc basis, it was sometimes difficult for privateers to keep up with politics and switch from one status to the other. While governments could dismiss privateers in peacetime, privateers could not afford to stop their activities, so they turned from privateering to piracy in order to survive. They went where the pickings were abundant. Thus, when France and England fought over trade supremacy in the West Indies and privateers were recruited on both sides, the end of the conflict signaled a huge increase of pirates in the region.

Their ambiguous situation and their fluctuation from legitimate to piratical endeavours are well illustrated through some famous sailors' biographies. For instance, George Dampier (1651-1715), explorer and three-time circumnavigator, frequently switched roles. First sailing with the buccaneer Bartholomew Sharp, Dampier haunted the Spanish Main, later sailing with the privateer John Cook. His reputation caused the Royal Navy to give him in 1687 the command of the warship HMS *Roebuck*. However, when the war erupted again in 1702 between England and Spain, funding for explorations ceased, and Dampier simply resumed his buccaneering activities until Queen Anne commissioned him as a privateer to prey once more on Spanish ships. His adventurous life continued (including being tried for cruelty), but he mostly holds our interest through the alternating identities he assumed according to available sponsors and the opportunities provided by the sea trade.

Promiscuous relations between the English crown, pirates, privateers, and legitimate traders were longstanding by then. A century before Dampier, two other navigators stood out as exemplars of the benefits of this ambiguous condition: John Hawkins (1532-1595), merchant, slave trader, and sometimes admiral, and Francis Drake (c.1540-1596), privateer, unrecognized circumnavigator, slaver, plunderer of the Spanish colonies in Chile and Peru, and vice-admiral during the reign of Queen Elizabeth I.

The situation was somewhat different with the French. Following several naval confrontations with the British, the French Government decided to put its resources into privateering and engaged in a successful *guerre de course*. Between 1702 and 1713, French privateers took almost 7,000 prizes, against 2,239 for the British. From these privately chartered privateers emerged national heroes, still celebrated today through the naming of modern vessels. Noteworthy among them were Jean Bart from Dunkirk (1650-1702), René Duguay-Trouin (1673-1736) and Robert Surcouf (1773-1827), both from St Malo, who all followed the same pattern of shifting roles.

Jean Bart, a man of low birth unable to get a commission in the navy, enlisted among the "Dunkirk privateers" serving the Spanish monarchy against the Dutch. Such was his success that he was recruited into Louis XIV's navy and became particularly active against Dutch vessels during the Nine Years War (1688-1697). His record is prestigious; he captured 386 ships and sank or burned many more.

René Duguay-Trouin, started as a corsair, became a privateer, and ended up as admiral in Louis XIV's navy. There was obviously no opprobrium attached to flirting with various aspects of command at sea.

Robert Surcouf, navigator and slaver, was particularly active in the Indian Ocean harassing British Indiamen. He had started sailing on different slave ships and continued to do so on his own ship *Créole*, even after the National Convention had prohibited slave trading in 1793 in the spirit of the French Revolution. Nevertheless, he remains one of the proud names of the French navy and several vessels, including a submarine cruiser and a stealth frigate, have borne his name.

However, French corsairs did not have the same origin as their British counterparts, even if their actions were similar. They had started under Huguenot auspices, their licences usually issued by the Protestant nations of England and the Netherlands. Variously based in La Rochelle (Brittany), Emden (Friesland), and Dover (England), they were known as the Sea Beggars, and their official role was to fight against Spain and the Catholic Rule. By the late 1560s, some eighty-four Sea Beggars ships, manned by crews of many nationalities and mostly based in La Rochelle, had been given letters of marque by William of Orange.

It was an interesting mix of privateering and religious drive, reminiscent of the Muslim Barbary Coast corsairs' actions against Christian vessels. The Spaniards were attacked for their Catholic faith as much as for the wealth of their New World colonies. The Spanish tribunals, in return, ignored the potential confusion between the captured corsairs' status as privateers, pirates, or ordinary prisoners of war, and simply sentenced them all to the gallows as heretics, the usual punishment for this crime.

The Peace of Westphalia (1648) officially put an end to the wars of religion, resulting in a much tighter control over letters of marque issued to privateers and effectively curbing the corsairs' activity. While they were involved in these religious conflicts, French corsairs had also wholeheartedly supported the slave trade. Between 1540 and 1578, some two hundred ships sailed from Normandy ports to Sierra Leone, connecting the "triangle trade" between Africa, Europe, and the New World.

Notwithstanding the limitations of the letters of marque brought in by the Treaty of Westphalia, French corsairs became again active during the Queen Anne's War (1702-1713) between England and her American colonies on one side and France, her settlers, and their Indian allies on the other. Known as the Sea Wolves and supported by the Acadians of Nova Scotia, they cruised in the Caribbean from their main base of Port Royal and attacked English colonies along the coast, occasionally reaching the Dutch settlements in South America. The Treaty of Utrecht (1713) put an end to their activities in the Caribbean, where they had inflicted serious losses to the Spanish treasure fleet.

For the crews, sailing on privateer ships brought few of the benefits enjoyed by those on pirate ships. Even when the vessels operated under letters of marque, the hierarchy and structure were the same as in peacetime. On the other hand, one of the great advantages (particularly for officers) of sailing under a letter of marque or a *lettre de course* was that they would be considered prisoners of war rather than suffer the pirates' hanging fate. Naturally, this privilege would not extend to peacetime.

The Americans eagerly fell on privateering during the American Revolutionary War (1775-1783), as investors heavily engaged in war-related activities. By the end of the war, the American Congress had issued almost 1,700 letters of marque or commissions, involving more than 1,300 ocean-going vessels, a significant contribution to what could be called the war effort. The War of 1812 saw a renewed activity and considerable engagement between the Royal Navy and American privateers. Among the latter, the well-equipped *Yankee* captured nine British ships, twenty-five brigs, five schooners, and one sloop, also destroying or seizing substantial property.

Public opinion often turned against privateering, particularly in view of the crimes committed against Spanish vessels in the Caribbean. But it was not until the Declaration Respecting Maritime Law, signed in Paris in April 1856 at the end of the Crimean War, that privateering was abolished. Spain, Mexico, and the United States abstained from signing, the latter arguing that the country possessed too small a navy to dispense with privateers. However, the U.S. agreed in 1861 to abide by the principles outlined in the declaration that also addressed the all-important matter of prizes during wartime engagements. Furthermore, it declared that passenger ships could not be attacked and hostile merchant crews had to be seen to safety before their vessels were sunk.

In modern times, the United States toyed again with issuing letters of marque. The submarine-hunting airships *Resolute* and *Volunteer* were assimilated to warships and were unofficially deemed to operate under letters of marque in World War II, although the commission was never authorized by Congress. Twice in our century, Congressman Ron Paul introduced bills to revive the practice, first against the perpetrators of the attack on the World Trade Center whom he likened to pirates, and next against the Somali pirates operating in the Gulf of Aden, arguing that ordinary military means were ineffectual against them. Neither bill was passed.

MODERN PIRATES

Many Somali pirates probably started out as fishermen short-changed by foreign fishing and trying to improve their income through straightforward piracy. It was a move that fitted with the atmosphere of violence and poverty present in the region. The average lifetime income of a Somali is $14,500, an amount easily doubled in a single piracy action.

The 2013 film *Captain Phillips* supposedly relates these pirates' attack against MV *Maersk Alabama* in 2009. Sixteen container ships had recently been attacked in the same area, and all captains had been advised to stay at least six hundred miles off the Somali coast. The protocol for such attacks is for the captain to radio a distress call, cut off the power, and take refuge with the crew below deck. Whether the film is accurate in its depiction of Captain Phillips's heroism (a version challenged by the crew), and whether the six-hundred-mile limit and the protocol were respected is of less interest here than seeing the ship's main defence against such attacks. In consists in powerful water jets designed to repulse the small pirates' skiffs and prevent them from getting close enough for the attackers to throw grappling hooks and ladders and climb aboard.

Rose George, who reports on the shipping industry, does not call these men "Somali pirates," as most media do. While they operate out of Somalia, they are of several nationalities: Somali, certainly, but also Yemeni, some Kenyans, and maybe even Tanzanians. Their self-identity is also in some doubt. According to Canadian journalist Jay Bahadur, who interviewed them, they call themselves *badaadinta badah* (saviours of the sea), rather than *burcad badeed* (ocean robbers), presenting themselves as the descendants of the eighteenth-century pirates and claiming kinship with this somewhat idealized company.

In fact, the pirates' living conditions are poor and when captured they sometimes seem to be starving, perhaps having been sent out without supplies. Equipped with weapons bought cheaply in Somalia's markets, they are often heavily armed youths high on drugs. They rely on the insurers to pay for the release of seized ships and cargo and usually do not harm the crew. These forays into piracy are profitable, even considering the cost of equipping and arming themselves (weapons and ammunitions, skiffs and outboards, curved ladders, GPS receivers, and radios). A British documentary by Neil Bell shows that it can cost as little as $30,000 to finance an attack in the Red Sea and $40,000 in the Indian Ocean. On the other hand, the cost to the shipping companies of having their ships and crews taken hostages is enormous. In 2005, it cost $150,000 a day to charter a tanker, whether the ship was sailing or being held for ransom, and a month of inactivity could cost the company $4 million. By 2012, the recession had reduced the cost to only $10,000 day and rendered the situation less urgent, which resulted in the ship and crew being held captive much longer.

These new pirates are reputed to spare crews and passengers from violence, yet the figures show a different picture. Between 2007 and 2010, sixty-seven hostages died, another twenty-three were killed in 2011, either by the pirates themselves or in navy crossfire during rescue operations. Atrocities such as amputation and keel-hauling were also committed on a captain and a crewmember, and a Chinese crewman was reported killed in 2007 when the owners refused to pay the ransom asked.

A multinational coalition, Combined Task Force 150, has been formed to patrol the Arabian Gulf and the Indian Ocean, the command of the operations rotating between the participating countries, causing the attacks to be both less successful and more numerous. There were 127 attacks in 2010 with 47 successes; a year later the numbers rose to 1511, but with only 25 successes. International monitoring and intervention have caused sea piracy to switch to more attacks and hostage takings on land.

Anti-conspiracy measures have only resulted in a few prosecutions. About four thousand pirates are thought to operate in the area; some fifteen hundred have been caught, several more than once, usually with little consequence.

19 SLAVES

For most of us, mentions of slavery evoke the human trade that brought Africans to the Caribbean and America over three centuries, from their first arrival in Santo Domingo in 1501 with the Spaniards to the official American ban on importing African slaves in 1808. The custom of using slave labour is far more ancient and other cultures have often relied on its economic value, but our focus is only on slaves who toiled at sea or were taken by sea to their final destination.

Rowers were the usual source of propulsion on Mediterranean galleys. A Greek representation from the middle of the fifth century BCE of Odysseus, tied to the mast to avoid the sirens' seduction, showed the rowers straining at the oars to propel his vessel. The three-tiered triremes became the dominant warships of ancient Greece, their rowers sitting in rows of benches. Their standard complement was 170 rowers, 14 soldiers, and 21 officers and crew. The rowers were usually free men, not chained to their benches, and the work ceased at night when the ships were beached and the rowers rested.

The Romans, on their way to dominating the Mediterranean, perfected the Greek model and increased the size of the vessels, often using slaves as crew. Their larger and slower war vessels served to ram the enemy, their smaller and faster ones to pursue their ships. Triremes and smaller vessels were almost exclusively used for chasing pirates and for individual transport, while the important trade fleet of slow merchantmen and faster galleys carried perishable and expensive goods—from fruit to exotic animals for the circus games. All required substantial manpower.

On the Barbary Coast, the Muslim fiefdoms mostly used as galley slaves prisoners taken from powerful western European and Christian nations, usually captured during religious conflicts, starting with the Crusades. Some were freed or ransomed, and a few escaped, but it is estimated that at least a third died at their rowing posts from exhaustion or disease within the first two years.

There were strongholds all across the Mediterranean, all requiring enormous manpower. Algiers had sixty to ninety warships at its peak; Tripoli, twenty to twenty-five; Tunis, fifteen to twenty; and Salé on the Moroccan Atlantic coast up to thirty. Through the sixteenth and seventeenth centuries, the Barbary Coast states alone needed between 25,000 and 35,000 rowers, only one part of the total number of slaves on Mediterranean galleys. Further east, the Ottoman Empire alone was said to require some 80,000 men for the ruler's galleys. Altogether, up to a million and a half European slaves probably went through North African prisons between 1530 and 1780. A single slaver from Tripoli or Algiers would perhaps seize more slaves in a raiding season than the average cargo of slaves transported from West Africa to the New World in a typical year.

This is how a Frenchman described the harsh conditions on such a galley in the sixteenth century.

> They were chained six to a bench; these are four feet wide, covered with sacking stuffed with wool, over which are laid shipskins... When the captain gives the order to row, the officer gives the signal with a silver whistle which hangs on a cord around his neck; the signal is repeated by the underofficers, and very soon all fifty oars strike the water as one... Sometimes the galley slaves row ten, twelve, or even twenty hours at a stretch, without the slightest rest or break. On these occasions the officer will go round and put pieces of bread soaked in wine into the mouths of the wretched rowers to prevent them from fainting.

Slavery and slave trading had long been established traditions in Asia and Africa, where slaves constituted a substantial element of the workforce. When Europeans became involved in the trade, the control usually remained in African hands. The Portuguese were among the first Europeans to organize a profitable commerce of this nature. The Treaty of Tordesillas (1494) had guaranteed them the exclusivity of trade with Africa, where a brisk business soon provided slaves for the New World. Ironically, this trade derived from Spain's royal prohibition on enslaving indigenous American peoples and the latter's decimation through new diseases. Both reduced the potential number of labourers and forced the Iberians to look to Africa for their work force.

The Congolese king Nzinga (renamed João when he became a Christian) and his successors were particularly active in this trade. In 1540, King Alfonso of Congo wrote to his Portuguese peer João III, "Put all the Guinea countries on one side and only Congo on the other, and you will find that Congo renders more than all the others put together... No king in all these parts esteems Portuguese goods as much as we do. We favor the trade, sustain it, open markets, roads, and markets where the pieces [prime male slaves] are traded."

Later, ships of all nationalities en route for the Americas and the Caribbean would specialize in carrying slaves to the New World or mixed cargoes of slaves and other equally profitable merchandise. It was easy to outfit a ship for the slave trade by simply building bulwarks to segregate decks and platforms equipped with shackles. Several of these ships became known through their disastrous endings. Some sank, their holds full of slaves; others became victims of slave mutinies, with equally dreadful outcomes. Ironically, some of their names spoke of other dreams. *Amistad... Hope...*

Two Spanish slave ships based in Cuba are noteworthy, less through the number of slaves they carried or their particularly dreadful conditions than through being the subjects of two well-documented court trials: the *Antelope,* captured near Florida in 1820, with 283 slaves on board, and *La Amistad,* a mixed cargo ship, whose slaves from Sierra Leone revolted in 1839 and were recaptured by the USS *Washington*. Another notable slave ship, British this time, the *Zong*, had previously come to public attention in 1781, when the captain was accused of having thrown overboard 132 sick and dying slaves, who could not be sold in their condition, to collect their cargo insurance.

Among those who most benefitted from the slave trade was John Hawkins, the British naval commander who worked as a merchant, shipbuilder, navigator, pirate, sometimes admiral, and also a successful slave trader in the late sixteenth century. He operated particularly in the Triangle Trade, where he sold Africans in the Spanish colonies of Santo Domingo and Venezuela. In 1564, he rented the *Jesus de Lübeck* from Queen Elizabeth I to transport four hundred Africans and then captured the *Madre de Deus* in 1567 with four hundred slaves on board and ran her himself. Hawkins was amply rewarded for his services to the crown, and when finally awarded a crest, it was that of a slave bound by a cord, which he proudly flew on the *Jesus of Lübeck* among the other heraldic devices displayed in the flotilla.

The "black ivory" trade made the wealth of a number of English ports, including Plymouth and London in the mid-seventeenth century, then Liverpool and Bristol—safe from enemy privateers and away from the Customs in London. Rather than being secretive, it had received a royal seal of approval in 1660 when the Royal Adventurers into Africa, later to become the Royal African Company, was chartered. It ran profitable ivory and slave trades from the Gold Coast from 1664 onward. By the 1740s, Britain was the world's leader in the busy traffic of human beings. Most other seafaring European nations were also actively engaged in this lucrative commerce.

So much for the money-makers, but we may wonder how the sailors felt about their cargo and the nature of a trade that required filthy and laborious work from them but also provided some private trading when the opportunity arose. Both the harsh work and the clandestine profits could have come from any other type of merchandise, so did they feel differently about that particular trade with Africa? They did, but only because they hated Africa. All sailors resented the tropical "Torrid Zones" and regarded Africa as the worst of them all. There was a well-known saying among sailors: "Beware and take care / Of the Bight of Benin / For one that comes out / There are forty go in."

The West African coast, where most of the traffic took place, was ill charted, with hostile populations and few safe harbours. The currents were unfavourable, the winds unpredictable, and the ships were poorly ventilated, baking under the tropical sun. The crews were often afflicted with dysentery caused by polluted water and they suffered from malaria and yellow fever. Their mortality rate was said to match that of the slaves, and may even have been greater. On the *Florida*'s voyage to Antigua in 1714, sailors tossed the corpses of three or four Africans overboard daily, losing 120 of them along the way, or one third of their cargo. At night, to hide their own losses, they similarly disposed of the crew's bodies, thus losing eight sailors out of twenty.

All sailors feared the possibility of slave mutinies, and much care was taken not to bring together human cargo from similar linguistic groups to avoid communication among them. Yet, in spite of this precaution, there were bloody mutinies, including the *Eagle Galley* in 1704, the *Henry* and the *Elizabeth* in 1721, and the *Ferrers* in 1722. In the last case, three hundred slaves had come from the same community; they revolted, killed the captain, were subdued, mutinied again, and by the time they reached Jamaica, were rejected out of fear by the planters, their prospective owners.

The sailors also hated being unable to use one of their traditional weapons: the threat of desertion. Where would they have gone, had they deserted in Africa? The Royal African Company ran the English settlements there, and the merchants' response to the threat of desertion would only have been a derisive invitation to "sit and rot." Their lot was not an enviable one, being trapped in a conflicting position as captors of slaves and captives of their own captains and merchants.

The slave trade also occurred in Polynesia, where Europeans needed workers for their coconut and sugar cane plantations because the native population had been decimated by foreign diseases and the survivors would not be willingly turned into toilers of the soil. Thus, plantation owners turned to the "blackbirders," slavers who came mostly from Peru and roamed the islands for supplies. In the early 1800s, over three thousand islanders were taken to Peru. Only 157 survived and after they were returned to the islands, many soon died. The Peruvian authorities could not be trusted to supervise their health conditions or to provide food on the return journeys. There were a few small victories, such as when the French authorities seized a Peruvian slave vessel in 1863, freeing two hundred islanders destined for guano mines and plantations. The same year, natives of Rapa-Iti and three Europeans seized the slave ship *Cora* and brought her to Tahiti where a French tribunal sentenced her officers to ten years in prison.

These islands were not under British jurisdiction, and the admiralty could do little to prevent the practices. However, in June 1872, the British Parliament passed the Act of the Prevention and Punishment with Criminal Outrages upon Natives of the Islands of the Pacific Ocean (also known as the Pacific Islanders Protection Act) at the request of the Australians, outraged that nothing was done to stop slave ships. The act authorized the Royal Navy to intercept slave ships and required masters to obtain a £500 bond against mistreatment and abduction of workers. In 1904, the Australian government finally succeeded in stopping blackbirding practices.

The nineteenth century saw a general awakening of anti-slavery sentiments. In France, the Revolution first produced an act against it in 1794, followed in 1848 by the abolition of slavery. Other treaties and acts were introduced elsewhere: the Anglo-Swedish Treaty (1807), the Anglo-Dutch treaty (1814); the Slavery Abolition Act (1833), passed by the Parliament of the United Kingdom. In the USA, a federal Act Prohibiting Importation of Slaves was passed in 1807, but the abolition of slavery had to wait until the end of the

Civil War. The slave trade and slavery were deemed to be different matters, the former considered "a commercial practice," difficult to abolish, particularly due to its international ramifications, and the latter "a domestic institution," falling into governmental purview.

We know that slavery has not been entirely abolished and remains—often glossed over—a source of cheap labour difficult to eradicate. The recent exhibitions of the International Slavery Museum in Liverpool, titled Broken Lives (slavery in modern India) and Oil Boom, Delta Burns (the Niger Delta oil industry), confirm that the system still exists profitably, but perhaps no longer on our oceans.

20 CONVICTS

Unlike the desperate slaves shipped against their will and impotent to change their fate save through mutiny or suicide, most convicts preferred transportation to the long imprisonment or even hanging they faced in England. After the discovery and annexation of Australia, whole cargoes of convicts sailed from British jails to establish penal colonies there.

Joseph Banks, who had been on James Cook's first voyage, identified Botany Bay as a possible penal settlement as early as 1779, basing his opinion on the propitious environment of mild weather, lack of savage animals, and a small, timid nomadic population. The Australian option came at a convenient time for Britain, as American independence had put an end to the shipping of prisoners to Virginia from overcrowded English jails. Banks's suggestion was adopted, and in 1788, eleven British ships brought 759 convicts, 211 soldiers, 30 wives, and 12 children to their new settlement in Botany Bay.

This was only the beginning. The Migration Heritage Centre in New South Wales estimates that approximately 160,000 convicts were sent to Australia between 1788 and 1868, when transportation effectively ceased. Few were hardened criminals; most were only guilty of some of the 220 crimes against property that would have otherwise carried the death penalty at home or were recidivists of many lesser misdeeds.

While the first Australian settlers had been convicts and soldiers, new people were soon needed to build roads, operate farms, and generally settle the country. By 1815, many men and their families were encouraged to emigrate, and some were offered positions of responsibility in the new land. The project was generally well received, but in 1819, there were still five times more convicts than free men and women. Slowly, the balance evolved, and between 1830 and 1850, about one third of passengers to Australia paid their own way. As their numbers increased, a budding Australian society wanted to discard the "convict stain," and the colonial government decided to stop transportation in 1852.

The history of French convicts is harsher. The French Mediterranean galley fleet was decommissioned in 1748, ending for prisoners what was tantamount to a death sentence. Thereafter, several galley hulks or *bagnes* were established in the military ports of Toulon, Brest, Lorient, and Rochefort, where prisoners (or *bagnards*) were put to work in such severe and dangerous conditions that public opinion forced them to be permanently closed by decree in 1852. *Bagnards* were then transported overseas.

Several locations had been considered, including Algeria, Haiti, Cuba, and the Dominican Republic—all far away from metropolitan France, and all possessing a climate hostile to undernourished and overworked prisoners. Finally, a *bagne* was established in Cayenne, French Guiana (1852-1953), which the French had unsuccessfully attempted to settle in 1763. Three-quarters of these 12,000 colonists died during the first year, and by 1852, few remained of the original settlers and their descendants.

Among those transported were common law prisoners and traitors. The *bagne* consisted of a labour camp on the Dutch Guiana border (today's Surinam), consisting of three islands in shark-infested waters: Ile Royale and its near impossibility of escape for the general prisoner population, Ile St. Joseph for those held in solitary confinement, and Ile du Diable (the infamous Devil's Island, a former leper colony) for a small group of political prisoners, Captain Alfred Dreyfus among them. Putting political prisoners together with violent offenders and murderers led to many abuses that, combined with the harsh climate and the endemic tropical diseases, resulted in few prisoners surviving long enough to return to France after they completed their sentences.

Naturally, the question of encouraging settlement arose. Freed convicts were required to remain there for the same length of time as their sentence, if it was under eight years. The others had to remain permanently, but they were given land to encourage settlement. By 1885, repeat minor offenders, including women, were sent to Guiana. This attempt at settling it met with little success and the practice was discontinued; the *bagne* was eventually closed in 1953.

A similar *bagne* was established in New Caledonia (1864-1924) for those sentenced from eight years to life (political deportees, recidivists, incorrigible felons). Forty families decided to settle there afterwards, farming within the penal colony.

21 EMIGRANTS

During several important emigration movements to America, most of the passengers on transatlantic crossings travelled in steerage or third class. There were notably one and a half million Irishmen (1840s-1850s), mostly suffering from the aftermath of the Potato Famine, and four million Germans (1840s-1880s) escaping from the economic depression at home, combined with political unrest.

They had often suffered utter misery. The Irish had been unable to recover from the famine of 1845-52 that killed one million people. The cheap potato crop on which a third of the population relied for their subsistence had suffered from a blight, leaving them starving in a country where wealthy landowners still regularly exported food. This was the second great famine for the Irish, whose crop had also failed in the terribly cold winter of 1740-41. Equally vulnerable were the crofters from the Highlands of Scotland, expelled from their traditional land tenancies during the Highland Clearances of the eighteenth and early nineteenth centuries, when landowners decided to turn from farming, which required crofters, to sheep raising, which did not.

Those afflicted people were subjected to further abuse when they boarded what were known as "famine ships" or even "coffin ships." Many deaths occurred at sea from diseases and starvation, even leading to a typhus epidemic in 1847. It was said that sharks followed those unsafe ships, attracted by the bodies regularly dispatched overboard. During this period, the enormous surge of emigration from Britain to Australia and America (two and half million people between 1846 and 1854) led to a shortage of passenger ships.

Other vessels were converted to carry people and many were unfit for the task, being overloaded and undermanned. In seven years, sixty of those newly reassigned vessels sank, at the cost of sixteen hundred lives.

Both the Passenger Vessel Act of 1828 and a revised act later the same year had attempted to offer some protection for these passengers, such as limiting their numbers on board and ensuring there was enough food and water for them. These legal provisions only applied to ships sailing from British ports and had no impact on others. It was only around 1867 that a modicum of safety was actually expected, and often delivered. Comfort, naturally, was another matter.

Emigration peaked during the 1880s-1920s, when ships brought in between 13 and 14 million Europeans to America. They were mostly Central Europeans (4 million), driven away from their home-lands by poverty and overpopulation; Italians (4.5 million), fleeing poverty, political problems, and uprisings; Jews from Eastern Europe (2.5 million), escaping from religious persecution; Scandinavians (1.5 million) facing poverty and lack of farmland in their coun-tries; and Poles (1 million), who had endured political repression, poverty, and a cholera epidemic.

Such were the great movements of population from one con-tinent to another. Emma Lazarus's poem reflects the response of America to these tired and poor "huddled masses" seeking a better life for themselves. The words, then fashionable, were inscribed on the Statue of Liberty and greeted the hundreds of thousands who reached America's shore on Ellis Island. Those steerage passengers, while of different origins, had similar needs as they crossed the Atlantic. Their fortunes would diverge after they arrived, but at sea the main difference among them came from the conditions of their voyage: weather and accommodations. Some quarters were better than others and some food more palatable, but while a number met with disaster, most reached Ellis Island and were soon absorbed into what is today's America.

More recently, since the Revolution (1953-59), Cuba has sent a constant trickle of political and economic migrants to Florida, made welcome by earlier Cuban expatriates. Even after Raúl Castro replaced his brother Fidel in 2008, the attempts continued. U.S. government figures show that about twenty-five thousand Cubans arrived mostly by sea and without visas in 2013-14. Many sailed on homemade and unseaworthy vessels and some may not have reached American shores.

Today's migrants come mostly from Africa, people trying to wend their way through Spanish, Italian, and Greek ports to other parts of Europe where they believe their chances of success are better. A man from Gambia, quoted by *Médecins sans frontières* in 2015, expresses the same needs as his Irish counterpart a century and a half earlier. "We go away from our country because we have no choice... We risk our lives to help our families, our neighbours, our friends, our parents, and our brothers. That's why we embark on this journey." Their route is dangerous and frightening, with constant threats of shipwreck, murder, imprisonment, and repatriation along the way.

During 2015, dismal reports of migrants crossing the Mediterranean figured almost non-stop in the media, making it almost impossible to keep up with the incoming data. There were documented deaths: slightly over 3,500 on the Mediterranean crossings in 2014, and reaching 3,440 by November 2015 (there have been many others since), with some notable and highly publicized disasters in overcrowded dinghies. Specific incidents, such as the deliberate capsizing of a migrants' boat in the Mediterranean on September 9, 2014, made the news all over the world. Heading for Italy, they first had to wade chest-deep into the water to crawl into two small boats and then transfer to two other boats, overcrowded with three hundred people. Following a conflict between smugglers, the larger and faster boat rammed into the migrants' boat, flipping it over. Some 150 people were able to grab life jackets, but only four were still alive three days later, when the *Antartica,* a tanker carrying crude oil through the Suez Canal, alerted by the Maltese authorities, was able to rescue them.

On September 2, 2015, a critical and emotional recognition of the migrants' plight followed the appearance in the world's media of a young Syrian boy's photograph. Aylan Kurdi's body washed ashore near the resort town of Bodrum in Turkey. From the same boat of twenty-three migrants, twelve had drowned, five of them children. Aylan Kurdi became the tragic poster child for a social and political situation that has dominated the news since 2014.

There is something new to this wave of migrants. While the earlier European crossings to the New World were often difficult, they were not publicized to the extent that are the events accompanying the current wave of refuge seekers and economic migrants. These are mostly from Africa and sailing to Western Europe, often at the hands of unscrupulous and sometimes murderous people smugglers.

As well, while we are far from the numbers of the earlier great European emigrations by sea to North America, the new numbers do not include the totality of the people seeking refuge, since much of the migration also occurs on land. Finally, unlike the United States, and to a lesser extent Australia and Canada, which were then able to absorb the emigrants' numbers, the European Union does not offer comparable opportunities in our century.

MARRIAGEABLE WOMEN

In Britain, roughly one-third of women between the ages of 25 and 35 were unmarried through the nineteenth century. Called "surplus women," they were encouraged to search for husbands in Australia and India, where men could be found in large numbers. These women's hopes for marriage, children, safety, status, perhaps even happiness were not always fulfilled by their male compatriots living in the colonies, but many succeeded through resourcefulness, hard work, endurance, and some luck.

Britain naturally was not the only country encouraging female emigration to settle their overseas territories, where men strongly outnumbered women. The Dutch in Java and the French in the

New World also did, at different times and with varying degrees of success.

Australia

In the 1800s, the British government was actively encouraging young unmarried women to immigrate to Australia. Those who responded were sometimes mocked, although marriage, even in the colonies, was the only legitimate way to better their conditions. Among those who made a life for themselves in Australia, some may have responded to such promotional tracts as the following, published on October 20, 1848, in the *Hastings & St Leonards News*, painting this hopeful picture of the life that awaited single women on the new continent.

FEMALE EMIGRANTS

There is an unlimited demand for wives of all ranks, from the shepherd to the gentleman squatter, with his 1,000 head of cattle and 20,000 sheep. The Colonists, as a body, whether emigrant or native born, make good husbands, kind, indulgent and generous. They are all rather rough in their language to each other, but no one ever heard of a bushman beating his wife. In the towns there is as much gaiety as in England. Rather more. The bush huts have not generally been very comfortable; but there is no reason why they should not be as well built and furnished as English farmhouses. Young widows and orphans of small means will find themselves in reality far safer than in any of the greatest towns of Europe, better protected, and with better prospects. Of course some caution is necessary before accepting the first offers made, but there is little difficulty in finding out an Australian's character. There are obvious reasons in two or more ladies joining to make a party for the sea-voyage, besides reasons of economy. There can be no more impropriety in going to Australia than to India for the same purpose...

For governesses, there is a moderate demand. We should only recommend those to think of emigration who are not comfortable here. Every lady thinking of emigrating should know how to bake, boil, roast, wash and iron, and then although she may not have to do these things, she will feel independent.

For domestic and farm-servants the demand is unlimited and will continue so for many years, as a good sober cook, housemaid or nurse is worth any wages, and may always have a house of her own within twelve months. A clever maid-servant is sure to better her position by emigrating to Australia, and will frequently have part of the passage-money by attending on one of the lady passengers.

Never stand out for good wages at first. Get a house over your head and then change if you can for the better.

Earlier attempts at convincing women to exile themselves to Australia had not met with much success. In 1788 (the first departures to Australia), twenty-three women were convicted in London of offences carrying the death penalty. Those who agreed instead to spend the rest of their lives in New South Wales were pardoned. Seven elected to die rather than sail to the unknown antipodes.

India

Mockery also greeted those hopeful British women who sailed to India as part of what was called the "fishing fleet," of those "fishing" for husbands. From the late seventeenth century, the East Indian Company had sent women out to India as potential brides for their officers. In all stations and colonies abroad, men grossly outnumbered women, and with such a strong ratio in their favour, women's looks or fortune did not matter as much as they would have at home. Both the company, anxious to pursue a profitable service, and families encumbered with "superfluous" women organized transport to more propitious grounds, and they were shipped off to India. The company paid for these prospective brides' passages and maintained them there for a whole year. Most were snapped up upon arrival; the occasional one unable to find a timely match was shipped back in a category known as "Returned Empty."

The establishment of the Raj in 1858 was a positive note, and the opening of the Suez Canal in 1869 greatly facilitated the women's emigration by reducing the perilous five-month long trip to India around the Cape of Good Hope. Jane Austen described their conditions on board as "a punishment that needs no other to make it very severe... Seasickness, weeks upon weeks of cramped conditions, stink from the bilge, coldness on deck and heat below." Travelling in the late 1850s, Minnie Blane wrote, "The eggs all went bad and had to be thrown overboard weeks ago and though there is dessert on the table every day I cannot touch a thing, as biscuits, figs, and ratafia are alive."

In search of marriage, seen as every female's entitlement, all sorts found their way to India, from experienced women seeking their fortune to naïve girls sent to stay with relatives, their parents tacitly hoping they would find husbands during their visit. The odds were in their favour, as single men outnumbered marriageable women by roughly four to one. Once married, they became part of the Raj hierarchy, their place in society dependent on their husbands' status.

Java

There were twenty women on the *Batavia* (some unmarried), an unusually high number since the *VOC* had learned from bitter experience not to let single women sail alongside so many young sailors for so many months. The company had earlier attempted to procure wives for lonely merchants in the Indies, and the then governor-general had personally escorted to Java thirty-six spinsters, who turned out to be prostitutes. His successor, anxious not to repeat this embarrassing mistake, looked for prospective wives in orphanages. He berated the company's governors in these terms: "You, Sirs, would only send us the scum of the earth, and people here will sell us not but scum either... Send us young girls, and we hope that things will go better."

These new girls, or "company daughters," as they were known, were given some clothing and free passage, and were expected to find husbands in Java. There was only one chaperone to supervise them on the voyage and, not unexpectedly, they soon found much favour among members of the crew.

The problem of finding appropriate wives for company men in Batavia continued to preoccupy those in charge. Prostitutes were still discovered on board, often as stowaways. The commander of the 1628 Christmas fleet wrote home, "We want for nothing save honest maids and housewives in place of the filthy strumpets and street wailers who have been found... in all the ships. They are so numerous and so awful that I am ashamed to say more about it." VOC's efforts continued to be unrewarded, which was a serious problem, as native women were usually deemed unsuitable as mates or found to be unwilling.

Quebec and Louisiana

Far more successful was the French attempt at settling her colonies in New France. Some 260 marriageable women first arrived in Quebec between 1634 and 1663, recruited privately or through religious groups who paid their passage and lodgings until they found a husband. This first attempt only succeeded in recruiting about ten a year, far below the demand. Men greatly outnumbered women among the 2,500 colonists, and many, unable to find wives, returned to France when their term of service expired, putting the growth of the settlement in jeopardy. When Louis XIV took control of New France in 1663, the project was reactivated, this time with royal support. Under the aegis of the efficient minister Colbert, it immediately became a resounding success. In the first decade, 768 young women sailed to their new homes: 560 remained in Quebec, 133 went to Montreal, and 75 to Trois-Rivières.

Far from relying on the earlier haphazard recruitment, the new selection method was designed to ensure success. The women were carefully selected for physical suitability (strength and endurance for hard chores, as well as presumed fertility) and good morals; then, they were properly endowed and equipped to contribute to their new household. There was also a guarantee that the "Filles du Roi" did not have to accept offers of marriage if the men were not suitable. While waiting for their suitors, they were housed in dormitories under the strict supervision of Ursuline nuns.

The cost of establishing these women was high: ten *livres* for their recruitment, thirty for their clothing, sixty for their passage, plus a number of practical items in the chest or *cassette* each of them received. Each new couple also received some livestock, two barrels of salted meat, and other goods to start them off in their married life. Once married, the women were expected to produce large families. An annual pension of three hundred *livres* rewarded the birth of ten children, rising to four hundred *livres* for twelve.

The project succeeded handsomely, and in November 1671, the New France *Intendant* already reported the birth of about seven hundred babies for that year. When France and England declared war on the Dutch Republic a year later, the cost of sending the Filles du Roi to Canada was re-evaluated against these new demands on the king's purse and declared too expensive to be continued. Moreover, the project had been so successful that the colony could now provide enough marriageable girls on its own. When the last arrivals came in 1673, the population had reached 6,700, an increase of 168 percent during the eleven years of the successful program.

Indeed, so successful had it been that it partly inspired another in Louisiana. Among the eighty Frenchmen who took possession of it in 1699 were twenty Canadians who remembered how the population of their own colony had been boosted by the arrival of women from France. A request for thirty women was sent to Paris and the first ones arrived in 1704. These newcomers to Louisiana (the "Filles de la Cassette," named after the same *cassette* that had been provided to the Filles du Roi) were not screened with the same exacting criteria that had been applied to the women selected for Quebec. They ranged from orphans brought up by nuns to prostitutes destined for Parisian jails, and all the recognition they received was a chest full of clothes and provisions to help them settle in the new colony. Several women came to Louisiana, but not enough to meet the demand. The half-hearted and ill-funded project never really took off, and local women, often African slaves, took over the task of encouraging the men to settle.

22 THE CUSTOM OF THE SEA

Au bout de cinq à six semaines, / Les vivres vinrent à manquer.

On tira à la courte paille / Pour savoir qui serait mangé.

Le sort tomba sur le plus jeune, / Qui n'avait jamais navigué.

(Old French children's song about a ship's boy who drew the short straw when rations ran short after a few weeks at sea, yet miraculously escaped being eaten).

This unrevealing title—the custom of the sea—hides one of the most troubling actions taken by sailors when no other method of survival was available: cannibalism. Naturally, it was not exclusively peculiar to the sea. Several cultures have done it for spiritual reasons, and starving people have also resorted to it, but we consider here the dire measure whereby, after drawing lots to ensure fairness, one sailor is sacrificed so that several may survive.

The custom was so well established that surviving castaways often indicated that, although they were starving when they were rescued, they had not resorted to it. Fictional accounts sometimes relied on it for dramatic effect. In the 1962 film version of the *Mutiny of the Bounty,* one of the starving and exhausted sailors in the open launch taking them to Timor begs Bligh to draw straws. Bligh, played by Trevor Howard, refuses to submit to the tradition and swears they will "behave like civilized men." They were saved by Bligh's fanatical rationing and superb navigation, and the only man they lost was one stoned to death by the natives of Tofua. Providentially, they caught several boobies that were shared according to tradition. For each ration, one man with his back turned answered the question, "Who shall have this?"

However, there are two well-documented cases: the Nantucket whaleship *Essex*, fatally rammed by a sperm whale (1820), and the British yacht *Mignonette*, wrecked on her way to Australia (1884). While theirs were not the only desperate crews to resort to eating some of their mates, what followed their discovery was unique. The sinking of the *Essex* inspired the enduring tale of Herman Melville's *Moby-Dick* (1851) and a Ron Howard film, *In The Heart of the Sea* (2015), while the political trial of the *Mignonette*'s three remaining crew members riveted England, from (it is said) Queen Victoria to the lowliest deckhand in Southampton. In both cases, a young man was killed to provide for others.

THE *ESSEX*

On November 20, 1820, some 1,500 nautical miles west of the Galapagos near the equator, the whaleship *Essex* was attacked and wrecked by an enraged sperm whale. Both her first mate, Owen Chase, and the cabin boy, Thomas Nickerson, later related the events that followed and the fate of her crew of twenty.

The story first emerged three months later, when the whaleship *Dauphin* found a small boat drifting off the Chilean coast. In it were two men, curled up at opposite ends, "their skin covered with sores, their eyes bulging from the hollows of their skulls, their beards caked with salt and blood. They were sucking the marrow from the bones of their dead shipmates." The two men were Captain Pollard and a sailor, Charles Ramsdell. The bones were those of sailors Owen Coffin and Barzillai Ray.

The irreparable damage to the ship occurred fifteen months after the *Essex* had sailed from Nantucket. Abandoning the wreck, the entire crew of twenty set off in three ill-suited whaleboats. They had scavenged the *Essex* for provisions and equipment for the boats, but the pickings were scant and their prospects seemed dim. "The misery of their situation came upon them with such force as to produce spells of extreme debility, approaching almost to fainting," Owen Chase recalled.

The three whaleboats stayed together until they reached the inhospitable shores of Henderson Island, rather than nearby Pitcairn Island, where survival would have been ensured. Finding little food and water, they sailed after a week, hoping to reach Easter Island. They left behind two sailors and one of the three boat-steerers, Thomas Chappel, who believed their chances were better there than at sea. Indeed, they were rescued four months later. Thus, the three boats sailed away together, under Captain George Pollard, Jr., First Mate Owen Chase, and Second Mate Matthew Joy.

The *Essex* was manned by sailors of three different origins: true Nantucketers bound by blood or friendship, white off-islanders, and blacks (as they were then called). In this regard, the third boat was particularly ill-favoured. Not only was Matthew Joy in poor health (he soon died), but of the other five in the boat, one was an off-islander and the other four were blacks; moreover, with Thomas Chapel's decision to remain on Henderson Island, there was no boat-steerer available.

The colour of the sailors' skin is not a gratuitous detail, and it is even more significant than their remoteness from the strong ties and mutual protection linking Nantucketers. Black sailors, often undernourished, with little body fat, and in poor health, were likely to die before the others. On both counts (skin colour and disconnection), the composition of the third boat's crew did not bode well for its chances of survival.

When Matthew Joy died, he was sewn into his clothes, weighed down with a stone at his feet, and consigned to the ocean. Boat-steerer Obed Hendricks transferred from the captain's boat and soon realized that the rationing had not been properly supervised by the dying Joy. After three days, the boat ran out of food. Pollard's boat shared a few provisions with them—reluctantly and resentfully, as all three boats had been initially issued the same share of provisions and, except for Hendricks, that particular boat was not part of the cohesive Nantucket group.

By then, they all realized they faced starvation. Chase described their dilemma: "Either... feed our bodies and our hopes a little longer, or in the agonies of hunger to seize upon and devour our provisions, and coolly await the approach of death." Their daily rations reduced to a cup of water and three ounces of hardtack per man, they now headed towards the islands of Juan Fernandez and Masafuera, off the coast of Chile. Then, with more than a thousand miles to go, a perilously strong gale separated Chase's boat from the others.

At this point, fifty-two days after leaving the *Essex,* they were dispersed as follows: three men left on Henderson Island, five on Chase's boat now drifting away, five on Pollard's boat after Hendricks's transfer, and six on Hendricks's boat—these last two boats still sailing together. One man had already died and been buried at sea. Let us follow their separate fates.

In Chase's boat, the rations reduced to an ounce and a half of bread daily, conditions were horrendous. The men were close to starving and too weak to harpoon the sharks and dolphins swimming nearby. The second to die, Richard Peterson, an elderly black man from New York, was also dispatched into the sea.

Chase and his three remaining men, their bodies covered in boils and their condition steadily deteriorating, were so feeble they could barely move and speak. Seventy-nine days after leaving the *Essex,* Isaac Cole died. As his friends prepared to bury him, Chase stopped them. "I addressed them on the painful subject of keeping the body for food." They agreed, and all three fed on Cole's heart and limbs, then sewed up the remains of the body and committed it to the sea. Chase, referring to the "dreadful dilemma," later wrote that they "knew not then to whose lot it would fall next, either to die or be shot, and eaten like the poor wretch [they] had just dispatched."

Chase and his two men, supported by strong winds but without food, had resigned themselves to death when the whaleship *Indian* came upon them, eighty-nine days after they had left the *Essex.* In an extraordinary feat of navigation, they had almost reached Juan Fernandez and Masafuera. Their condition brought tears to the eyes of the *Indian*'s captain. In later life, Chase was still haunted by the dreadful events, and he was plagued by terrible headaches before he was finally judged insane.

Hendricks and Pollard's boats were still sailing together when another black man, Lawson Thomas, died. For the first time, Hendricks and Pollard decided to save the body for food. Ironically, two months earlier, the men had decided to avoid the Society Islands, particularly the Marquesas, because their populations were reputed to be cannibals.

On Hendricks's boat, the next to die after Joy (who had died of sickness) were three black men. They were eaten, as was Samuel Reed, the only black on Pollard's boat. Between the two boats, four black sailors had died and been eaten within eight days. Only one remained, in Hendricks's boat. Even if devastating hunger had turned the men from shipmates into cannibals, the Nantucketers still seemed to benefit from their strength and solidarity.

Hendricks's boat drifted away sixty-nine days after leaving the wreck, with only three men on board and without compass or quadrant. When the boats separated, the four weakened Nantucketers in Pollard's boat had been unable to handle their sails and look for their mates. Nothing was heard of Hendricks's boat again, although a whaleboat with four skeletons (possibly the three men and the body of the last sailor to have died) was found on Ducie Island, near Henderson. If this was Hendricks's boat, it had drifted more than a thousand miles.

Pollard's boat, with eighteen-year old Owen Coffin, sixteen-year-old Charles Ramsdell, and nineteen-year-old Barzillai Ray, all Nantucketers, was still some 1,500 miles from the South American coast. They were without food, apart from the remains of Samuel Reed. Ramsdell first brought up the need to cast lots and decide who would die so the other three could survive. He was merely following the custom of the sea, which the others had been loath to bring up. By then, all were close to death. In spite of the horrified

Pollard's offering himself as a substitute, the lot fell to Owen Coffin, who was then killed. Five days later, Barzillai Ray died, serving the same purpose only a few days before they were rescued.

From the twenty who left Nantucket, only eight returned: three from Henderson Island (rescued by the *Surrey*), three from Chase's boat (rescued by the *Indian*), and two from Pollard's boat (rescued by the *Dauphin*). Of the men who died after they left Henderson Island (excluding those on Hendricks's boat, whose fates were unknown), all but the first two, buried at sea, had served as sustenance for the others. Of much greater impact, one of them (even if he was already close to death) had been designated as victim by drawing lots.

Captain Pollard's later career was unsuccessful. After another disastrous outing, he had become a "Jonah," and his bad luck prevented him from ever commanding another ship. Later, talking about the *Essex* to a missionary he met in Raiatea, he said, "I can tell you no more, my head is on fire at the recollection; I hardly know what I say."

THE *MIGNONETTE*

The *Mignonette,* an older but seemingly serviceable yacht, was bought in England by an Australian, who asked to have her delivered to Sydney. She sailed in July 1884 from Southampton with Captain Tom Dudley, mate Edwin Stephens, able seaman and ship's cook Edmund "Ned" Brooks, and ordinary seaman Richard Parker.

They were beset by monstrous waves off the coast of Africa, and the *Mignonette,* having shown signs of weakness and aging from the beginning (even requiring caulking until the last minute), sank as the four men escaped in a small boat. Without provisions or water, they eventually resorted to sacrificing the sickest and weakest—seventeen-year-old Richard. They were all family men, a status that perhaps weighed in their choice of Richard, who, it should also be said, was already comatose and suffering from the effects of drinking seawater.

After drifting for twenty-four days, they were rescued by the *Montezuma,* whose captain described them as living skeletons. His wife, who bathed their wounds, gasped when she saw their thin bodies, covered with sores, and their immensely swollen legs.

On their return, their decision was at first accepted as normal; everyone understood it. In fact, when the accused were examined, the young victim's brother publicly shook their hands and stood by them. So why would these men be charged for what was deemed to be an understandable act in such dire extremities?

When Tom Dudley appeared at the Custom House to report the loss of the ship, an official told him that another report would be needed for the Board of Trade, as was customary after a death at sea. Since the death was that of a seaman and not a passenger, no one apparently thought it would constitute a problem. While no follow-up was expected from the Board of Trade, a copy of the report was routinely sent to the Home Office. This is when the order came to arrest the three astonished men.

A local solicitor, Arthur Tilley, offered to take their case. Public opinion was immediately divided. Port people strongly supported the three men, while the London press (the *London Standard,* the *Times,* and the *Spectator)* only wrote about "revolting" actions, "cold-blooded" narratives, "damning" features, "callous" tragedy, "brutal" destruction, and "diabolical" traditions, inflaming their urban readers with indignation. Even Captain Dudley's honest relation of the events and his evident sorrow were apparently held against him. His defence, self-evident to him, was that they had only followed "the custom of the sea."

Other newspapers, notably the *Southampton Times* and the *Daily Telegraph,* later showed more understanding towards the men, reflecting public sympathy and their readers' opinion. When the case went to trial and the men were shown to be destitute, the local *Falmouth & Penryn Weekly Times* supported them effectively. It was a case of those familiar with the terrible demands of the sea siding against urban landlubbers and their cold judgement.

There had been a similar case ten years earlier involving the *Euxine*'s five survivors, who like the men of the *Essex*, had neither denied killing one of their own nor hidden the evidence. After much argument, the accused were brought from Singapore to London, where neither the Board of Trade officials nor the Marine Department assistant secretary were anxious to charge them. However, the Home Office and the attorney general were strongly in favour of prosecuting—until politics intervened. The *Euxine*'s owner was Sir Edward Bates, a Conservative M.P., and the Disraeli government hated the prospect of facing once more Mr. Plimsoll, the "Seamen's Friend." He had previously addressed the House of Commons on the conditions imposed by unscrupulous ship owners, and he had even called the same Edward Bates "a ship-knacker" for the three ships he owned that had sunk the previous year with the loss of eighty-seven lives. Thus, the trial did not take place, and the men were allowed to return to sea after signing a pledge not to seek legal redress against Edward Bates.

Dudley and his men, kept without bail, were charged in September 1884, the complaint stating that they "feloniously, wilfully and of their malice aforethought, did kill and murder one Richard Parker." Brooks decided to turn against his companions and struck a deal to act as witness for the prosecution. Thus, only Dudley and Stephens were formally charged with murder rather than manslaughter, as they had expected. They pleaded not guilty when their trial opened in November 1884 at the Western Circuit Winter Assizes in Exeter, where popular support for the accused was strong. Presiding was Baron Huddleston, who dismissed from the start the possible defences of necessity and self-defence. At trial, he suggested to the jury that a special verdict would be appropriate in this case, leaving it to the judge to rule on points of law and determine the guilt of the defendants. We will not follow the details of a complex trial, otherwise well documented in legal archives and studies. However, it established the precedent that necessity was no defence to the charge of murder, thus outlawing what was known as the custom of the sea. In spite of the defence's best efforts (Arthur

Collins, QC, retained with funds raised publicly) and the evidence that Huddleston had tampered with the wording of the special verdict, Dudley and Stephens were sentenced to the statutory death penalty with a recommendation for mercy. All appeals failed, even to the queen. Their sentences were commuted to six months in jail and they were released on May 20, 1886.

In the years following Stephens and Dudley's sentence, there were only two other recorded cases of crews following the custom of the sea: the *Teckla* (1893) and the *Drot* (1899), without legal consequences for the survivors. Whether unrecorded cases have occurred is difficult to know, as foreseen by Tom Dudley, who remarked to his lawyer, "Never again will men return to these shores and freely confess what they have done." Indeed, none other than the *Teckla* and the *Drot*'s crews have.

THE PROTOCOL

The real argument was not against eating the body of a mate to survive but in killing him for it in accordance with an unwritten custom. And why kill him, since most were already at death's door? Why not wait a few extra hours, let nature take its course, and avoid the dreadful moral condemnation and natural remorse that would follow such a deed? An eminently practical reason argued against it. Hunger certainly had to be satisfied, but even more pressing was thirst. When water supplies were gone and condensation or rain were not enough, only three liquids were available to those desperate crews: seawater, urine, and blood. Many resorted to drinking their own urine, as seawater was believed to lead to madness and death, and men were forcibly restrained from consuming it, but blood could only come from living bodies. Sometimes, shipwrecked sailors were lucky to catch a sea turtle and slashed the animal's neck to collect its blood. This happened to the crew of the *Essex*, who felt immediately restored from drinking the fast congealing liquid and eating the liver and heart, but the relief did not last long, and the eyes once more turned to the weakest among them.

In the long ordeal of starvation at sea, had the survivors waited for the designated victim to die naturally, they could not have collected the blood on which they relied to survive. Everyone understood this, and everyone respected the decision; records exist of victims willingly baring their chests to the knife. Those were shipmates, sometimes of longstanding, and often friends. Even when drawing lots may have seemed unnecessary because one sailor was already close to death, the act was not committed casually. The deed was usually done quickly, as painlessly and efficiently as possible, and whatever blood could be collected was shared equally. Some later said that the memory of the killing haunted them until the end of their lives. Others, more pragmatic, simply accepted the necessity of it. It was a recognized fact of sea life, one evoked in Walt Whitman's grim poem: "I observe a famine at sea, I observe sailors casting lots / Who shall be kill'd to preserve the lives of the rest."

The custom has been admittedly practised on at least twenty vessels, including the famous *Medusa*, whose raft was recreated in Géricault's painting. Even worse, some ships were so poorly provisioned that it even happened outside of shipwrecks. Rather than perish through thirst and starvation, the men cast lots, and the victim was bled, his blood consumed at once with the heart and liver, while the rest of the body was later butchered.

It is sometimes mentioned in narratives that passing vessels had refused to help shipwrecked sailors. This was not necessarily done from cold-heartedness, and there may have been other reasons: accosting the boat might have endangered the passing vessel, or the other ship's provisions might not have supported a few extra starving men.

One may also wonder about the fairness of drawing lots. Were all sailors included in this lottery, or were only a few—predisposed by age or low rank—expected or even forced to participate in it? On the *Francis Spaight* (1835), for instance, out of fifteen survivors, only the four young apprentices were deemed suitable for selection. The captain even remarked, "They had no families and could not be considered so great a loss to their friends as they that had no wives and children depending on them." Two of the four were killed to provide for the others (against their protestations that the process had been unfair), and one died naturally.

The custom of drawing lots was almost universally accepted: if the deed had to be done, the choice should be left to fate and the guilt fall on no one. However, when we consider the identity of the victims, we observe a slant. We saw on the *Essex* the predominance of black victims. Undernourished and often weaker than the white sailors, they were the first to succumb in a form of natural selection. However, it would also seem that the weakest were frequently picked first, together with the most disliked or the most isolated in the following order: slaves before anyone else, black men before white, women before men, passengers before crew, and unpopular crew-members before the others. Informal hierarchies also seem to have evolved in the selection of victims among the crew: cabin boys or apprentices first, then those described as "idlers" (carpenters, cooks, sailmakers, boatswains, and all specialists not usually mixing with the crew), finally ordinary seamen, before officers. The consistency of the records is, to the say the least, both suspicious and alarming.

23 SURVIVAL AT SEA

Happy cruisers, drink in hand and with the facile companionship of a first-night get-together, toast the ship's departure and watch the shore recede. They may have temporarily forgotten that sailing is not always an easy matter. What emerges from reading about human experience at sea is both a story of courage, excitement, and discovery and a tale of hardship, destruction, and despair. Tragedies and accidents are as much a part of maritime history as the eventless sailing we take for granted. We never clap, as perhaps we should, when our ship successfully pulls into port, which is a common occurrence in some countries when pilots land their planes. A ship's safe arrival into port is usually closely observed by only a small group, perhaps old navy men, who watch from the deck and mentally guide her progress to the pier. What others merely see is the arrival in a foreign port with its promises.

LEST WE FORGET

Hostile human actions, such as mutinies, have occasionally destroyed ships (the *Bounty*, deliberately set on fire), but nothing equates the dimensions of warfare. The willful sinking of ships remains outside the ordinary sailing experience because nothing in the nature of ships predisposes them to this end. However, we cannot dismiss it without mentioning briefly two ships whose destruction were of heartbreaking magnitude. The British *RMS Lancastria* and the German *MS Wilhem Gustloff* were both passenger ships conscripted during WWII, on opposite sides of the conflict, with a combined loss of fourteen to fifteen thousand lives.

The *Lancastria* (sunk in the English Channel, June 17, 1940)

Barely off the coast of Brittany near St Nazaire, Cunard's *Lancastria* sank in less than twenty-five minutes under a Luftwaffe's attack. A luxury ship designed to carry 2,500 passengers and crew, she was boarded by five to seven thousand soldiers ("they stopped counting at six thousand," said a witness who believed the higher number). She was part of the operation Ariel, ordered to remove British nationals two weeks after Dunkirk, mostly from the evacuating British Expeditionary Forces, as well as others trying to leave on June 17, 1940, after France had signed an armistice with Germany. The exact number of lives lost is unknown, but there were few survivors and the loss of the *Lancastria* ranks among the worst naval disasters. The number considerably exceeded the combined total from the *Lusitania* and the *Titanic.*

The *Lancastria's* records were sealed for one hundred years, so they will not be released until 2039. Much of what we understand about her sinking is based on contemporary opinion and on speculation. It is thought, for instance, that her captain's decision to wait until the smaller crafts were filled with soldiers and civilians before setting out as a convoy contributed to the ship's fatal outcome. Had she sailed earlier, she might have reached the nearby English coast before being attacked by enemy planes flying from Belgium. The convoy formation of navy and merchant ships enlisted in the war, while useful against German U-boats in the Atlantic, may have caused this dreadful outcome in the case of an attack from the air, but this is only speculation.

The *Wilhem Gustloff* (sunk in the Baltic Sea, January 30, 1945)

Built as a cruise ship for 1,800 passengers and crew and intended to serve Hitler's propaganda and reward Nazi partisans, the *Wilhem Gustloff* was put to sea in 1938. First conscripted as a hospital ship, then as a troop transport ship, and finally, fleeing advancing Russians troops, she left the Baltic port of Gdynia, heading for Kiel, with one escort, the torpedo boat *Löwe*. She was carrying over ten thousand wounded soldiers, naval personnel, and refugees—among the latter some four thousand children of all ages. All on board were ordered to wear life jackets at all times, and the ship's lights were extinguished as the officers guided her through a mine-swept channel. The *Löwe's* submarine detector did not work and both ships were relying on lookouts. Suddenly, the *Wilhem Gustloff* was hit by three Russian torpedoes in rapid succession. The watertight doors were immediately shut down to isolate the front of the ship, unfortunately locking behind them off-duty sailors who might have assisted in lowering the lifeboats. Her distress calls only reached the *Löwe*, who relayed them and rushed towards her. On board, chaos reigned, stairwells were jammed, and desperate people used their guns either on themselves or in attempts to control the situation. On the icy decks, sailors could not at first lower the lifeboats, as the davits were frozen. The ship sank seventy minutes after being hit. Bodies trapped in their lifejackets, particularly ill-fitting for the younger children, floated everywhere, as the *Löwe*, quickly joined by another vessel, attempted to rescue all they could, fighting heavy seas and using nets to lift people out of the water. In this manner, 472 people were rescued. Another ship, the *Admiral Hipper*, arriving soon afterwards, was able to rescue another 179. By the time two later freighters arrived on the scene, they only found frozen bodies in the icy water. Some escaped in lifeboats and in total about 1,230 survived, while some nine thousand were lost in the frigid Baltic. Others assess the loss of life at a lower number, but it still reaches into the thousands.

It is of course a terrible story, with its equally terrible counterpart four years earlier. The Russian hospital ship *Armenia,* evacuating refugees and staff from Crimean hospitals, was struck by a German torpedo in November 1941. Eight people were rescued. An estimated seven thousand died.

Some patterns emerge with the loss of ships and human lives incurred during peacetime, WWI, and WWII. First was the enormous increase in human losses per ship. Peacetime liners require cabin space and large common rooms; thus, their passenger ratio is below that of war ships, particularly those transporting troops. Similarly, the ships used during WWII were larger than in WWI, also meaning the fatalities would be much higher. The list of disasters is so long that I arbitrarily considered only ships that suffered a minimum loss of fifty lives for peacetime sinking, one hundred for WWI, and five hundred for WWII. The remaining list of ships sunk with lost lives below those numbers runs into the hundreds.

Some countries paid a much higher price than did others. Among 280 ships sunk in peacetime disasters throughout recorded history with a minimum of fifty lives lost (a number eliminating many earlier ships), ninety-five came from Britain and the English East India Company. Britannia definitely ruled the waves and proved it through the high number of her losses.

In wartime, two countries were particularly noted for their losses. Among about a hundred ships from several nations sunk worldwide during WWI with a loss of at least hundred lives each, forty-five were British. During WWII, topping the list of the 112 naval losses suffered by both the Allies and the Axis from ships sunk with a minimum loss of five hundred lives were forty-five Japanese vessels, including the battleship *Yamato,* carrying 152 guns, some among the largest ever mounted on a ship. En route to Okinawa in April 1945, she was attacked by nearly three hundred American planes and sunk with her 2,500 sailors. Again, we should remember that the total losses are far greater when smaller ships are included.

Many peacetime disasters could have been avoided. The recent *Costa Concordia* springs to mind, but another blatant example, far more costly in human lives, is that of overloaded ferries, with some countries particularly prone to this type of abuse and their disastrous and criminal consequences. The worst example is the 1987 collision between the *Doña Paz*, a ferry from the Philippines, and the oil tanker *Vector,* which caught fire, resulting in the official loss of approximately 4,386 people (the ferry was grossly overloaded and not all passengers were recorded).

While the above data from various sources may contain omissions and inexactitudes, they present a reasonable idea of the magnitude of the loss of ships and lives both in normal sailing circumstances (storms, collisions, shoals, etc.) and in times of war. These ships and our own twenty-first century cruising vessels, both distant relations of the triremes and caravels of old, all belong to various stages of the same ongoing maritime history.

THE CUNARD DISASTERS

Encounters with an iceberg and a German submarine would presumably exempt the Cunard Line from responsibility in the accidental sinking of two large and luxurious ships at the beginning of the twentieth century. Nature and war may seem beyond the remit of mere humans, whether bureaucrats, vessel owners, or ship captains, but records show that some lethal aspects of both encounters could have been avoided. As in many tragedies, arrogance and complacency, not to forget incompetence, led to far greater destruction than the circumstances warranted. Reliance on shipbuilding innovations *(Titanic)* and speed *(Lusitania)* blinded those who flaunted them before concerned passengers and made a mockery of the reality they were unwilling to face.

The *Titanic*.

Until the fatal night of the ship's sinking, the number and location of lifeboats seemed of little concern, provided they did not impinge on the view from first-class cabins and decks. Yet, there being only twenty of them disturbed no less a passenger than Mrs. John Jacob Astor (who survived, but whose husband did not), to whom the ship's designer, Mr. Andrews, replied that, indeed, there were not enough of them for the number of passengers on board. He reassured her, "Don't be afraid, Mrs. Astor, we don't really need the lifeboats because the *Titanic* can never sink. It is the safest ship in the world." In the end, it mattered little that there were only twenty, since only eighteen went properly into the water and many were only half-full. Of the last two, one went in upside down, and only a handful managed to clamber inside the other.

The lifeboats had been reserved for women and children, but those in third class did not always manage to reach them. More than a thousand people were left attempting to escape from the icy black waters of the North Atlantic, and most of them died. Many moral lessons were drawn from the *Titanic*'s fate, as well as a drastic reappraisal of the essential requirements for passengers' safety. But more on the *Titanic* later.

The *Lusitania*

The day passengers were embarking in New York, newspapers carried a warning from the Imperial German Embassy to deter Americans, not yet at war, from sailing on British rather than neutral ships. It alerted them to the presence of German submarines in the war zone, including "the waters adjacent to the British Isles," which the *Lusitania* would be entering in a few days. Seeing the many children getting on board, onlookers worried. Passengers themselves asked what the warning meant for their safety, and the ship officers' pat answer was not to worry because the *Lusitania*'s speed would foil any pursuing submarine. Indeed, submarines' speed did not exceed nine knots and the *Lusitania* had won the Blue Riband and could easily outdistance them. Even with one boiler room shut down to economize on fuel, she could still achieve a top speed of twenty-two knots. Time and again, her speed would be the officers' response to the increasing concern shown by passengers.

After the sinking of the *Titanic,* Cunard and other companies transporting passengers reassessed the need to provide sufficient lifeboats for all. Indeed, it had been one of the self-evident recommendations of the inquiry report on the disaster: "The provision of life boat and raft accommodation on board such ships should be based on the number of persons intended to be carried in the ship and not upon tonnage." Thus, three years later, the *Lusitania* was well provided with them. Twenty-two were lined up along the Boat Deck, capable of holding 1,322 people, with a further twenty-six collapsible boats fitting beneath them and able to carry another 1,238 people. On this return voyage, the *Lusitania* carried 1,264 passengers and a crew of 702, certainly well within the lifeboats' capacity, but the latter was still insufficient had the ship been completely filled with 3,025 people, its full complement of passengers and crew.

At eleven every morning, the sailors conducted a lifeboat drill. Ten would arrive, climb into a single boat, sit down, and hoist the oars. A few seconds later, they would replace the oars, stand up, and climb back onto the deck. None of the ropes holding the boats were ever tested. None of the boats were ever raised or lowered. None of the passengers were ever involved in the exercise.

It is worth remembering that by 1915, the most experienced Cunard sailors had joined the Royal Navy, and the crew hired for this voyage was poorly trained, with no particular loyalty to Cunard, the captain, or the ship herself. Even Captain Turner complained that the new crew were not proficient in handling the lifeboats, yet he did nothing to rectify the situation. When passengers suggested they too could participate in the drill, their request was ignored. Finally, passengers were never assigned to any specific lifeboats.

Life belts would also become a serious problem. Each cabin had them, but many were out of reach or locked in overhead compartments. When the liner was struck, passengers who rushed back to their cabins for their life belts often found that others had taken them instead of fetching their own, and they too had to grab any they could find elsewhere. They had never been shown how to put them on, and when panic-stricken passengers sought help from the crew, they often found them standing idly by, all wearing lifebelts, often refusing to assist them. Some passengers thrust their heads through the armholes, or put them on upside down, and even tried to tie them around their waist rather than their shoulders. Many male passengers helped others, particularly women and children, by giving them their own lifebelts. Finally, when the first torpedo struck and the ship started listing, there was no public address system to direct the passengers.

Those who reached the boats were shocked to find them in terrible condition. "The tackle was utterly stiff from paint and want of use, and so complicated that only capable seamen could have handled the boats. I regarded only a few of the men I saw as able seamen," wrote a survivor. Some lifeboats "lacked plugs, oarlocks were rusted, oars were missing, and ropes were frayed" and the collapsible boats stowed underneath were of little use, some of them badly rusted.

Captain Turner's actions made the sinking of the *Lusitania* a particularly tragic affair. He consistently ignored the admiralty's warnings and directions, particularly the injunctions to keep at high speed, zigzag, and avoid headlands. Once, he even slowed down to fifteen knots and when the ship was torpedoed, she was only eleven or twelve miles from shore. He did not believe that a zigzag course was necessary, and he did not even bother ensuring that all portholes were properly closed. Worst of all, as he approached waters where submarines had been reported, he decided to take a four-point bearing to confirm the ship's position, thus slowing her down further and keeping her in a straight course, which made her an easy target. Coming upon her and seeing her unescorted, the *U-20* captain, Walther Schwieg, gave the order to dive and increase the submarine's speed to nine knots, ready to strike the *Lusitania*. He later said, "She was coming directly at us. She could not have steered a more perfect course if she had deliberately tried to give us a dead shot."

A small flotilla of fishing trawlers, steamers, tugboats, and tenders from the nearby town of Queenstown came to the rescue.

Altogether, 768 passengers and crew survived while 1,198 perished. Captain Turner, the Cunard Company, and the Royal Navy all were sued, but they were eventually absolved of any negligence.

SURVIVAL

In the face of the enormous losses suffered at sea, we may well wonder at our own chances of surviving a shipwreck. Let us consider again the case of the *Titanic*. While the tragic and bungled affair remains a lesson, this modern catastrophe came at the end of centuries of reported disasters occurring in a different context of priorities. Whereas today's accepted behaviour is to evacuate women and children first and expect the captain to be the last to abandon ship, earlier skippers were much more likely to save themselves than to remain at their post until all had been evacuated. What we see now as cowardly behaviour might not have made an eyelash bat in previous centuries. We remember that the captain of the *Costa Concordia* (2011), Francesco Schettino, admitted to having inadvertently "fallen" into a lifeboat as he abandoned ship. Similarly, when the *Oceanos* (1991) sank off the South African coast, Captain Yiannis Avranas was among the first to leave, abandoning 225 passengers, who were lifted off by helicopter just before the vessel sank. He later declared, "When I give the order to abandon ship, it does not matter what time I leave. If some people want to stay, they can stay." On both ships, the entertainers and musicians assisted in the evacuation or radioed for help.

In past centuries, the strongest and ablest, usually the sailors, would commonly rush to the boats (of insufficient number to save anyone but a few) and commandeer them, often leaving behind the sick, the feeble, the wounded, the women, and the children. Even on the *Titanic*, the symbol of manly heroism and self-sacrifice, there was the odd lapse. Whereas all the engineering officers lost their lives, many among the lesser ranks (stokers, wipers, oilers) found their way to the lifeboats. Regular crewmen sometimes allowed their mates to board the boats they were supposed to be guarding.

By contrast, Commodore Edward Smith remained on his sinking ship, perhaps last seen by a Mrs. J. J. Brown of Denver, Colorado, who had already sailed twice with him. From her lifeboat, she looked up and saw the "benign, resigned countenance, the venerable white hair and the Chesterfieldian bearing of the beloved Captain Smith... He peered down upon those in the boat, like a solicitous father, and directed them to row to the light in the distance, all boats keeping together."

As maritime traditions evolved, passengers' safety had definitely become primordial by 1912, and every effort was made to save women and children first. Mores had changed over the centuries, and naval tradition reflected more humane priorities. As well, passengers had replaced gold, spices, and other treasures, and become the new precious cargo to be salvaged at almost any cost. At least in theory.

In reality, the response to the question of survival odds is perhaps little more than a roll of the dice, best illustrated by the events on two ships, the *Birkenhead* (1852) and the *William Brown* (1841). The troopship *Birkenhead,* carrying 648 sailors, soldiers, wives, and children, hit a reef at night in shark-infested waters off the coast of South Africa. As the rock pierced the hull, all but sixty of the men asleep in the lower deck drowned in their hammocks. Some of the survivors were sent to the pumps, while the rest lined up with heartbreaking gallantry and military discipline (even if the captain may have had to draw his sword to achieve it) and watched the women and children being helped into the ship's two cutters. The horses were pushed overboard, some making it to shore. Only sixty-nine men survived, but all 124 women and children were saved.

The American ship *William Brown,* with sixty-five passengers, a crew of eighteen, and a full cargo struck ice floes off the Newfoundland coast. In the ensuing chaos, thirty-two passengers, many of them children, were left behind while a jolly boat and a longboat were lowered. The first held Captain Harris, eight seamen, and one female passenger, the second nine crewmen and thirty-two passengers. As the boats separated, it became obvious that the longboat was not only overcrowded but also leaking. Able seaman Holmes took over and directed the other seamen to toss some passengers overboard to lighten the boat. Fourteen men and two women were thus disposed of, with all the seamen remaining on board. They were rescued soon afterwards by the *Crescent.*

When the facts became known, Holmes—the only sailor still in Philadelphia—was arrested and charged with murder. There was no doubt that he had participated in the murders, but the question was whether the act had been justified by necessity and the argument was that all would have perished if a few had not been killed—an argument we also saw in the case of the *Mignonette.* Even if such had been the case, the custom of the sea (drawing lots) had certainly not been observed. The jury returned a verdict of guilty and Holmes was sentenced to six months' imprisonment.

The year 1841 saw another case of heartlessness on the *Hannah,* a coffin ship carrying 180 Irish men, women, and children fleeing the Potato Famine. Captained by Curry Shaw and sailing for Quebec, she hit an ice reef off the coast of Newfoundland, tearing a long gash in her keel. During the forty minutes it took the ship to sink, the captain boarded the only boat with some of his possessions and a few crewmembers, leaving the passengers behind. All would have perished, had a sailor not freed them after observing the captain and the carpenter nailing down the trap door to their quarters below deck. The survivors were rescued seventeen hours later by the *Nicaragua,* another famine ship. The *Hannah's* surgeon, William Graham, reported the matter, but he died from his wounds before he could testify. Curry Shaw was accused and tried but he disputed the allegations and was exonerated.

There is no moral to be drawn from what happened on these ships, save that circumstances differ and human nature varies. The *Birkenhead* has remained, even more than the *Titanic,* an exemplar of manly and gallant behaviour—no doubt of little comfort to the women and children who reached shore alive. The *William Brown* stands instead as an image of cold-hearted pragmatism, and the *Hannah's* sad memory would have been obliterated, save for the efforts of some of the emigrants' Canadian descendants to bring their story to light.

We believe today that passengers hold a privileged position with regard to survival—mostly relying on anecdotes to form our opinion. Two researchers from the University of Uppsala, Mikael Elinder and Oscar Erixson, have actually reviewed the data from eighteen maritime disasters between 1852 and 2011. The ships were mostly British and American, and naturally the list includes the better-known disasters (*Birkenhead, Titanic, Lusitania, Empress of Ireland*), for a total of 15,166 passengers and crew on board. Of these 15,166 people, only 5,667 survived. In other words, the odds are strongly stacked against us.

The authors were interested in finding out whether women fared better than men in such instances, and so they took six common assumptions as their hypotheses:

- Survival advantage for women over men in maritime disaster;

- Survival advantage for passengers over of crewmembers;

- Increase in women's chances when the captain orders "Women and Children First";

- Lower survival difference between men and women after WWI;

- Greater advantage of women over men when disasters occur on British ships;

- Less difference between women and men's survival rates when the ship takes longer to sink.

Only the fourth proved true because, as the authors note, women's clothes were much less restrictive and women had become more athletic. The study's general conclusion is that "the sinking of the *Titanic* was exceptional in many ways and what happened [there] seems to have spurred misconceptions about human behavior in disasters." The *Titanic* has indeed often served as the model of exemplary behaviour, but the reality is otherwise. In the samples reviewed by Elinder and Erixson, the typical order of survival is, starting with the highest: the crew, followed by captains and male passengers, while women and children generally lag far behind.

On the latter point, several survivors of the *Lusitania*'s sinking reported coming upon the floating bodies of women tightly clutching dead infants in their arms. Similarly, during the 2008 cyclone Nargis in India, most of the fatalities were women. They had held on to children while the men had clung to coconut trees. Young children are not an enhancement to women's odds when speed and agility are required for survival.

What are we to conclude from these findings? Probably nothing more profound than acknowledging human nature for what it is. Some individuals are heroic, others think of themselves first; some people do better than others; and survival is mostly due to circumstances.

On the other hand, we now enjoy safer conditions on board, as each disaster has served to improve our chances. The creation of the United Nations in 1948 led to the decision to promote international rules for safety at sea and to the creation of the Intergovernmental Maritime Consultative Organisation, becoming in 1982 the International Maritime Organisation.

From a practical point of view, the sinking of the *Essex* led to having lifeboats adequately stocked with a reserve of food and water. That of the *Titanic* forced the provision of an adequate number of lifeboats on passenger ships, and the sinking of the *Lusitania* showed that lifeboat and life jacket drills need to involve passengers and to assign them to specific lifeboats. Since the wreck of the *Costa Concordia*, compulsory passenger drills now occur in port before departure rather than one or two days into the cruise, and are routinely practiced once a month on long voyages.

Similarly, some security measures followed the sinking in May 1987 of the car ferry *The Herald of Free Enterprise* as she left Zeebrugge in Belgium on her way to Dover, with 473 passengers, 80 crewmembers, and a load of 124 large vehicles. Much tighter safety checks were required afterwards, as her capsizing and the death of approximately 193 was the result of the bow doors being accidently left open. Loading techniques were also reviewed on the sensitive roll-on, roll-off (RORO) ships, where vehicles drive on one end and exit the other. While the concept of vehicle-carrying ferries is recent, there were costly RORO ship disasters even before the sinking of *The Herald of Free Enterprise*. Several occurred while the ferries were still in port, usually with few or no casualties, but others involved a significant loss of lives: the British *Princesss Victoria* (1953, in heavy seas, 133 dead), the Greek *Heraklion* (1966, in heavy seas, 264 dead), the New Zealander *Wahine* (1968, in port, 53 dead). Ferries have usually come to grief either through the shifting of their loads or being flooded through stern or bow doors. By 1987, it was high time to review both safety routines and loading techniques.

Oil tanker spills also led to some improvements. The *Exxon Valdez* accident on March 24, 1989, had a dramatic and visible impact on the Northwest Pacific coast fauna. It ranks thirty-sixth in the world, spilling *only* eleven million gallons of crude oil (one fifth of her capacity), against, say, the 206 million spilt in April 2010 in the Gulf of Mexico. However, the destruction inflicted on animal life had long-lasting effects, killing an estimated 250,000 sea birds, 2,800 sea otters, 300 harbour seals, 250 bald eagles, 22 orcas, and losing billions of salmon and herring eggs. The *Exxon Valdez* was barred from ever sailing along the coast of Alaska (although still plying her trade elsewhere under a different name). More importantly, the US Congress passed an Oil Pollution Act (1990) instituting the gradual implementation of a double hull design for oil tankers by 2015. Double hulls do not prevent accidents, but they considerably reduce the amount of spilled crude into the ocean.

VII
TOMORROW'S SHIPS

I don't know why all of us are so committed to the sea, except I think it is because, in addition to the fact that the sea changes and the light changes, and ships change, we all came from the sea... All of us have in our veins the same percentage of salt in our blood that exists in the ocean, and, therefore, we have salt in our blood, in our sweat, in our tears. We are tied to the ocean. And when we go back to the sea, whether it is to sail or to watch it, we are going back whence we came.

J.F. Kennedy (1962 speech in Newport R.I.)

My original question had been, how did sailing in the Age of Discovery evolve into cruising in the Age of Tourism, or perhaps more simply: how have the events that shape a voyage evolved over time? There have been some important changes. Knowing both our longitude and latitude, we now know where we are at sea and where we are going, and we no longer depend on the elements to get there. We no longer compel civilian ships to fight in our wars. Communication between sea and shore is instantaneous. The displacement of goods and people far exceeds anything we might have anticipated only a century ago. Scurvy and food shortage have made place to omnipresent consumption. Being entertained at sea is no longer a matter of passing time but an end in itself. For many, being at sea has become its own idle purpose. Sailing qua sailing, as it were.

Coming after past maritime endeavours, many of a heroic nature, some may see this modern progression as an entropic devolution, definitely a passage from the greater to the lesser—even as the size of the vessels continues to increase and their numbers continue to grow. Seeing how far we have come, the next question is, where are we going?

SEA TRADE

Modern working ships (tankers, freighters, container ships, and so on), in spite of their enormous scale and unusual shapes, continue to serve the same purpose as their earlier counterparts and remain, in spirit at least, close to the trading ships of the past. The technological advances on which they rely were impossible to conceive a mere century ago, and the quantity of freight they transport has no match in history. They carry most of our requirements, including food, clothes, cars and the gas they consume, along with many of the unnecessary trappings of our modern lives. Given the size of some of these ships, we may assume they have more or less achieved their maximum capacity.

Their future may entail more economical and ecological propelling energy. The shipping industry relies on fossil fuels (bunker fuel, the sludgy left over from oil refining) and contributes 2.4 percent of global emissions. In this context, we should note several alternative initiatives that cut down fuel consumption, like the company SkySails, a technology leader in this field, and Yves Parlier's Beyond the Sea experimentation with wind power at the technology park near Bordeaux, France. Cancelling the drag and easily stored when not in use, the new method uses enormous kites, fitted with position and motion sensors and adjusted through hydraulic computer-controlled hoists. The results have been positively tested at sea, and a Quebec-based shrimping vessel currently uses this method. Wind power is also used by *Tres Hombres,* the only transatlantic sail-powered cargo vessel so far.

Even when the lower price of oil does not make alternative fuels significantly more economical, the power of wind remains the cleanest of all, it and should become a source to consider for shipping companies regulated by standards that can only become stricter.

CRUISING

Today, cruising for the masses no longer provides the exclusive access to leisurely and elegant travel it once did. So commonplace has it become that the various companies must find ways to reinvent their identity and differentiate themselves from their competitors. They diversify by offering cruises as short as two days and as long as several months. A new trend seems to emerge, combining cruising with other activities, such as extended land treks or opportunities to do volunteer work locally, thus broadening the basic cruise pattern and increasing its attractions to people with different interests. For those attracted to more intense urban tourism, river cruises provide an opportunity to visit famous and historical cities, and the competition is fierce there as well, with ever more exclusive sites and shore visits consistently offered.

The choice of destinations, distant and exotic, is increasing all the time and soon there will be few parts of the world that cruise ships will not visit, as only political strife, war, the threat of piracy or terrorism, epidemics, and the like (including canal widths and port facilities for the giants of the seas) will restrict their access. In an ironic twist, the Northwest Passage, for centuries a nearly mythical quest, was the destination for over a thousand passengers and seven hundred crew members on the *Chrystal Serenity* in August 2016. Cruisers sometimes complain that a former pristine place visited earlier has now been "spoiled" by tourism, and the same fate may eventually apply to the passage itself. In the meantime, how could cruisers not feel embarrassed when reading the advertisement, "To sail the Northwest Passage is to join the ranks of fearless adventurers and explorers who came before."

The cost of cruising is already low for ordinary passengers, and it is unlikely that any changes will take a significant downward curve, even with a further reduction of the current amenities. Instead, the upward trend towards more specialized types of cruising (sail, river, luxury, and exoticism) is likely to continue, as those with means will demand to distance themselves even further from *hoi poloi* filling lower deck cabins. Rather than sail in the same vessels at different levels of cost and comfort, they will tend to separate themselves into different types of cruising even more than they already do. The worldwide trend of an increasing gulf between the moneyed classes and the less fortunate is also present in the cruising world, even if it goes against the original intention for cruise ships to have a levelling influence and make everyone feel similarly pampered. This has become a less valid premise and we can anticipate an even greater range of facilities and destinations.

As well, vessels will probably tend to diverge even more, from the behemoths herding several thousand passengers with different levels of comfort to destinations limited by their sizes, to the "niche" yachts with only a few dozen people enjoying the delights of exclusive privacy in extremely luxurious conditions and visiting the most remote or unusual parts of the world. One such is the *Europa 2* (Hapag-Lloyd Cruises, the highest rated cruise ship in the world, with six stars from the *Berlitz Guide to Cruising and Cruise Ships*). On some sailing ships, vying for ever greater variety of experiences, a new trend is for passengers to have fun acting as deck hands for a while, like Marie-Antoinette tending her well-groomed sheep at the Petit Trianon.

Even more than with working ships that do not have to justify their existence, the cruising industry will need to show much environmental awareness. Both Princess Cruises and Holland America are already recognized for their outstanding recycling efforts and Holland America was awarded in 2011 and 2012 the U.S. Coast Guard's Benkert Gold Medal for outstanding achievements in marine environmental protection. Others will need to follow in the same path.

PARALLEL USES

In Victorian England, hulls were used as jails. There was even a later attempt at doing so when the British government bought a U.S. vessel, the *Weare*, in 1977 to ease overcrowding in Her Majesty's prisons. Anchored near Weymouth, she served as a jail, but closed down eight years later, with mixed feelings and mixed reviews.

Other pragmatic uses for cruise ships have been suggested. In 2004, two geriatricians proposed using cruise ships sailing to the tropics as an alternative to retirement homes. They calculated that the costs would be only marginally higher than those of private nursing homes and assumed it would be easy to adapt the ships' facilities to meet the requirements of aged but still active people. This solution would also probably assuage their children and grandchildren' consciences: grandpa would not be put in a "home," he'd be *cruising*.

Cruising almost year around is already happening for a small number of elderly people in good health who have sold or rented their house and use the income to spend most of their time at sea. They usually report being satisfied with their current way of life and their *ad hoc* arrangement. They have companionship, regularly enjoy entertainment far superior to that available to ordinary retirees, go on the odd shore excursion, relish much better meals than if they lived alone or in a residence, and, more importantly, they spend time with people of different ages. What is there indeed not to like about the arrangement, since they usually visit their families between cruises? When their health deteriorates and they can no longer do without additional assistance, they will do what they would presumably have done anyway and resort to residential care.

The model proposed by the geriatric physicians a dozen years ago is one that a number of elderly people have already adopted informally. Would there be any drawbacks? We assume that one of the attractions of cruising is its distance from the exigencies of real life. However, we need to re-enter our real everyday experience to appreciate being away from it, and we may wonder how long the excitement of full time cruising could be sustained. The realities of old age, infirmity, and mere boredom may not be deceived for long by the accoutrements of a maritime residence.

Another type of exclusive residential cruising also exists, intended for a different clientele. These "condo-ships" are described in promotions as "real estate with mobility." The first of these privately owned yachts is *The World*, completed in 2002. At 644 feet (224 metres) she contains 165 beautifully appointed homes, ranging in size from 1,450 square feet to an imposing 5,320 (135 and 494 square metres). As with any condominium, residents have a say in the affairs of the community. They determine each year's itinerary, select expedition sites and events, and deal with on-board activities. Should they tire of being in their spacious quarters, their floating condo offers the choice of three restaurants, luxury shops, a 6,000 square foot golf club, casino, spas, cafés, observation centres, and three swimming pools. Another such grouping of luxurious, ocean-going homes is *The Utopia*, planned for 2016, catering to some four hundred residents and featuring amenities of outstanding elegance and comfort.

We can rest assured that entrepreneurs are actively developing new and always more seductive ways to lure people into spending time at sea, even if in so doing the sea need no longer be anything but a mere background to a way of life.

We have covered much ground in this foray into the many aspects of sailing, from earlier times to today, from the dire constraints of unavoidable voyages full of peril and discomfort to the alluring luxury of first-class liners. We moved from caravels of exploration and trade to enormous container ships plying their way across the oceans, from the horrors of slave trading to the terrors of naval warfare, and each time a new topic is broached we can only marvel at humanity's ingenuity, courage, and determination in dealing with the inescapable sea.

From my windows in Vancouver, I see the black and white Holland America ships waiting in English Bay before sailing into the Strait of Georgia, and several plainer cargo ships at anchor waiting to be loaded with grain or other merchandise. The men on board are perhaps only pale imitations of those who sailed earlier, or they may be the same and equally harassed by the brutality of their lives.

I feel distressed when reading about catastrophes at sea, from the loss of life of a few lonely men to crowds of hundreds and sometimes thousands, but it is the ships that fascinate me. Swept on a wave of anthropomorphism, few things sadden me more than imagining the great creaking groans of agony emitted by the carcasses of those enormous beasts of burden as they are swallowed by the sea. But it is in the natural order of things and all must come to an end. Perhaps it is better that they be engulfed in the waves and rest on the ocean floor, becoming one with the sea as artificial reefs, rather than be broken in the largest ship graveyard in the world, on the infamous wrecking beaches of the Gulf of Khambat.

For most of us, ships remain symbols of temptation, departure, and escape. In Gabriel García Marquez' *Love in the Time of Cholera*, Fermina Daza said she "would like to walk out of this house, and keep going, going, going, and never come back. 'Take a boat,' said Florentino Ariza. [She]looked at him thoughtfully. 'Well, I might just do that.'"

NOTES AND SOURCES

Frequently Quoted Works:

- Alexander, Caroline. *The Bounty. The True Story of the Mutiny on the Bounty*. London: Viking Penguin. 2003.

- Allen, Benedict, ed., *An Anthology of Worlds Revealed by Explorers through the Ages*. London: Faber and Faber. 2015.

- O'Brian, Patrick, ed. *A Book of Voyages*. New York: W.W. Norton & Company. 2013.

- Dash, Mike. *Batavia's Graveyard*. New York: Crown Publishers. 2002.

- Cordingly, David. *Pirates. Terror on the High Seas from the Caribbean to the South China Sea*. Atlanta: Turner Publishing. 1996.

- Deakes, Christopher and Tom Stanley. *A Century of Sea Travel. Personal Accounts from the Steamship Era*. Barnsley: Seaforth Publishing. 2010.

- Dear, I.C.B. and Peter Kemp, eds. *The Oxford Companion to Ships and the Sea*. Oxford University Press, 2nd edition. 2005.

- Druett, Joan. *Rough Medicine. Surgeons at Sea in the Age of Sail*. New York: Routledge. 2001.

- Fussel, Paul. *The Norton Book of Travel*. New York: W.W. Norton & Company. 1987.

- George, Rose. *Ninety Percent of Everything. Inside Shipping, the Invisible Industry that Puts Clothes on Your Back, Gas in

Your Car, and Food on Your Plate. New York: Henry Hold and Company. 2013:69.

- Hale, John R. *Age of Exploration.* New York: Time Incorporated. 1966.

- Hanson, Neil. *The Custom of the Sea.* London: Doubleday.1999.

- King, Greg and Penny Wilson. *Lusitania. Triumph, Tragedy, and the End of the Edwardian Age.* New York: St Martin's Press. 2015.

- Maxtone-Graham, John. *The Only Way to Cross.* New York: MacMillan Publishing. 1972, and *Liners to the Sun.* New York: MacMillan Publishing.1985.

- Moorhouse, Geoffrey. *Great Harry's Navy. How Henry VIII Gave England Sea Power.* London: Weidenfeld & Nicolson. 2005.

- Paine, Malcolm. *The Sea and Civilization. A Maritime History of Europe.* New York: Alfred A. Knopf. 2013.

- Rediker, Marcus. *Between the Devil and the Deep Blue Sea.* Cambridge University Press. 1987.

- Sobel, Dava. *Longitude. The True Story of the Lone Genius Who Solved the Greatest Scientific Problem of his Time.* New York: Walker & Company. 1995.

- Stevenson, Robert Louis. *The Amateur Emigrant.* (First published 1896). New York: Carroll & Graf Publishers. 2002.

- Withey, Lynne. *Voyages of Discovery. Captain Cook and the Exploration of the Pacific.* Berkeley: University of California Press. 1989.

- Worth Este, J. *Naval Surgeons. Life and Death in the Age of Sail.* 1997; *Stephen Maturin and Naval Medicine in the Age of Sail,* Digital Library, http://booksos.org/book/245414/3068d4 and in Dean King (ed.) *Sea of Word.* 1995.

Prologue

Henry Hudson, whose ship is shown on the logo of the Holland America Line, served the Dutch until being arrested by his English compatriots and charged with sailing under a foreign flag to the detriment of his country. The same Henry Hudson discovered in 1610 the Bay that bears his name, on a ship aptly named *Discovery*, sponsored this time by the British East India Company. The following year, a mutiny arose on board and Hudson, his son, and seven sailors were sent adrift in James Bay and never heard of again.

I-PRELIMINARIES (1-48)

1-A Eurocentric Vision (3-18)

The main source for European ships is Dear and Kemp (rigging, 2005:467-70; sails, 484-5; shipbuilding, 519-523; steam power, 559-561; also: *245, the Great Britain,* 245; 261-62; *Henry Grâce à Dieu* and Henry the Navigator; the *Vulcan,* 616). More specifically for England, see Geoffrey Moorhouse (2005).

An excellent source of information on the longitude is Sobel (1995) from which I draw freely–from sailing on an unknown longitude, e.g. the Portuguese galleon *Madre de Deus* (15) or Commodore Anson's *Centurion* (17-20)–to Sir Isaac Newton on the importance of determining the longitude (60), and to John Harrison and the Royal Navy's use of the chronometer (163-4).

The Longitude Act, proclaimed by Parliament in 1714, was to award a prize of £20,000 for determining the longitude to an accuracy of half a degree of a great circle (one degree the equivalent of 68 geographical miles at the Equator). There were two other prizes: £15,000 for an accuracy of two-thirds of a degree, and £10,000 for accuracy within one degree (Sobel, 1995:53). These apparently small differences translate into significant margins of errors at sea.

In 1569, the Flemish cartographer Gerardus Mercator introduced a map shown as a cylindrical projection. Intended for navigators because it preserved the linear scale in every direction, the distortion near the poles was too extreme to make the Mercator map useful until the longitude could be calculated.

The Phoenician trade is described in Benedict Allen (2015:3) and the Italian city-states in Malcolm Paine, notably the marriage ceremony between the Doge and the Adriatic Sea (2013:316-8). Marco Polo's original accounts have been lost, but many books relate his experiences, such as *The Travels of Marco Polo* (London: Thomas Wright Publishers, 1926).

Paine (2013) describes the expansion of the Chinese trade (304-5), the ship building methods (311), and the navigational system, quoting Zhu Yu, a contemporary specialist (351), as well as the development of the impressive Chinese fleet, as does Moorhouse (2005: 161-2). Information on Emperor Zhu's fleet is found in Joseph Needham, *Science and Civilization in China* (Cambridge University Press,1954:484). A documentary by Hagihara Keiko Bank, *Emperor of the Sea: Zheng He* (Bang Singapore Pte. Ltd. 2006), also contains information on the Chinese fleet.

Descriptions of Polynesian outriggers are from James Cook, *Captain Cook's Journal During the First Voyage Round the World Made on H.M. Bark "Endeavour" 1768-71* (London: Elliot Stoke 1893 (also at http//www.gutenberg.org/files.8106-h/8106-h-htm#ch2); Joseph Banks, *The Endeavour Journal of Sir Joseph Banks from 1768 to 1771* (online at http://gutenberg.net.au.ebooks05/051141h.html); Hank Driessen, "Outrigger Canoes and Glorious Beings." *The Journal of Pacific History*. XVII, 1982. Finally, the comments by Spanish explorer Ignacio Andia y Varela during his 1774 expedition to the Society Islands are found in G.B. Corney, *The Quest and Occupation of Tahiti by Emissaries of Spain During the Years 1772-6* (London: Haklyut Society, 1913-1919), Vol. II, 282-287.

290

For the Jomon migrations, see Jon Turk, *In the Wake of the Jomon: Stone-Age Mariners and a Voyage Across the Pacific* (New York: McGraw-Hill. 2005: 7, 12-13). The motivation for exploring and migrating is discussed in Clive Gamble, *Time Walkers: The Prehistory of Global Colonization* (Harvard University Press. 1993:16).

2-How Cruising Came to Be (19-26)

Two acts notably curtailed emigration to America from certain parts of Europe: the Emergency Quota Act (1921) and the Immigration Act (1924). While immigration continued, it ceased to be the great waves of earlier times.

On the improved quality of transoceanic crossings, see Paul Fussel (1987:273) and for recent developments in cruising, Kay Showker, *The Unofficial Guide to Cruises* (John Wiley & Sons, Inc. 11th edition, 2010:8).

On pre-Edwardian travel to Italy and Margate, see Roy Hattersley, *The Edwardians* (New York: St Martin's Press. 2004:320).

3-Travel, Tourism, Cruising (27-44)

Sources on women travellers are: Benedict Allen (comment by Abigail Adams: 2015:xvi); Dea Birkett, *Off the Beaten Track. Three Centuries of Women Travellers* (London: National Portrait Gallery Publications, 2004) on unescorted ladies (59); Mary Morris, *Maiden Voyages* (New York: Vintage Departures 1993); Jane Robinson, *Wayward Women. A Guide to Women Travellers* (Oxford University Press, 1990) and *Unsuitable for Ladies. An Anthology of Women Travellers* (Oxford University Press, 1994) for various celebratory statements by women travellers, and more specifically the unfortunate Emeline Lott (1994:17).

On women pilots and sailors: Jacqueline Auriol, *I live to Fly* (New York: E.P. Dutton & Co, 1970); Sally van Wagener Keil, *Those Wonderful Women in Their Flying Machines. The Unknown Heroines of World War II* (Rawson, Wade Publishers, 1979); Ellen MacArthur,

Taking on the World (London: Michael Joseph, 2002) and *Race Again Time* (London: Penguin Books, 2006).

Various conceptions of travel are addressed by Paul Theroux, *The Happy Isles of Oceania. Paddling the Pacific* (London: Hamish Hamilton,1992:31); R. L. Stevenson, (2002:80); James O'Reilly, *The Best Travel Writing* (Travel Tales, 2005). See also newspapers articles by Wade Davis, "Travel is a privilege, not a right," *Globe and Mail* (June 2, 2015), Desmond Morris," Why I love cruises," *Mail Online* (March 14, 2013), and Rick Steves, "Cruises perfect for sampling a continent," *Vancouver Province* (April 29, 2014).

For the difference between sailing and cruising: Simon Schama, "Sail Away" in *Scribble, Scribble, Scribble* (New York: HarperCollins Publishers, 2010), and John Maxtone-Graham (1972, 1985).

4-Coastal Communities (45-47)

The attempted rescue of the *Lusitania* passengers is reported in King and Wilson (2015) and the unsuccessful ones of the *Princess Sophia* off the coast of Alaska in Ken Coates and Bill Morrison, *The Sinking of the Princess Sophia. Taking the North Down with Her* (University of Alaska Press, 1991:70-1).

The *Leviathan II* story comes from *CBC News* (October 25, 2015) and other local media. The British Columbia Medal of Good Citizenship was awarded in August 2016 to the members of the Ahousaht band for doing what these communities have always done in such circumstances, usually without medals or other official rewards.

II-STYLE, COMFORT, SAFETY (49-86)

5-Ships That Struck the Imagination (51-70)

Don Eugenio de Salazar's report on his crossing to the colonies is extensively quoted in Paul Fussell (1987:102-10). The voyage of Captain Charles May on the *Terra Nova* is related in Patrick O'Brian (2013:106-33).

Sources for the *Santa Maria*'s crew are "The Columbus Navigation Homepage" and Appendix C of John Fiske, *Discovery of America*, first published in 1892 (Kessinger Publishing Legacy Reprint Series, 2005). For the grounding of the ship and Columbus's navigation and log keeping practices, see Cesare Giardini, *The Life and Times of Columbus*, (New York: The Curtis Publishing Company, 1967:38, 44). For the conditions on board, see John Hale (1966:80-81, 83).

Numbers for the *Mayflower*'s crew vary between 30 and 50. Caleb Johnson *(The Mayflower and Her Passengers,* Indiana: Xlibris Corporation, 2006), proposes the lower number, while Charles E. Banks *(The English Ancestry and Homes of the Pilgrim Fathers Who Came to Plymouth on the "Mayflower" in 1620,* first published in 1929, reprinted by Genealogical Publishing Co, 2006) suggests that there were 36 sailors and 14 officers. Other reports vary between 17 and 30. See Caleb Johnson's "Inside the Mayflower" and "Her Passengers" on line at *Mayflower History,* http://mayflowerhistory.com
For the plans of the ship and her navigation, see John Hale (1966:93). Regarding the conditions of board and upon arrival, there is only one account of the voyage by a passenger, William Bradford, in William T. Davis (ed.), *Bradford's History of Plymouth Plantation, 1606-1646* (New York: Scribner, 1908), but Caleb Johnson is a good source of information on the first winter (2006: 34).

The story of the Dutch East Indiaman *Batavia* was much publicized at the time. Many have compared its enduring haunting of maritime history to that of the *Titanic.* See Mike Dash's excellent book (2002), from which were drawn, inter alia, the description of the ship and the conditions on board (53-54, 60-62), the mutiny, and dreadful fate of both victims and survivors (404).

Sources for the *Nonsuch* come from The Manitoba Museum promotional material. A companion ship, the *Eagle*, loaned by the Navy, with Pierre Radisson on board, was damaged and had to turn back (hbcheritage.ca Our History).

Information for the *Titanic* is drawn from Tim Vicary, *Titanic. Factfiles* (Oxford University Press, 2009) and on line at *The Titanic: Facts and Summary*, as well as Nigel Bryant, *The Nooks and Crannies of First-Class Onboard the Titanic, on* line at http://www.google.ca/#9=nooks+crannies+first+class+on+board_the_r.m.s.+titanic. Paul Brown's conference "Life Aboard Titanic" on board the *Maarsdam* (Nov. 13, 2013) provided a description of the daily events on board, and singular details (e.g. a cross-section of the ship). Also useful is Simon Mansfield's documentary, *Titanic: And the Band Played On* (UKTV New Ventures, 2012).

Sources for the *Lusitania* are on line at *Lusitania Resources.* (www.mslusitania.info/people/statistics). Eric Larson. *Dead Wake* (New York: Broadway Books, 2015). See King and Wilson (2015:36-38) for a detailed description of the various accommodations.

For *Normandie*, the question was whether the ship would be called *Le Normandie* (ships often use the masculine gender in French) or *La Normandie* (to reflect the feminine appellation of the province that inspired the ship's name). The country was soon divided into two ardent political groups: those supporting the feminine article which the Right was somehow reputed to prefer, and those advocating the masculine article, apparently belonging to the Left. To avoid splitting France in half it was officially decided that *Normandie* would never be attributed any gender. This, and much else is discussed in Eric Lange's 2012 documentary, *Normandie. Une croisière en couleurs*, from *The Great Days of Sailing/Le Monde des croisières* (Thalassa series, Lobster Films, 2012).

The intended war time use for the ship and the inferno that consumed her in the port of New York in 1942 are described in François Reinhardt in *Incendies suspects: Normandie*, a *Mystère maritime* series (Grand Angle Productions, 2011).

The articles about the *Andrea Doria's* sinking are from the *Boston Daily Globe* of July 25, 1956. On the sinking and its causes, also see Pierette Domenica Simpson, "*Andrea Doria:* The Sinking of the Unsinkable," from *Alive on the Andrea Doria. The Greatest Sea Rescue in History* (Purple Mountain Press, 2006). The Italian waiters and stewards' "rescue" is found in Richard Goldstein, *Desperate Hours: The Epic Rescue of the Andrea Doria* (London: John Wiley & Sons, 2003:304).

6-The Class System and Segregation (71-80)

For the *Titanic*, we return to Tim Vicary (2009) and Paul Brown (2013). The argument that a democratic passage for all was the goal of shipping companies comes from Maxtone-Graham (1985:53).

R. L. Stevenson described the visit of first-class passengers to steerage (2002:33) and the deplorable conditions on the *Devonia* (47).

The class system on various ships is described in Deakes and Stanley (2010), who collected samples from passengers' writings, such as Robert Roberts, *Diary of a Second Voyage to Australia* (31), Rudyard Kipling, *From Sea to Sea* (28), William Morris, *Letters Sent Home* (46).

For conditions on a migrant ship from the West Indies, *the Francisco Balboa*, see V.S. Naipaul, *The Middle Passage. The Caribbean Revisited*, first published 1962 (London: Vintage Book Edition, 2002:5-7).

Paul Fussell relates the second-class voyage of Evelyn Waugh (1987:511-2) and Claude Lévi-Strauss his own in *Tristes Tropiques* (Bibliothèque de la Pléiade, Paris: Gallimard, 2008:8-9).

The description of luxury liners' various accommodations and divisions is drawn from John Maxtone-Graham (1985). Quotes are in 1985:66,52.

7-Yachts (81-86)

For the history of yachting in Britain, see Maldwin Drummond, *Salt-Water Palaces* (London: Debrett's Peerage Limited, 1979), where the limerick is also quoted. Elizabeth Ribgy's *Quarterly Review* article of 1845 is quoted in Dea Birkett (2004:59). Dear and Kemp also devote several sections to yachts and yachting (2005:638-649)

Much of the information on modern yachts comes from Eric Reguly's article, "A superyacht sensation: Peter Munk's great sea adventure" *(The Globe and Mail,* Aug. 30, 2014).

III-FOOD (87-126)

8-From Scurvy to Entertainment (89-108)

Description of scurvy symptoms from Magellan's sailors is found in John Hale, (1966:83), Malcolm Paine (213:402), and from Admiral Anson's *Centurion* crew in David Cordingly, *Pirate Hunter of the Caribbean* (New York: Random House, 2011:54-55). Thomas Pascoe describes his condition in *A True and Impartial Journal of a Voyage to the South Seas and Round the Globe in His Majesty's Ship the Centurion* (London, 1745:142).

Kenneth Carpenter *(History of Scurvy and Vitamin C)* is quoted in Charles W. Johnson, *Ice Ship. The Epic Voyage of the Polar Adventurer* (University Press of New England, 2014) as is the Inuit diet (2014:59). Dutch voyages particularly affected by scurvy are related in Mike Dash (2002:80).

On proposed remedies, see Joan Druett (2001:143), Mike Dash quoting John Woodall (2002:296), and Lynne Withey (1989:86). There was great reliance on natural remedies. A number of postage stamps were issued by the Falklands in 1972, featuring the scurvy grass, whose virtues were appreciated by seamen already suffering from the diseases by the time they reached these islands.

The Irish physician David McBride propounded in his *Experimental Essays* the use of a popular concoction, the "wort": one part malt and three parts boiling water, steeping for several hours, then mixed with sea biscuit or dried fruit to form a paste. Cook firmly believed in its merit, "The encomiums on the efficacy of malt cannot be exaggerated, and this useful remedy ought never to be forgotten on board of ships bound on long voyages" (Allen, 2015:67).

On the Copley Medal being awarded to Captain Cook, see Daniel Conner and Lorraine Miller, *Master Mariner. Captain James Cook and the People of the Pacific* (Toronto: Douglas & McIntyre Ltd, 1978:18-19). Cook, a great believer in the benefits of a dehydrated "portable soup," was always on the alert for replenishing his stock.

On a personal note, I should mention that sauerkraut juice still figured among the drinks listed on the menu of some Cunard ships crossing the Atlantic in the mid-1950s. I tasted it once and sympathized with Cook's sailors.

On provisions for the voyage, see Thomas Forrest's article on victualing ships in warm waters is quoted in Allen (2004:67); provisioning ships in the seventeenth century in Hale (1966:82); Hanna Acton, ed., "Food at Sea in the Age of Fighting Sail," *British Food in America*, No 6, Fall 2015; and Lynne Withey, *Voyages of Discovery* (particularly on the *Endeavour*, 1989:86). More notes on rations come from Marcus Rediker (1987:127-8), Nicholas Rodger, *The Command of the Ocean. A Naval History of Britain, 1649-1815* (London: Penguin, 2004:305). For Bougainville's provisions, see Diderot, *Supplément au voyage de Bougainville* (1796), available at http://www.inlibroveritas. net (Collection Philosophie).

The references to eating dog meat come from Sydney Parkinson, *A Journal of a Voyage to the South Seas in His Majesty's Ship the* Endeavour (London, 1773:122), and Anne Salmond, *The Trial of the Cannibal Dog* (Yale University Press, 2003:8); and J. C. Beaglehole, *The Journal of Captain Cook* (Cambridge University Press for the Hakluyt Society, 1969:Vol.3, 333-4).

For the crews' food served on Dutch ships and the passengers' richer fare, see Mike Dash (2002:72-75). Calling preserved meat by the name of famous murderesses is from Taffail (Henry Tapprell Dorling) "The Language of the Navy" in A.C. Spectorsky, *The Book of the Sea.* (New York: H. Wolff, 1954:126).

The fair method of distributing food on the *Terra Nova* is found in O'Brian (2013:106-133), and the benefits of St. Helena's climate in Rediker (1987:41).

Fictional captains Hornblower and Aubrey are quoted on provisioning and favourite recipes in C.S. Forester, *The Happy Return* (London: Michael Joseph, 1937:246), and Patrick O'Brian, *Post-Captain* (London: HarperCollins Publishers, 1972), respectively. Those interested in these recipes would enjoy Anne Chotzinoff Grossman and Lisa Grossman Thomas's book, *Lobscouse and Spotted Dog, Which It's a Gastronomic Companion to the Aubrey/Maturin Novels,* (New York: W.W. Norton & Company, 1997).

The menu rich in comfort food served in cold weather on the *Fram* is found in Charles W. Johnson. *Ice Ship* (2014:58).

On livestock: the Duchess of Albermale's stores on the *Terra Nova* are described in O'Brian (2013:106). The instructions for butchering in Richard Bond's *The Steward's Handbook* (Glasgow: J. Munro, 1918) come from Neil Hanson (1999:25).

Comments on livestock from passengers (Joseph Sams on the *Northumberland,* Ernst Haeckel on the *Helios,* and others) come from Deakes and Stanley (2010:25-26, 92) and from *POSH,* the quarterly publication of the P. & O. Lines, Inc. (Los Angeles, CA: Infoplan, 5(1) Vol. 5, 1964:5).

The Cunard Line's cow figures in Simon Schama (2010:6), the 150 rambunctious dogs heading for Canada in Keith Foster, "Grit & Gumption" *(Canada's History,* 2015:41), and the shipwreck cattle in George (2013:69).

The exigencies of preparing such large numbers of meals are reflected in the staff employed. For instance, eighty people work in the kitchen of the *Statendam,* a mid-size ship: an executive chef, a second executive chef, 2 sous-chefs, 9 chefs de partie/demi chefs, 2 butchers, 18 assistant cooks and apprentices, 15 pantry workers, 3 crew cooks (two Indonesians, one Filipino), one chief steward, one kitchen foreman, and 19 general purpose attendants. Four bakery and 5 pastry cooks prepare daily around 250 loaves of twenty different kinds of bread, 4,000 dinner rolls, 800 croissants, 800 Danish and sweet rolls, etc. Nineteen crew member, supervised by a dishwashing foreman, wash approximately 3,000 dinner plates, 7,000 dessert plates, 2,400 side plates, 5,000 glasses, not to mention ramekins, plate covers, silver cutlery, trays, etc. (*Statendam* Data).

Don Eugenio's description of the food served on board is in Fussel (1987: 102-113).) The list of staples taken abroad by British travellers is from Henry Knollys, *Sketches of Life in Japan* (1887), quoted in Hugh Cortazzi, *Victorians in Japan* (London: The Athlone Press, 1987:256-59), who also describes the meal served in Japan to Ernest Satow (1987:209). On the consumption of meat by Europeans during the Renaissance, see Fernand Braudel, *The Structure of Everyday Life* (London: William Collins Sons & Co Ltd, 1981:190-97); on caviar, Margaret Visser, *The Way We Are* (London: Faber and Faber, 1996:117-18). Finally, on the different appreciations of the smell of cheese, Claude Lévi-Strauss, *The Origins of Table Manners* (London: Jonathan Cape,1978:478).

Evaluation of the quality and amount of food served on board varies from the superfluous (various passengers cited in Deakes and Stanley, 2010) to the barely acceptable (K. Forster, "Grit & Gumption," 2015:41).

Passengers' comments on food and meals are in Deakes and Stanley (2010: 88-97), from Annie Beauchamp, *Victorian Voyage* (Wilson & Horton, 2000); D. G. O. Baillie, *A Sea Affair* (Hutchinson, 1957); John Finch, *To South Africa and Back* (Ward Lock, 1890; Ernst Haekel, *A Visit to Ceylon*, Eckler (undated); Rudyard Kipling, *From Sea to Sea* (McMillan, 1900); Robert Roberts, *Diary of a Second Voyage to Australia, 1897-8*, (Christadelphian Scripture Study Service, undated); and Joseph Sams (Simon Braydon and Robert Songhurst, eds), *The Diary of Joseph Sams*, (National Maritime Museum, HMSO 1982).

The provisions stored on cruise ships reflect the use of food as entertainment. They denote abundance and variety, are intended for long cruises, yet are far below provisions on luxury liners, whose crossings only lasted a few days. See *Titanic Facts* and King and Wilson (2015:4) who end the *Lusitania*'s list with 100 lbs of caviar, three barrels of live turtles, boxes packed with rare truffles, pâté, crab, and lobster.

9-At the Dinner Table (109-126)

Mr. Quilp is depicted in Charles Dickens, *The Old Curiosity Shop*. Don Eugenio's description is found in Fussell (1987:102-110).

Branislav Malinowski's breach of etiquette is mentioned in *Argonauts of the Western Pacific* (New York: Dutton, 1961:7-8). The other breach of etiquette is found in Bee Wilson, *Consider the Fork. A History of How We Cook and Eat* (New York: Basic Books, 2012:189).

The Prioress's good manners are described in Geoffrey Chaucer, *The Canterbury Tales. A Retelling by Peter Ackroyd*. New York: Viking, 2009:6).

Thomas Coryate's discovery of the Italian fork is related in Bee Wilson (2012:193) and Fernand Baudel charts the evolution of table manners in Europe (1981:207), where he also quotes the Baron de Tott.

The "proper" way of eating is described in Wilson (2012:60-61, 194-95). Alice Munro's "Real Life" is from *Open Secrets* (Toronto: A Douglas Gibson Book, 1994:52-53).

For a discussion on the value of living together, see Norbert Elias, *The Civilizing Process: Sociogenic and Psychogenetic Investigations* (Oxford: Blackwell, 2000).

The Frenchman C. Colviac's description of various European eating habits is from a 1560 French imitation of Erasmus's *Civilitas*, quoted by A. Franklin, *La Vie Privée d'autrefois. Les Repas* (Paris, 1889:201-2) and Lévi-Strauss, *Origin of Table Manners* (1978:498).

Lévi-Strauss alludes to Jean-Paul Sartre's *Huis-Clos (No Exit)*, his 1944 play, where the proposition "hell is others" is taken in the context of the German occupation of France during WWII. It would be considered differently today. The current trend, particularly in North America, is towards distancing ourselves from others. See Robert D.Putnam, *Bowling Alone: The Collapse of American Community* (2000), a study of our increasing disconnection from one another.

Michael Ondaatje describes Table 76 and its occupants in *The Cat's Table* (Toronto: McClelland & Stewart, 2001

Erving Goffman's inescapable study of social interaction is *The Presentation of Self in Everyday Life* (New York: Anchor Books Doubleday, 1959). His remark on couples' behaviour is on p.79. On the same topic, Lyn Lofland, *A World of Strangers. Order and Action in Urban Public Space* (New York: Basic Books, 1973).

Anthropologist Radcliffe-Brown was the first to describe the connection designed to release social tension in traditional societies in "On Joking Relationships," (*Journal of the International African Institute,* July 1940, 13 (3): 195-210).

IV-ENTERTAINMENT (127-168)

10-Whiling Away the Days (129-142)

On the pros and cons of ocean gazing, see Don Eugenio on *Nuestra Señora de les Remedios* (Fussel, 1987:102-110); Ralph Waldo Emerson on the *Washington Irving* (Fussell, 1987:365-66); Simon Schama on the *Queen Mary 2* (2010). Other opinions are found in Deakes and Stanley (2010): Harry Clark on the *Cassandra* (105); Julian Huxley, writing in *Africa View* (116); Frederic Treves, author of *The Other Side of the Lantern* (65), and Lewis Upcott on the *Arabia* (116).

See Mike Dash on the treatment inflicted on sharks aboard the *Batavia* (2002:81). On physical contests among sailors or between sailors and passengers, see Rediker (1987:250-51). It is also mentioned in Margaret Meredith.

The potentially licentious adventures of the Prince de Nassau-Siegen in Otaheite (Tahiti) appear in John Dunsmore, *Monsieur Baret. First Woman Around the World* (Auckland, NZ: Heritage Press Ltd, 2002:95).

On dancing and singing on earlier ships, see Dash (2002:75). On later passages, R. L. Stevenson's endearing accounts (2001:20-21). Mrs Beauchamps looked forward to the ball that would mark the crossing of the line on the *Ruahine* (Deakes and Stanley, 2010:101-2).

On games, see Stevenson (2002:32); on reading: Ralph Waldo Emerson (Fussell, 1987:365-66), Maurice Baring (Deakes and Stanley, 2010:115) and Margaret Meredith's travel log. Entertainment provided by the crew is reported in Meredith and in Annie Beauchamps in Deakes and Stanley (2010:173).

On shore excursions: Margaret Meredith's article on a visit to Saint Helena was published in an undated Australian newspaper, *The Hopetoun Courrier,* as "A Trip to England on the Hesperus," and in *The Lady* under the title, "A Visit to Saint Helena," on September 10, 1896. Unlike today's excursions on cruise ships, her visit to Saint Helena belongs to an era when going ashore truly meant discovering the endless possibilities of life elsewhere. The *Ormond*'s captain injunction to passengers to behave while in Lisbon is in Deakes and Stanley (2010:80).

11-Romance (143-148)

The reference to Mrs Collins comes from Caroline Alexander, *The Bounty. The True Story of the Mutiny on the Bounty* (London: Viking Penguin, 2003:413). For more on the often unacknowledged presence of women onboard, see Suzanne J. Stark. *Female Tars: Women Aboard Ship in the Age of Sail* (Annapolis, Md: Naval Institute Press, 1996).

Roderick W. Cameron, *The Golden Haze. With Captain Cook in the South Pacific,* (London: Weidenfeld and Nicholson, 1964: 129-30) quotes historian John Mansfield on the "boatload of women" rejoining their seafaring men.

Re-Article 28: The two officers, Cpt. Allen and Lt. Berry, are mentioned in Paula Byrne, *The Real Jane Austen* (2013:241-43). Two books relate the end of the unfortunate Hasenbosch: Alex Ritsema, *A Dutch Castaway on Ascension Island in 1725* and Giles Milton's *Castaway: A Dark and Terrible Tale*. The Dutch historian Michiel Koolbergen researched Leendert Hasenbosch's life but died before he could publish his findings.

12-Crossing the Line (149-168)

Descriptions of the ritual during the sixteenth, seventeenth, and eighteenth centuries can be found in

- Joseph Banks, entry of 26 October 1768, *The* Endeavour *Journal of Sir Joseph Banks,* online at http://gutenberg.net.au/ebooks05/050114h.html;

- John Bechervaise, *Thirsty-Six Years of a Sea-Faring Life* (1839:62-63, 146-150), available from Kessinger in facsimile.

- Bernardin de Saint Pierre, *Journey to Mauritius* first published in 1768 (New York: Interlink Books, 2003);

- Patrick O'Brian *(The Far Side of the World,* 1984:133);

- Commerson's Memoirs, entry of 22 March 1767, quoted in Dunsmore (2002:62-63);

- *Captain Cook's Journal During his First Voyage Round the World Made in H.M. Bark "Endeavour," 1768-71* (W.J.L. Wharton, ed. London: Elliot Stocke, 1893);

- Charles Darwin, *A Naturalist Voyage Round the World,* available on line at www.gutenberg.org/catalog/word/readfile?fk files=2966362;

- Henning Henningsen, *Crossing the Equator: Sailors' Baptisms and Other Initiation Rites* (Copenhagen, 1961);

- Marcus Rediker (1987) quotes from the Journal of Francis Rogers (187), describes the movement of sailors among ships (155-56), and also quotes from Captain Pennycook's 1698 *Journal* (188);

- Otto von Kotzebue, *A New Voyage Round the World*. London: Henry Colburn and Richard Bentley, 1830 – Project Gutenberg ebook;

- Hans-Jörg Pust "Equatorial Baptism" (1970) http://www.pust-norden.de aequ.qb.htm, who kindly authorized me to quote from his relation;

- Finally, Penelope Lively gives her own version in *Making it Up* (Penguin Group, 2005:22-23).

The dunking sketch described here is taken from an 18th-century edition of Woodes Rogers, *Cruising Voyage Round the World* (1711) and is now in the National Maritime Museum.

Saint Brendan's vision is related in Allen (2015:15-16). The hodgepodge of sailors' beliefs is described in Rediker (1987:184); the Nantucket comet appears in Nathaniel Philbrick, *In the Heart of the Sea. The Tragedy of the Whaleship Essex* (Penguin Books, 2000: 4-5).

Among the monsters of the sea, Gustave Doré's engraving of the "Destruction of the Leviathan" gives an idea of the horror generated by the monster, as do the 1801 and 1810 drawings by Pierre Denys de Monford of the *"poulpe collosal"* attacking a three-masted vessel, its tentacles reaching to the top of the masts, ready to wrap around the ship and drag her into the sea. The continuation of these myths into modern literature and games is mentioned in Marina Warner, "Here Be Monsters," *The New York Review of Books* (December 19, 2013).

It is said that only one sailor in six could swim, perhaps as a preference for succumbing swiftly rather than being left swimming among shark-infested waters or facing a long slow death on an island devoid of food or water. I resort several times in this book to the cliché "shark-infested sea/ocean/waters," particularly in relation to the sailors' fear of these animals–because well tried clichés best convey the intended meaning through the weight of repetition and connotation. On August 6, 1945, following the sinking in only twelve minutes of the USS *Indianapolis* by a Japanese submarine, a nightmarish scene ensued. Of the 1,196 men on board, 900 were able to escape in life rafts or wearing life jackets in the water. Drawn by the sound of the explosion and the wounded's blood, sharks (mostly the aggressive oceanic whitetips) came and attacked the men relentlessly during the four days they waited for rescue. When it finally came, only 317 men were still alive. The others died of many causes, but the sharks probably accounted for some 150 deaths. A short version of the ordeal is found in the *Smithsonian Magazine* article by Natasha Geiling, "The Worst Shark Attack in History: (August 8, 2013) at http://smithsonianmag.com/history/the-worst-shark-attack-in-history-25715092/?no-ist

For the various steps in the socialization process, see Arnold van Gennep, *The Rites of Passage,* first published in 1909 (New York: Routlege, Chapman & Hal, 2010).

V-ILLNESS AND MISERY (169-200)

13-Medics on Board (171-184)

For early medicine at sea, I have relied on the works of Mike Dash (2002); Joan Druett (2001); J. Worth Estes (1995); Andrew Lambert. *Life in the 18th century Royal Navy.* http://www.thedearsurprise.com/an-introduction-to-life-at-sea-in-aubreys-navy/; Christopher Lloyd and Jock L. S. Coulter. *Medicine and the Navy, 1200-1900* (1961, Vol 3: 1714-1815); Geoffrey Moorhouse (2005); and William Turnbull, *The Naval Surgeon Comprising the Entire Duties of Professional Men at Sea* (RareBooksClub.com, 2012) from which comes the information of ship surgeons' training and duties.

More specifically, Edward Barlow *(Barlow's Journal. His Life at Sea in East and West Indiamen)* is quoted in Rediker (1987:93); the description of the plague in the Royal Navy is found in Moorhouse (2005:259-60, 268), and the information on Dutch surgeons and apothecaries is drawn from Dash (2002:118-19). Worth Estes (1997) provides the figures showing the positive results on scurvy after the introduction of limes in the sailors' diet.

The importance of Batavia for 18th century navigators cannot be underestimated. Most eventually ended up there, and it was unanimously condemned as being pestilential and fever-ridden. "A Painted sepulcher, this Golgotha of Europe," wrote George Hamilton, *A Voyage Round the World, in His Majesty's Frigate* Pandora (London, 1793).

Jane Austen's mockery of the bathing fad is found in Chapter II of *Sandiston* (1817), and Fanny Burney's comment on tuberculosis in Anne Salmond, *Bligh: William Bligh in the South Seas* (University of California Press, 2011: 109).

Captain Wallis on the introduction of venereal diseases to Tahiti is often quoted, notably in Robin Hanbury-Tennison, *The Oxford Book of Exploration* (Oxford University Press, 2005:412).

Some war injuries are described in Moorhouse (2005:123) and Worth Estes (1997) reports on operating during battle and on the progress in surgical techniques. Robert Young's operations on the *Ardent* are related in Lloyd and Coulter (1961:58-60). Maturin's views on medicine are taken from Patrick O'Brian, *H.M.S. Surprise* (London: HarperCollins Publishers, 1993) and are reviewed in J. Worth Estes (1995). Finally, the disgusting conditions on the Russian ship *Maria* are described in Owen Matthews, *Glorious Misadventures. Nikolai Rezanov and the Dream of a Russian America* (New York: Bloomsbury, 2013:208).

On health hazards on cruise ships, see G. H. Bledsoe et al. "Injury and Illness Aboard an Antarctic Cruise Ship," *Wilderness Environmental Medicine* (Spring 2007, 18(1):36-40); E.H. Crammer, et al. "Diarrheal Diseases on Cruise Ships, 1990-2000," *American Journal of Preventive Medicine* (April 2003, 24(3):227-233); M. Flemmer and E.C. Oldfield, "The Agony and the Ecstasy," *American Journal of Gastroenterology* (September 2003, 98(9):2098-99).

14-The Elements (185-196)

Hesiod is quoted in Allen (2004:3); the limitations of travel time in the Mediterranean are explained in Fernand Braudel, *The Mediterranean and the Mediterranean World in the Age of Philip II* (New York: Harper Colophon Books, 1976:263-4).

The Dutch ships engaged in a race over time are mentioned in Dash (2002:69), and the overland crossing predating the construction of the Suez Canal is described in *POSH* (1964:5).

On the difficulties of sailing and on the elements, Peter Whitfield, *Mapping the World* (London: The Folio Society, 2000:126); *The Columbia Electronic Encyclopedia*; C.S. Durst. "The Doldrums of the Atlantic," *Geophysics Memoirs*, (28(8), 1926:228-38).

The Romans' use of the monsoon for navigating to India is described in Jeremy Jeffs's documentaries, "Beginnings" and "Spice Routes and Silk Roads," *The Story of India* (Maya Vision International Ltd. 2007).

There are numerous descriptions in the literature of horrendous storms at sea. We quote from the following: Allen (Vasco da Gama: 2004: 34); O'Brian (the *Terra Nova*, 2013: 231-302; Col. Norwood on *The Virginia Merchant*, 231-302); and Richard Lawrence's *The Mammoth Book of Storms, Shipwrecks and Sea Disasters* (New York: Carroll & Graf Publishers, 2003 - the *Serica*: 160-83). Uncharacteristically, the *Serica*'s master and owner, Thomas Cubbin, was the last to leave the ship.

The *Empress of Ireland*'s story is retold in Antoine Laura, "Bateaux Maudits" [The *Empress of Ireland* and the *SS Eastland]* *Mystères Maritimes. Affaires Classées*. (Grand Angle Productions, 2011). The ravages of the tropical heat are found in Maxtone-Graham (1985:194).

The story of the *Fram* comes from Charles Johnson's *Ice Ship* (2014). A new *Fram* was launched in 2007 by the Norwegian line Hurtigruten, in the old tradition of naming new vessels after past ones.

15-Mal de Mer (197-200)

Charles Dickens's comment appears in Peter Orford, ed. *On Travel* (London: Hesperus Press, 2009) and is quoted in George (2013:54). Don Eugenio's distress is described in Fussell (187:103). The "rail" cartoon of seasick passengers comes from Maxtone-Graham (1972:191). Kipling's humorous description is from his book, *From Sea to Sea,* quoted by Deakes and Stanley (2010:150-51), as are William Bastard, S.J. Perelman, and others. Contradictory advice is reported by Maxtone-Graham (1972:192).

Keith Foster (2015:41) relates the misery of Canada-bound passengers on the *Lake Manitoba.*

VI-THE DARK SIDE OF THE SEA (201-278)

16-Crews (203-212)

For general background, the following were consulted:

* Dear and Kemp (1976);

* Craig V. Fisher, *Royal Navy and Customs and Traditions,* www.hmsrichmond.or/avast/customs.htm (retrieved September 22, 2015);

* Andrew Lambert, *Life in the 18th Century Royal Navy,* www.thedearsurprise.com/an-introduction-to-life-at-sea-in-aubrey-royal-navy/;

* Christopher Lloyd and Jack L.S. Coulter "Life at Sea in Nelson's Day," in Peter Kempt, ed. *History of the Royal Navy* (New York: G.P. Putnam's Sons, 1969);

* Nicholas, A. M. Rodger, *The Command of the Ocean. A Naval History of Britain, 1649-1815* (London: Penguin, 2004); and

On the special status of sailors, see George (2013:47) and the perils at sea (148). Ian Urbina reports on the high losses at sea in

"Stowaways and Crimes Aboard a Scofflaw Ship," *The New York Times,* July 17, 2015.

The Maritime Labour Act covers most aspects of hiring and employment, notably the Occupational Accident Insurance Fund. It considers, inter alia, the age and fitness for service to sea, the right to wages, the presence of monitoring doctors, manning levels, qualifications, the obligations of the ship owners. It reviews compulsory presence on board, shore leave, maritime hours of work and hours of work in port, rest periods (maximum hours of work and minimum hours of rest), entitlement to leave and its duration, notice and termination of engagement, entitlement to repatriation, urgent family matters, vocational training on board. Criminal prosecution is also indicated for any infringement to these rules.

However, those among us who reside in port cities (Vancouver, in my case, overlooking Burrard Inlet) are sometimes made aware of flagrant dereliction to the duties outlined in the Act (unhealthy conditions on board, unsafe vessel, withheld wages, refusal to repatriate, etc.) on cargo ships waiting at anchor.

The shortcomings of seventeenth-century diet in the Royal Navy is discussed in Rediker (1987:126); Hannah Acton describes food preparation and distribution in "Food at Sea in the Age of Fighting Sail." *British Food in America,* No. 6, Fall 2015: 2-3, 7), and Captain Dudley's reference to "salt-horse" is from Hanson (1999:26).

The data on discipline at sea come mostly from Rose George (2013); Neil Hanson (1999); and Craig Fisher, *Royal Navy and Maritime Customs and Traditions.* For discipline in the US merchant navy until 1951, see L.A.G. Strong's history of the Missions to Sea Farers, quoted in George (2013:168).

For the daily woes of a seaman's life, see in particular Hanson (1999: 35-37, 40-43, the *Epaminondas*: 44, 50), George (2013:167-69), Fisher (2015); David Cordingly (1996:12). Plimsoll's actions are described in Hanson (1999:44-50).

17-Mutineers (213-218)

The main sources for this section are:

- the Royal Navy: Dear and Kemp (2005:374-75) and Olivier Chaline, "Les mutineries de 1797 dans la *Navy*," *Histoire, Economie & Société* (2005/1:51-61);

- *Batavia*: Mike Dash (2002) and "Batavia's History," *Western Australian Museum* (museum.wa.gov.au);

- *Bounty*: The aftermath of the mutiny and the construction of the *Resolution* are described in Alexander (2003: 31), who quotes from *The Journal of James Morisson,* (edited by Owen Rutter, London: Golden Cockrell Press, 1936); a good account is also given by Douglas Linder, "The Story of the Court-Martial of the *Bounty* Mutineers" (law2.umkc.edu, 2004); and Anne Salmond, *Bligh* (2011), who quotes Bligh on the causes on the mutiny.

- Canadian Navy: Richard Gimblett, "What the Mainguy Report Never Told Us: The Tradition of 'Mutiny' in the Royal Canadian Navy Before 1949," *Canadian Military Journal,* (Summer 2000:85-91); reference to the *Morale Study* and previous incidents, 2000:87;

- *Potemkin:* Dear and Kemp (2005:374).

18-Pirates (219-230

Article 101 of the U.N. Convention of the Law of the Sea defines piracy as:

a. any illegal acts of violence or detention, or any act of depredation committed for private ends by the crew or the passengers of a private ship or a private aircraft as direct

(i) on the high seas, against another ship or an aircraft, or against persons or property on board a ship

or aircraft;

(ii) against a ship, aircraft, persons or property in a place outside the jurisprudence of any State;

b. any act of voluntary participation in the operation of a sip or an aircraft with knowledge of facts making it a pirate ship or aircraft;

c. any act of inciting or intentionally facilitation of an act described in para (a) or (b).

For this section, I am mostly indebted to the following:

- David Cordingly (1996), particularly chapters by David Marley (16-35), Jenifer Marx (36-62)), David Cordingly (63-64), Richard Platt (78-79), Marcus Rediker (122-23, 125-27);

- David Cordingly, *Pirate Hunter in the Caribbean* (New York: Random House, 2011);

- Rose George (2013);

- Lynne Withey (1989);

- The Shady Isle Pirate Society, *Privateer History – French Corsairs*, (http://bbprivateer.ca); and

- David J. Starkey, *British Privateering Enterprise in the 18th Century* (Exeter, 1990).

Marcus Rediker (1987), was particularly useful for the Blight of Benin quatrain (106) Chapter 6, "The Seaman as Pirate. Plunder and Social Banditry at Sea," 1987:254-287 and Appendix E: "Mutiny at Sea, 1700-1750," :308-311). Noteworthy among Rediker's own sources are Charles Johnson [actually Daniel Defoe], *A General History of the Pyrates*, ed. Manuel Schonhorn (1724,1728; reprint Columbia, S.C.,1972) and Hugh F. Rankin, *The Golden Age of Piracy* (New York, 1969);

References to Anson and Dampier are found in Withey (1989:39 and 34, respectively), to Drake in Allen (2015:53). The buccaneers' background is provided by Jenifer Marx (in Cordingly, 1996:38-44, 46-48, 50, 102).

The French reliance on privateers is related in Cordingly (2011:34), by the Americans in James Bradford (in Cordingly, 1996:172, 181). Modern Somali pirates are examined in George, 2013:115, 132-33, 149), including the violence against crews (140-41), and Wikipedia. *Piracy Off the Coast of Somalia.*

19-Slaves (231-238)

Wikipedia (Slave Ships) provides a general idea of various countries' general involvement in slave shipments to the Americas. More specifically, I consulted:

- Marcus Rediker (1987: 44-49);

- Robert C. Davis, *Christian Slaves, Muslim Masters* (New York: Palgrave, 2003);

- H. Lewis-Jones, "The Royal Navy and the Battle to End Slavery," 17 February 2011, www.bbc.co.uk/history/british abolition/ royal navy article 01.shtml;

- Reynart Unwin, *The Defeat of Sir John Hawkins: A Biography of His Third Slaving Voyage* (London: Allen & Unwin, 1960); and

- Stephen Hahn, "A revised history of the slave-trade," *Le Monde Diplomatique*, Mai 2016:8-9).

The French galley slave's experience is from Platt (in Cordingly, 1996:84). Stewart Gordon's *A History of the World in Sixteen Shipwrecks* (University of New England Press, 2015:111-12) examines the religious conflict that resulted in thousands of captured Christian slaves toiling and dying in the Muslims' Mediterranean galleys.

Jonathan Bryant's *Dark Places of the Earth. The Voyage of the Slave Ship* Antelope (New York: Liveright Publishing, 2015) relates a significant ideological quandary of the 1820s in America with the trial of the *Antelope*'s owners. The ensuing court case, pitting the insurance company against the slave ship owners, is the theme of Amma Asante's film *Belle* (2013). Similarly, Steven Spielberg's *Amistad* (1997) is inspired by the slaves' mutiny on that ship (1839) and the ensuing court case (1841).

The Congolese king's correspondence with his Portuguese counterpart is quoted in Paine, (2013:410), and John Hawkins's crest is described in Reynart Unwin (1960:51). For the profitable ivory and slave trades, see Marx (in Cording, 1996:92), and for the sailors' hatred of Africa, see Jonathan Bryant (2015:31) and Rediker (1987: 47-48, 50).

For "blackbirding" in the Pacific, see Robert W. Kirk. *History of the South Pacific since 1513. Chronology of Australia, New Zealand, New Guinea, Polynesia, Melanesia and Robinson Crusoe Island* (Denver, Colorado: Outskirts Press, 2011: 332-34, 370).

The distinction between slavery and the slave trade in the USA is found in J. Bryant, (2015:xv-xvi).

20-Convicts (239-242)

The arrival of convicts in Australia is documented in Julian Holland, "Lands of the Southern Cross." *Pacific Voyages. The Encyclopedia of Discovery and Exploration III.* (Garden City, NY: Doubleday and Company Inc, 1973: 385, 408) which draws on data from the Migration Heritage Centre in New South Wales. See also Debbie Cuell and Philip Smith's documentary, *Coast Australia: Torres Sound* (Foxtel. Great Southern Film and Television, 2015).

The history of the French hulks and *bagnes* can be found in *Encyclopedia Quillet* (Paris, 1937); *Bagne de Nouvelle Calédonie* (fr. wikipedia org); and Pierre Belet's documentary: *Nouvelle-Calédonie. Les Sentinelles du Patrimoine* (Archipel Production, Grand Angle Productions, 2015). The French Guiana *bagne* was not as escape-proof as ordinarily assumed; at least one man got away, Henri

6

6

6

66

MONIQUE LAYTON

Charrière *(Papillon,* Paris: Robert Laffont, 1969) who, after several failed attempts succeeded in 1941. Carried on a makeshift raft of coconuts and riding the tide out of the island, he eventually reached Venezuela where he settled.

21-Emigrants (243-252)

Alan Kraut, *The Huddled Masses: The Immigrant in American Society, 1880-1921* (1982) breaks down the emigrants' origins (quoted in Richard Vinen, *A History in Fragments. Europe in the Twentieth Century.* Da Capo Press, 2000:17).

I did not include countries with a much smaller number of emigrants to the United States: France, Romania, and Greece (although the later started showing a substantial increase after 1900).

The losses of the "coffin" or "famine" ships are considered in Neil Hanson (1999:42) and in Brian McKenna's documentary, *Famine and Shipwreck, an Irish Odyssey* (From Famine to Freedom Productions, Inc. 2011).

Often referred to as *balseros* (rafters), many Cubans attempted crossing to America on a great variety of crafts. One who eventually succeeded on his eighth attempt in 2014 was a young man who led twenty-one of his friends from Havana on a vessel made of scraps of stainless steel and plastic foam, powered by a Toyota motor, and guided by a pocket-size Garmin GPS (Frances Robles, "Cuban Migrants in Boats Again Fleeing to the U.S." *Times Digest,* October 10, 2014.), an illustration of the Cubans' reputed touch with anything mechanical.

It is almost impossible to keep current on the waves of African migrants making their way to Europe. A snapshot at the end of August 2015 produced the following facts from a number of sources (the refugee organization UNHCR, the BBC, the International Organization for Migration, and the European Union Agency, Frontex) for that year so far:

314

- Number of illegal border crossing by sea for the first six months on the various routes: Western Africa (150), Western Mediterranean (6,698), Central Mediterranean (91,302), Eastern Mediterranean (132,240), or about 230,400, a number already higher than the total crossings for 2014 (218,000). In Italy alone, the numbers for the month of January had grown from 2,171 arrivals in 2014 to 3,528 in 2015.

- People crossing the Mediterranean to Southern Europe from January to July 2015 came from Syria (85,150), Eritrea (25,657), Afghanistan (25,556), Nigeria (11,899), Somalia (7,538), Sudan (5,658), Iraq (5,616), Sub-Saharan Africa (5,306), Gambia (4,837), Bangladesh (3,962), Senegal (3,694), Mali (3,475), Other (33,277). All are countries destroyed by war or desertification and consistently figuring among the poorest on earth.

They were headed for Greece (601,079), Italy (140,200), Spain (2,797), and Malta (99), as shown by the latest figures. In 2014, they consisted roughly (rounded numbers) of 14% women, 20% children, and 65% men. In the month of October 2015 alone, 218.394 arrived by sea (210,265 in Greece, 9,129 in Italy), with 315 dead or missing.

The media have been covering the migrant problem in detail, from 2014 to the present (2016). My information comes from innumerable articles, mostly from *The Guardian Weekly*, *The Globe and Mail*, *Reuters*, and *Times Digest*.

On the topic of women's passages to distant settlements and colonies, the specific references are:

* for Australia, the same sources as for general emigration and, on the women being mocked, Julian Holland, "Lands of the Southern Cross" (1973:409);

* for India: Anne de Courcy. *The Fishing Fleet: Husband-Hunting in the Raj* (London: Weidenfield & Nicolson, 2012). Jane Austen is quoted in Paula Byrne (2013:33).

* for Java: Mike Dash (2002:101-102)

- for Quebec: Irène Belleau, "Les Filles de la Cassette." *Société d'histoire des Filles du Roi,* June 2010. http://lesfillesduroy-quebec.org/publications/articles/de-la-sociee-d-histoire/78-les-filles-de-la-cassette; Peter J. Gagné. King's *Daughters and Founding Mothers. Les Filles du Roi, 1663-1673* (Pawtucker, RI: Quinton Publications, 2001).

22-The Custom of the Sea (253-264)

The two sources for the events following the wreck of the *Essex* are Owen Chase, *Narrative of the Most Extraordinary and Distressing Shipwreck of the Whale-Ship Essex of Nantucket* (New York: W. B. Gilley, 1821) and Thomas Nickerson, *The Loss of the Ship "Essex" Sunk by a Whale and the Ordeal of the Crew in Open Boats* (Nantucket, Mass.: Nantucket Historical Association, 1984).

All the references I use come from Nathaniel Philbrick, *In the Heart of the Sea. The Tragedy of the Whaleship* Essex (Penguin Books, 2000): the boat's discovery (xii), Chase's emotions (94, 156, 181) and Pollard's (210); the black sailors' condition (146).

The trial of the *Mignonette*'s crew is related in Neil Hanson (1999): rescue by the *Montezuma* (154), the inflammatory articles in the press (181-83), Tom Dudley's skepticism on further reports (316-17); and the case of Edward Bates's *Euxine* (197-98).

For other cases of cannibalism at sea: on the *Medusa* and the *Francis Spraight* (Hanson:127 and 137, respectively) and the selection of victims (140).

Of the two liquids available once fresh water was gone, urine and sea water, the latter was deemed the worse and thought to cause delirium, insanity, and eventually death. In 1952, Dr. Alain Bombard attempting to prove that shipwrecked sailors could survive without fresh water, tested his theory on an Atlantic crossing. He lost over fifty pounds and affirmed that his diet had consisted exclusively of seawater for fourteen days and fish juice for forty-three days. He also caught some fish and added plankton for vitamins. He believed it was essential to start drinking small amounts of sea water *before* becoming dehydrated. The validity of his findings was contested. Hanson (1999:106) argued that Bombard's intake of salt was much less than believed because fish excrete salt from water, thus the fish juice he consumed was diluted compared to the salt from the sea water he drank.

23-Survival at Sea (265-278)

The general data on ships sunk during peacetime and the two World Wars come from Wikipedia. The information on the *Yamamoto* is from Paine (2013:571).

1. Sources for Lest We Forget

- *Zoltan Moll, "Bateaux Martyrs," (The Lancastria) Mystères Maritimes.Affaires Classées.* (Grand Angle Productions, 2011).

- D. Krawczyk, *Wilhelm Gustloff,* (2007) http://www.wilhelmgustloff.com/sinking.htm.

- Marcus Kolga. *Sinking the* Gustloff. *A Tragedy Exiled From Memory* (A Realworld Pictures Production, 2008).

2. the *Empress of Ireland*: Antoine Laura, *"Bateaux Maudits [The Empress of Ireland and the SS Eastland]. Mystères Maritimes. Affaires Classées.* (Grand Angle Production, 2011).

3. The Cunard Disasters:

Titanic: Simon Mansfield, *Titanic: And the Band Played On* (UKTV New Ventures, 2012). The response to Mrs Astor is quoted in Vicary. *Titanic* (2009:7).

Many more passengers could have been saved. Unfair as it may seem to single out those who thought of themselves first, the following statement was taken from Charles Hendricksen, a fireman in No.1 lifeboat: "When the ship sank we picked up nobody. The passengers would not listen to our going back. Of the twelve in the boat, seven were of the crew. Symons, who was in charge, said nothing and we all kept our mouths shut. None of the crew objected to going back. It was a woman who objected, Lady Duff Gordon, who said we would be swamped. People screaming for help could be heard by everyone in our boat. I suggested going back. Heard no one else do so. Mr. Duff Gordon upheld his wife."

Another fireman in the same boat, R. W. Pusey, confirmed: "After the ship went down we heard cries for a quarter of an hour, or twenty minutes. Did not go back in the direction the Titanic had sunk... I was surprised that no one suggested going back. I was surprised that I did not do so, but we were half dazed. It does occur to me now that we might have gone back and rescue some of the strugglers." He also mentions hearing Lady Duff Gordon sympathize with another woman on the loss of her beautiful nightdress (Lawrence, *The Mammoth Book of Storms, Shipwrecks and Sea Disasters*, 2004:206).

Lusitania: King and Wilson (2015).

On the proper number of lifeboats, see Lawrence, (2004:214). See King and Wilson about the dreadful conditions on board (2015: 67-8, 192-96) and the submarine captain's comments (179-81).

The theory that the *Lusitania* was used as "live bait" is supported by Colin Simpson, *The Lusitania* (1972) and historian Patrick Beesley, *Room 40: British Naval Intelligence, 1914-18* (1982), [both in King and Wilson (2015:263)], as is the letter of February 12, 1915 written to the then Liberal MP Walter Rucinman by First Lord of the Admiralty Winston Churchill: "It is important to attract neutral shipping to our shores, in the hope especially of embroiling the United States with Germany... For our part, we want the traffic–the more then better, and if some of it gets in trouble, better still."

Although we may be more familiar with the fate of the *Lusitania*, a similar sinking occurred on September 3, 1939. The *Athenia*, a passenger ship carrying evacuating children, Jewish refugees, and American heading home, was torpedoed by a German submarine off the coast of Ireland. One hundred and eighteen of her passengers perished (George, 2013:219).

For the *Oceanos* see George (2013:77) and Nicola Cennac and Jérôme Mignard's documentary, *Les colères de la mer* (Antipode,

2012). The odd slip on the *Titanic* is mentioned in Maxtone-Graham (1972), and Mrs Brown's last sight of Captain Smith in Lawrence (2004:193).

The fates of the *Birkenhead* and the *William Brown* are described in Hanson (1999:142-46). That of the *Hannah* in Brian McKenna, *Famine and Shipwreck, an Irish Odyssey* (From Famine to Freedom Productions, Inc. 2011).

The Swedish article reviewing the pattern of survival at sea is Mikael Elinder and Oscar Erixson, "Every Man for Himself! Gender, Norms and Survival in Maritime Disasters." *Research Institute of Industrial Economics.* Working Paper Series #913, 10 April 2011. Online at IDEAS. http://www.ifnse/wfiles/wp913.pdf. The typical order of survival is found on p. 18.

The very nature of some rescues was beyond the strength and agility of anyone but the sailors. The *Atlantic* was running out of coal when her captain decided heading for Halifax to avoid an approaching storm. The ship hit a half-submerged rock near Mar's Island and broke apart. Of the 938 people on board (345 of them women and children), 565 perished, including all the children and all but one of the women. This heavy loss among the weakest ones was due to the conditions of the rescue–a rope linked to the land by the ship's heroic quartermaster who swam ashore. Most of the 141 sailors survived.

For ferries, see Ian Yardly, *Ninety Seconds at Zeebrugg. The Herald of Free Enterprise Story* (Stround: The History Press, 2014).

For the ecological devastation from the Exxon Valdez and others: Laura Moss, "The 13 Largest Oil Spills in History." *Mother Nature Network*, 16 July 2010.

http://www.mnn.com/earth-matters/wilderness-resources/stories/the-13-largest-oil-spills

VII-TOMORROW'S SHIPS (279-286)

On cruise ship characteristics: Kay Showker's *Unofficial Guide* (2010) and trends in cruising: Candyce Stapen, "Anthem of the Seas: On a cruise, bigger doesn't automatically mean better," *National Post,* March 22, 2016).

Patricia Jolly writes about the ecological use of power in "Driven by the wind and the waves." *The Guardian.* 194(2-3), December 2015, and Lucy Siegle in "Ethical living: The echo guide to cargo ships." *The Guardian* 195(3:4), June 2016.

On hulks, see Lee Jackson, ed. *The Victorian Dictionary.* "Victorian London, Prison Hulk," from the *Illustrated London News,* 1846, and "A Convict Hull" from the *Leisure Hour,* 1896. http:www.victorianon-don.org/prisons/hulks.htm; and Steven Morris, "Britain's Only Prison Ship Ends up on the Beach." *The Guardian* (12 August 2005).

Using cruise ships as retirement residence is considered by Lee Ann Lindquist and Robert Goluc. "Cruise Ship Alternative: A Proposal to Assisted Living Facilities." *Journal of American Geriatrics Society,* 52(11):1951-54. November 2004.

Fermina Daza's thoughts on sailing are mentioned in Gabriel García Marquez, *Love in the Time of Cholera* (New York: Penguin Books, 1988:325).

CPSIA information can be obtained
at www.ICGtesting.com
Printed in the USA
LVOW12s1134190317
527715LV00002B/364/P